Launcelot Fleming: A portrait

Giles Hunt was an undergraduate at Trinity Hall, Cambridge, at the time when Launcelot Fleming was Dean of the college. He later served Fleming as bishop's chaplain in Portsmouth and Norwich dioceses.

He has been a contributor to *Theology* and *New Fire* and lives in north Norfolk.

Launcelot Fleming

A portrait

Giles Hunt

Introduction by
Owen Chadwick

CANTERBURY
PRESS
Norwich

© Giles Hunt 2003

First published in 2003 by the Canterbury Press Norwich
(a publishing imprint of Hymns Ancient & Modern Limited,
a registered charity)
St Mary's Works, St Mary's Plain,
Norwich, Norfolk, NR3 3BH

www.scm-canterburypress.co.uk

British Library Cataloguing in Publication Data

A catalogue record for this book is available
from the British Library

ISBN 1-85311-523-1

Typeset by Rowland Phototypesetting Ltd,
Bury St Edmunds, Suffolk
Printed and bound in Great Britain by
Biddles Ltd, www.biddles.co.uk

Contents

Acknowledgments

After Launcelot Fleming died his widow Jane asked me to go through all his papers. These are now all lodged at the Scott Polar Research Institute in Cambridge (with the exception of any royal correspondence which is at Windsor). Jane originally wanted me to select some of Launcelot's talks, speeches and sermons for publication, but it soon became apparent that this would not do him justice since it would be impossible to convey what he was like, what he meant to people, and what he thought and believed without a good deal of background material; and Jane understandably did not want anything of a biographical nature published during her lifetime. Nor indeed is this book a proper biography; but I hope it is a portrait which gives a true likeness.

As a vicar I always tried to avoid thanking people by name, knowing I would surely forget to mention someone; but I must acknowledge help given so willingly by so many people, hoping that anyone who has been omitted will understand and forgive.

Dr Owen Chadwick not only contributed an introduction, but made many valuable suggestions from his first-hand knowledge, and has allowed me to quote him freely. Lord Runcie gave me the typescript of the address he wrote but could not deliver for the Windsor memorial service, as well as his address at Poyntington with which this book ends. Donald Lindsay most generously supported the writing of this book and has allowed me to quote freely from his *Friends for Life* (now out of print) which was invaluable for piecing together Launcelot's early life; but it was difficult for him to describe the later years since most of those concerned were still alive and each chapter had to be submitted to Launcelot and Jane for approval.

Jane herself was immensely kind and helpful to me; she of course knew Launcelot during the last twenty-five years of his life better than anyone. Colin Bertram and Alfred 'Steve' Stephenson were fascinating and very informative about Antarctica. Christopher Fleming, and Richard and Margaret Morgan, gave insights from a family angle. Several people helped fill in gaps not covered by Launcelot's papers; Alastair Gold and Norman Crowder helped over the Portsmouth era; Frank Telfer, John Kirkham and Richard Hanmer (chaplains), the very Revd Alan Webster, Dr Stuttaford, Michael Handley, John Giles, Colin Bodkin, Sir Bernard Feilden, Dorothy Bartholomew, Gordon Tilsley, and Lady Harrod helped over the Norwich years; Bishop Michael Mann, Patrick Mitchell, Dominick Harrod, Kenneth Adams and Bishop Stephen Verney helped over Windsor. Jocelyn Poulton and others at Trinity Hall, and at the Scott Polar Research Institute, were very helpful over looking for photographs.

In fact, all sorts of people, many of whom had never met me in their lives, went out of their way to be helpful in a way which is really a great tribute to Launcelot; his name opened doors in a marvellous manner. It was thanks to Bishop Peter Nott impressing on Jane the importance of Launcelot's papers that she asked me to sort through them, and his successor, the present Bishop of Norwich, gave me his own assessment of Launcelot's influence on the diocese; and it is largely thanks to the Dean of Norwich, Stephen Platten, that this book is seeing the light of day.

In conclusion, I am grateful to Richard Morgan, Launcelot's literary executor, for giving his blessing to this book. I want to thank my daughter Elizabeth for having shown me various arcane aspects of word-processing that saved much time and aggravation. Last but not least, I am enormously grateful to my wife for encouraging me, for reading each chapter and pointing out the more obvious defects, and for being so patient and tolerant while I was being of no help whatever in house or garden.

Giles Hunt

A Note on Sources

Launcelot Fleming's papers – a voluminous archive that took years to examine – are the main and essential source for this book, supplemented by correspondence and conversations with those mentioned in the Acknowledgments and others, together with personal knowledge.

Archbishop Fisher's correspondence concerning the appointment to the bishoprics of Portsmouth and London is in Lambeth Palace Library, who were most helpful.

Published sources include (in order of appearance):
A History of the Trinity Hall Boat Club 1949–87 by D. I. Sparkes with an Introduction by Launcelot Fleming, printed for the College by Cambridge University Press (1988)
Antarctica & Cambridge by Colin Bertram (privately printed)
Meredith Dewey (diaries, letters and writings) ed. A. V. Grimstone, M. C. Lyons and Ursula Lyons, published by Pembroke College, Cambridge (1992)
The War at Sea by S. W. Roskill, Volume 1 (HMSO, 1951)
History of the University of East Anglia by Michael Sanderson (Hambledon and London, 2002)
Friends for Life by Donald Lindsay was published by Lindel Publishing Company in 1981. Unfortunately the publisher subsequently went out of business and all remaining stock was lost or destroyed (second-hand copies sometimes come on to the market, particularly in Norfolk where many copies

were sold); it gives a much fuller account of the early part of Launcelot's life than this present book.

The Director of the Royal Geographical Society kindly gave permission to reproduce an abridged version of the paper written by Launcelot Fleming and Alfred Stephenson in the 1940 issue of the *Geographical Journal*, with its map, as well as quotations from the account of the Society's meeting on 11 February 1938.

Launcelot Fleming's own papers contain a good deal of printed material; a few of his talks and speeches were printed, as were the proceedings of several Diocesan Conferences and other gatherings, and his House of Lords speeches are of course printed in *Hansard*. But nothing was actually published under his own name.

Launcelot's portrait, used on the cover, and a photograph of him as Dean of Trinity Hall, are reproduced by kind permission of the Master and Fellows. The Antarctic photographs, including those used on the cover, are reproduced by kind permission of the Scott Polar Research Institute, Cambridge. The remaining photographs were supplied by family members: Jane Fleming, Margaret Morgan, Christopher Fleming and Robert de Pass.

The cover design is by Leigh Hurlock.

Introduction by Owen Chadwick

The human being can go into words, but some are less easily described than others. There are people whose personality is so unique and we ought to be able to say why, and so describe them for those who did not know them. Sometimes we can almost do that, especially when the life has been filled with action. But there are others in whom the uniqueness depends on an indefinable quality in the personality. These are the men and women who are known and loved and revered in their own time but whose memory is bound to fade because we who knew them have not got the words to say why they mattered so much.

The people of this kind who are usually the most difficult are the pastors and teachers. Their life was quiet. Their work might (or might not) have been important, even life-transforming to a few people or many. But that is impossible to know. It is secret between four eyes, or a long succession of private encounters soul to soul; and we are helped very little, in knowing what we want to know, when someone says 'I did owe him (or her) such a lot.'

Still, we ought at least to have a try at painting their portraits even when we know that both the paint brush and the camera are liars.

Launcelot Fleming was one such. It was the personality that mattered; and when people ask us why, it is not easy to explain. It had grace. It had more than charm, it had enchantment. It had shyness, even, amazingly for one so outgoing, nervousness about what other people might think. The mind was not exactly questioning, for during his university career and as an explorer in the Antarctic (not fully before then) he reached a frame of principle, religious and moral, which never left him and which he never afterwards varied and which he applied to our world and society. That makes him sound like a closed mind, which he was not. He listened to people, respected them when he could not agree with them, tried to learn from them. This openness, willingness to listen, and not merely to pretend to listen, was part of the intellectual quality which drew a lot of people to want to discuss with him the problems that troubled or tormented or only interested them.

Fleming crossed out more things in draft than any other professional speaker in England. He could be absurdly diffident. He preferred to preach other people's sermons if he could, and his reason was unique to himself and unlike the motive of the speakers all down the ages who have preferred to save themselves trouble by making speeches drafted by someone else. He preferred other people's addresses because he was sure that they must be better than anything he could himself achieve. When he took someone else's draft, he made it his own and in doing so might make it better and incidentally more religious and more directly intelligible. But when perforce he had to write his own sermon, which was less often than with other bishops, he was almost comic in the way he went round to friends less qualified than himself and cajoled them to read the draft and consider it and reconsider it. Hence pages speckled with crossings out which will be like museum pieces in the history of sermonology. They reminded the reader of Helen of Troy if she caught measles.

He never said, and he never thought, as some others have said boringly, 'I am only a scientist and have not been educated to write or speak properly like you arts people have.' For in his mind the problem was nothing to do with style. He knew that he could write clearly, that he could avoid jargon and long-windedness and gas and seven-syllable words. The problem was nothing to do with the nature of his education. It was the mystery of the world and of mankind and of God. In these clouds that gird Mount Sinai, how shall we express the truth that we see? The result of his contortions was a direct, graphic, staccato quality which was powerful, realistic, and intentionally comic.

A quotation from a sermon of his about his fifteen great aunts – an 'unusual blessing . . . best encountered one at a time' – has just this humorous directness, but it will be observed in it that while the description is perfect and incontrovertible, the lesson which he drew from it is more of a bet – the one who loved Loretto school, where he was delivering this sermon, owed her zest and her vitality, he said that he believed, to her faith. He was not afraid, as some speakers would be, of bringing his personal feelings into a public address – how much he loved his sister, he told everyone at her funeral. He had a vivid memory of people and places and incidents and could talk about them in language that could be spell-binding. No one can read his descriptions of Iceland and the Antarctic without *feeling* the cold and the ice and the fresh winds. His judgment on people was discriminating. He did not say unkind things about people, but his geese were not all swans and he was a man to consult for references on people who applied for jobs. He did not allow his affections for people, who were more numerous than any single person has a right to have affections for, to bias him into backing someone for a job for which they were unqualified or unsuitable.

This book raises the question whether nowadays it would be possible for such a person to become a bishop – without any parish experience whatever, not even as a curate, although with pastoral experience in the Navy and in a Cambridge college. Probably even when he became a bishop in 1949 he could only have come to the see of Portsmouth. That see was full of the Navy and looked out to sea; and if they needed someone who would get on with naval ratings as well as admirals they could hardly have a cleric with better experience in war or a more proven record. But someone considered for a see in 2002 would not have had a war to serve as chaplain in, and his record would only have been that he was the least 'remote and ineffectual' of dons. It was a closed world, at first sight small; 'the establishment'. The ex-Communist Franciscan Michael Fisher wrote of Ken Carey, with whom for a time Launcelot shared a lodging and who was always a friend, that he came from a 'familiar and restrictingly self-conscious world of the people who, it is sometimes said, really ran England. Politically Tory, public spirited, "born to rule"' and educated at a few of the greater public schools, Carey fostered, said Fisher, the mood that the ordinands were a closed world of 'gifted amateurs'. It was a sort of club or network – but, asked Fisher, why not?

A gifted amateur was what Launcelot gave the impression of being. He was trained as a geologist and as such went on the tough Graham Land expedition, three years away on the ice studying rock formations and glaciers and fossils and his fifteen companions; and was one of the three who went on the long sledge journey of discovery where they mapped 450 miles of coastline that no one had ever seen before, and ran so short of food for the dogs that they had to kill seven of them. Because of all this he rose at a young age to an eminent position in the academic world of science, that is, to be head of the Scott Polar Research Institute. He won acclaim in the House of Lords for his speech on the Antarctic Treaty which is still remembered though it was made more than thirty years ago, and it is said that you do not win acclaim in that House unless you know about the subject as an expert.

He was one of those not so rare scientists for whom the search for the truth about God and the truth about this physical realm were not two separate endeavours but a single quest. One of his private ways of praising God was through the psalms, and probably this was because the glory of God in his creation keeps coming through those ancient words.

Launcelot Fleming had a puckish humour which no weight of mitres could suppress. He had a genius for friendship; open to everyone, accessible to everyone, outgoing to everyone, wise in what he said if they brought him a trouble. Each individual was unique in his eyes. He was a happy person, and in the later half of his life Jane brought him new forms of happiness and new dimensions to his work.

Giles Hunt knew him well and worked with him and had a unique opportunity to study his personal archive. This book is to be welcomed as a portrait of one of the rarer Christian souls of the twentieth century.

I

Upbringing

We can't help being influenced in our beliefs by the culture and environment in which we've been brought up, and by our parents, families and friends; probably more of our beliefs than we may imagine came to us at second-hand.

Launcelot Fleming

William Launcelot Scott Fleming was born on 7 August 1906 at 10 Chester Street, Edinburgh. Neither 'Launcelot' nor 'Scott' were family names, and Scott of the Antarctic had not yet become famous, but Launcelot's mother was a devotee of Sir Walter Scott. Launcelot (or, to his family, Lance) was the name by which he was always known, and will be called from now on.

His father Robert Fleming was a Scot, born in Dundee where the family fortunes were derived from jute; he was wealthy, and with a medical practice in the fashionable part of Edinburgh could have become much wealthier, but as well as fee-paying patients he looked after others who could afford to pay little or nothing. He was an honorary physician to Edinburgh Royal Infirmary, and also devoted much time to the Criminal Lunatic Asylum at Peterhead where he earned a high reputation for his enlightened views on the treatment of offenders. He became President of the (Edinburgh) Royal College of Physicians, an honorary LL.D., Fellow of the Royal Society of Edinburgh (FRSE), and Surgeon to the Royal Company of Archers (the King's Bodyguard for Scotland), and last but not least was an Elder of the Presbyterian Church. He had taken a first class honours degree at Edinburgh University and won a gold medal when he took his M.D. degree in 1896; he had, in fact, a first-class intelligence.

Launcelot's mother was Eleanor, daughter of William Holland, Rector of Cornhill-on-Tweed. There was a strong clerical tradition in her family; her maternal grandfather Canon Tristram had been the first occupant of the 'Golden Stall' in Durham after the Ecclesiastical Commission removed its gilt, and two of her brothers were ordained – one of them was Dean of Norwich not very long before Launcelot became its bishop. The third brother was Sir Henry Holland, whose skill as an eye surgeon when a medical missionary in India restored the gift of sight to tens of thousands.

Robert and Eleanor's eldest son, Bob, had been born in 1898; next came Jean, who married Captain Dan de Pass, Royal Navy; then a son who died at the age of five months (on All Saints' Day 1902); then Archie, born in 1904, who went into the Royal Navy via Dartmouth and had to retire as a Commander in 1946 as a result of deafness caused by gunfire. Launcelot, born two years later, was the youngest, and his upbringing and childhood were typical for a child of an upper-middle-class family in those days before two world wars changed the old order so completely. There was a nanny, and an under-nanny, Nellie Gittings, with whom Launcelot kept in touch until she died, long after he had become a bishop; she took him for walks with Archie when he was old enough.

A photograph of the two brothers with their mother in the nursery gives us a picture of a secure and utterly reliable childhood, and we can imagine what life for those little boys in 10 Chester Street was like. In the background, and taken for granted, were some half-dozen domestics – cook, scullery-maid, parlourmaid and housemaids – a rather large staff for such a household, but then Dr Fleming held his surgeries in the house. Mrs Fleming ran the household very efficiently, sometimes almost too efficiently; when she demanded higher standards than her minions felt reasonable her husband's tact and good humour had to defuse the resultant domestic crisis – as an old lady Mrs Fleming would recount how her husband would always say 'Oh dear, I'm afraid that was my fault' even when it could not possibly have been his fault at all. Robert Fleming was, indeed, an outstanding example of what a Christian gentleman should be; generous, patient, genuinely concerned for others' needs. He also possessed a good sense of humour which, coupled with a very good brain, an enquiring mind and freedom from prejudice, gave him a sound judgment and an aptitude for scientific work.

It would be wrong to picture Eleanor Fleming as a domestic tyrant. Launcelot's mother, like her husband, was generous and kind, she was a demanding employer, but a considerate one too; and she was devoted to her husband and family. In her old age she looked forbidding, and never hesitated to express definite and forcible opinions (which could embarrass her youngest son), but if gently mocked would unexpectedly hoot with laughter at herself; she was good company although her rigid, rather bigoted Low Church upbringing made her very strict both with herself and with her children (and servants!). Robert Fleming the Scots Presbyterian was paradoxically less dour and Calvinistic than his English Anglican wife, but her upbringing had given her a faith which, though sometimes narrow, was deep and sincere.

In addition to his parents, Launcelot (as he later recalled) 'had the unusual blessing of fifteen Great Aunts, all on my mother's side'.

They were a formidable bevy, best encountered one at a time. They were all devoted to good works; pious; penniless; long lived; and in various ways eccentric. Most of them were spinsters, remaining unmarried. One exception was Great Aunt Ella . . .You could never say of her that she was dull or boring. She had zest; she was very much alive; and this I'm sure was a product of her faith.

That would not be a bad description (apart from 'penniless' and 'eccentric') of Great Aunt Ella's niece, Launcelot's mother.

There is no doubt that he was very strongly influenced by both his parents; he admired his father and strove to emulate him, and although it would not be entirely true to say that he was dominated by his mother, there is some truth in that judgment. Like many sons of dominating mothers he did not marry until after his mother had died; on the other hand, it was mainly his mother who, humanly speaking, was responsible for his being ordained, and after his father died in 1948 he felt it was his duty to look after her. He never rebelled against his mother's wishes as his eldest brother did; but there again, he never really had any reason to want to.

Launcelot's upbringing was privileged, but quite spartan. There were servants to light the nursery fire (and if one was ill a bedroom fire as well), but that did not prevent one's sometimes having to break the ice in the water-jug before washing in the basin. Children had to be seen and not heard, and do what they were told – it is difficult today to appreciate the extent to which, before the chaos and carnage of 1914–18 brought their wisdom into question, those in authority were respected and looked up to. We also find it difficult to come to terms with the idea of privilege. Children like Launcelot accepted the fact that they enjoyed many advantages that were denied to most people; it did not occur to them that 'the system' was unfair and should be changed, but on the other hand it was very firmly drilled into them that privileges carried with them duties. The Catechism (which they had to learn) made it clear that 'My duty towards my Neighbour' includes 'to love, honour and succour my father and mother; to honour and obey the King, and all that are put in authority under him . . . and to do my duty in that state of life, unto which it shall please God to call me'. Launcelot never felt guilty at having enjoyed so many privileges, but he saw it as his duty to help as many other people as possible to enjoy them too.

It was lucky for him that he was the youngest in the family. Bringing up the elder children had blunted the edge of their mother's strictness, and the death of an infant son had made her softer and more compassionate towards the two younger boys born after him. Bob had suffered, as so many firstborn sons do, from having too high demands and expectations placed on him. Jean never forgot how her eight-year-old elder brother, who had loathed his first term away at a prep school in the south of England, stood howling, with tears streaming down his face, on Waverley Station, pleading not to be sent back there again. But his mother was adamant, and back to school he had to go. In later life Bob became something of a black sheep, getting into various matrimonial and financial scrapes; Jean dated his troubles from that moment on Waverley Station. Even as a schoolboy Bob seems to have been deemed unsatisfactory, and since Archie, being two years older than Launcelot, would have tended to get the blame for any mischief he and his young brother got up to, it is not surprising that Launcelot became his mother's favourite, her Benjamin. This often happens to the youngest child; but what is remarkable is that his parents commissioned a full-length portrait of Launcelot at the age of six by Croeber, a well-known artist of the period.

Being the favourite child did not, however, mean that Launcelot's upbringing was exactly soft; years later he recalled:

When I was a small boy, I was given lessons in boxing, presumably because it was considered desirable that I should learn how to defend myself – and also I suspect because it was thought good for my character. The experiment was not a great success. I couldn't get out of the habit of shutting my eyes when delivering or receiving a punch – and this tactic proved a distinct disadvantage in the noble art of self-defence, and the boxing lessons were eventually dropped. . . . [But] at my public school I was conscripted for a House Boxing Competition. . . . In the course of the bout, which needless to say I lost, I broke my arm. Then, to my astonishment, I ended up a hero – for having continued the fight to the end despite my arm being broken – a fact of which I was unaware. In point of fact I was scared stiff – far too frightened to expose myself as the coward I felt. This incident made me reflect on the quality of courage – for it helped me to realise how it can be misjudged and misdirected.

Jean often shielded Launcelot, six years younger than herself, from the full blast of parental storms. At her funeral in 1983 Launcelot spoke of his early memories of Jean's 'goodness and affection' and 'sense of humour', and how she was one of those 'people who have in some way ministered to us, made a difference to our lives, helped us and influenced us'.

> I would find it impossible to describe what influence she had on me, and the way I valued and loved her from childhood onwards. . . . She meant a great deal to me as a child, and as the years have passed I have increasingly realised how lucky I have been to have such a sister.

It would be quite wrong, though, to think of Jean having to protect her young brother from constant parental wrath. The structured environment in which he grew up provided stability and a sense of security that enabled self-confidence to grow, and his dominant childhood memories were happy. In his late fifties a photograph of a house in Scotland where as a small boy he used to stay with his grandmother 'brought back all kinds of memories'.

> I remember the stone staircase; a little window at the top from which one night we saw the Northern Lights; the tall chestnut trees; and the tragedy when a box kite caught on the top of one of them in a high wind. I remember a particular plum tree in the garden – great round soft yellow plums. And I remember family prayers in the dining room every morning and the quiet, awe-inspiring voice of my grandmother whom I regarded as very old reading from a large Bible.

When he was nine, Launcelot was sent off to boarding school – Stubbington House, near Fareham. He did not much enjoy it, but soon learned to adjust – it was a great help that Archie was already there. When he was Bishop of Portsmouth he some-times had to drive past Stubbingon, and he certainly showed no nostalgia for his old prep school, but neither did he give any suggestion that he had hated it. He went there in 1916, the middle of the Great War which cast its shadows over the school with rationing, black armbands when old boys were killed (no fewer than 258 of them), and most of the staff too old or physically unfit to serve in the forces. Most boys had fathers who were serving; Launcelot's own letters to his father, who was serving as a doctor in Salonika, show that anxiety was never far away.

Two years after the war, in 1920 when he was fourteen, Launcelot went to Rugby. He was happier there than at Stubbington, but never shone either in work or at games. During one of his many prize-giving speeches after he had retired (it was at Bristol Cathedral School) he said:

> I have been warned that I mustn't say 'I never won a prize at school and look at me now'. Well, I *did* win a prize – a Form Prize not regarded as worthy of public presentation, but a prize all the same. Admittedly the form was near the bottom of the school and by virtue of longevity I had floated to the top, but this did not take away my pleasure. That this was the sole star in an otherwise empty firmament I attributed to being a late developer.

In reply to an invitation in 1968 to join the Old Rugbeian Committee as a 'Distinguished Old Rugbeian' he said he was 'glad that recognition has been given in this way to the one and only prize I have ever won, and to my elevation as Sergeant in the OTC'.

These self-deprecating accounts of an undistinguished school career are only slightly exaggerated. Why was Launcelot so undistinguished at Rugby? During his first year it was probably because he was rather small, and not much good at the games which would have conferred prestige and popularity. Then during his second year, just when one would have expected his less obvious personal qualities to enable him to blossom, he went down with a bad case of scarlet fever. The illness took its toll; it left him permanently unable to sweat on one side of his body (which would divert him from tropical to polar exploration) and probably caused the mysterious weakness that some forty-five years later left his legs semi-paralysed. He missed a complete term, and never fully caught up during the rest of his time at Rugby. Paradoxically, from an academic point of view that turned out to his advantage; in the 1920s the brightest pupils were invariably channelled into the Classical Sixth, and Launcelot was eternally grateful that because he was not in the top flight academically he was allowed to do sixth-form science so that after he left Rugby in 1925 he was able to go to Cambridge to read Natural Sciences.

The reason why Trinity Hall was the college chosen for Launcelot was that a friend of his parents, B. K. Cunningham, the Principal of Westcott House, suggested it on the grounds that the Hall was a small college which, thanks largely to having a pastorally minded Dean in George Chase (later Bishop of Ripon), was a very friendly one. Launcelot's diffidence might have made him feel lost in a larger college, and Trinity Hall was an inspired choice. The *History of the Trinity Hall Boat Club 1928–49* tells how

> Launcelot came to the Hall in 1925, ignorant of rowing, a poor athlete and a fair scholar, pale and determined. He was fortunate to come in a vintage year and to have had the background to know the meaning of the term. He began to row, got his oar in his second term in the Third Lent Boat, and rowed with the Second May Boat at Cambridge and at Henley . . . he usually rowed Bow, and never said it was the hardest place in the Boat in which to row. . . . He enjoyed rowing as a game and as a means to companionship. He was as influential as an undergraduate as he later was as a Fellow. Everyone knew Launcelot; everyone loved Launcelot.

The Boat Club played a large part in Launcelot's development. In other sports you have to be reasonably proficient to represent your College, but in rowing each Boat, be it the First Boat or the Fifth Boat, is a College Boat. The Boat Club's *esprit de corps*, its complete acceptance of a new member regardless of whether he had rowed for his school at Henley or had never touched an oar before, gave Launcelot the assurance that he had lacked at school so that his innate friendliness, openness and engaging sense of humour came out, and he blossomed and flourished like a stunted shrub that has been transplanted into more congenial soil.

By this time Innerhadden, a house near Kinloch Rannoch in Perthshire, had become the family home. The game book shows that Innerhadden was a fine sporting estate, and with Bob in Australia (having gone there with his second wife and bought a sheep station that unluckily failed during an exceptional drought) and with Archie away in the Navy, Launcelot could freely invite friends to shoot. He eventually gave up shooting when he presented a brace of grouse to the clergyman who was doing holiday duty at Kinloch Rannoch, and saw his look of horror at the thought that his bishop should have shot them.*
But he loved the Highlands, just as he loved Trinity Hall, to the end of his life; until he could no longer manage it physically, his great delight on holiday was to take long walks in the hills.

It took him some time to get into his stride academically at Cambridge. In Part One of the Natural Sciences Tripos he only got a good second-class degree, but he had shown enough promise for his tutor to encourage him to stay on for a fourth year to read geology. By the end of his third year there was even talk of a possible Fellowship, and at the end of his fourth year he duly obtained a first in Part Two of the Tripos – having already been awarded a Commonwealth Scholarship to go to Yale.

---

* Launcelot had never shot except on holiday, unlike his predecessor at Norwich. It is told of Bishop Herbert that he was once given a loader at a shoot late in the season, who could not remember how to address him and was completely tongue-tied until a cock pheasant got up, when unable to contain himself he shouted 'Cock, your holiness, Cock.'

2

Yale and Ordination

There is obviously only one career possible for him – the
Church. He has the manners of a gentleman, even when
speaking to a policeman.

(Felix Greene the film director, a Commonwealth Fellow
friend of Launcelot)

By the end of his third year at Trinity Hall, Launcelot had
become engrossed with geology and was beginning to wonder,
rather wistfully, if he might be able to stay on at Cambridge as
an academic. The Dean, George Chase, wrote to him in August
1928.

You write about plans for the future. At one time I know you
said you would like an academic life. . . . But even if you got
your First, geology is not a crowded subject and few Colleges
can afford to give a Fellowship for that alone. But if it could
be combined with another office it might be quite different.
Quite apart from that question, I have sometimes wondered
whether you would ever think of taking Orders. I believe you
are well fitted for it. If you were ordained, you might well get
the position of Dean, either here or elsewhere. Don't laugh –
or swear at me. I know it sounds as though I were suggesting
Ordination as a means to a Fellowship. That I am sure you
would despise, and so should I. But I do honestly think you
are fitted for it and could do really good work among undergraduates. And it is a possible way of combining pastoral
work with geology in a way that is hardly possible anyhow
else. . . . Think it over and, if you like, come and have a talk

about it next term. I know the way I have put it sounds like an ulterior motive; but I know you don't want to drop your geology so I thought I would suggest the two in combination.

In later years as a bishop, Launcelot would talk of 'casting a fly over' some priest he hoped to lure into his diocese; by that token George Chase was no mean fly-fisherman. Launcelot's mother had always secretly nourished a hope that he might be ordained as two of her brothers and her father had been, but neither of her elder sons had shown any inclination for it, and Launcelot himself when he went up to Cambridge had no idea of becoming an ordinand. The unquestioning faith that he had learned at his mother's knee never entirely disappeared, but – to put it in his own words in a talk at Atlantic College in about 1980 – 'I seemed to have a lot of demolition to do – tearing down beliefs, or the forms that belief had taken, and trying to construct what I felt I could and did believe in.' The 'demolition' included a literal belief in the inerrancy of Scripture – the world being created in six days flat, or Jonah and the whale – that still largely held sway in the 1920s, and also the repressive Puritanism of his Edinburgh childhood – no games on Sundays, and a sense that anything enjoyable was likely to be sinful. Evangelical enthusiasm also put him off, as he admitted in a sermon just after the war in St Benet's Church Cambridge:

Have you been saved? That question was put to me on two occasions which are vivid in my mind. The first was during my first term as an undergraduate. I had asked a school friend to lunch. I did not suspect him of being religious and was therefore taken by surprise when in the middle of general conversation he asked if I was saved and followed this up by asking if he might then and there pray for this to happen. I gave an embarrassed assent. My own prayer was that none of the heartier members of the college might choose that moment to burst into my room, and to my intense relief my prayer was answered. . . . [The other occasion was in America when touring in the Rockies and] we were approaching a

sharp corner at a speed which made its successful negotiation
a matter of considerable doubt. On the face of a bare granite
rock were splashed in large white letters the words 'Have you
been saved?' I was alarmed lest the driver's consideration of
that question might lessen the chances of getting round the
corner – but we managed.

The reason why he abhorred evangelical enthusiasm of the
'Have-you-been-saved?' type was not that he had a low opinion
of born-again Christians, many of whom indeed he liked and
admired, but because their enthusiasm seemed to be bound
up with the literal interpretation of the Bible that he found
untenable.

Many of Launcelot's closest friends, clerical and lay, were
mystified as to why he was ordained. It was not that they felt his
Christianity deficient, but that he was utterly 'unchurchy' – it is
doubtful if he ever in his life read a single page of the *Church Times*
for pleasure. By the 1920s it had become rare for public school
boys to 'go into the church' – Dr Arnold would have been horrified
to see how few ordinands Rugby produced between the wars.
Felix Greene, quoted at the head of this chapter, was rare in
perceiving that Launcelot was 'very different' from his other
companions – 'delightful, gentle and kindly to a fault. I do not
believe that in all his life he ever thought hardly about anyone'.

The conviction that he ought to be ordained came to
Launcelot gradually. In his Atlantic College talk on 'Vocation'
he described how his 'religion went through a period of
reception'.

Many things seemed wrong about the Church; I questioned
everything; but this led to renewed belief in Christ. A friend
suggested that you would do most by trying to work for the
reform of the Church from inside, not from outside . . .

It was largely thanks to George Chase, and the worship and
preaching in the College Chapel under his direction, that
Launcelot came to realize that the scientific lessons taught by

geology were perfectly compatible with religious faith – Christianity made sense. As he told a group of sixth-form Norwich schoolboys in the early 1960s:

Almost by chance I chose Geology as my subject at Cambridge – a fascinating subject. The history of the world until human history began; it makes the countryside 'live' as you trace the effects of past changes in sea level, ice ages, volcanic eruptions, on the topography. There was nothing I could see in Geology at variance with Christian teaching; though this was not so for the freshman who gave up geology because its teaching conflicted with what he thought was Biblical belief that the world was made in seven days.

By the end of his time at Trinity Hall Launcelot had come to terms intellectually with the Christian faith, and the possibility of ordination was definitely in his mind, though he 'was a bit scared of it'. He welcomed the chance of going to America as a Commonwealth Fund Fellow 'chiefly because it gave me time to think'. With six others, who included Geoffrey Crowther, who later became editor of *The Economist*, and Eric Ashby, a future Master of Clare, Launcelot sailed from Greenock on 15 September 1929. The crossing to New York took ten days; they spent two days there and were invited to meet Edward Harkness, who had founded the Commonwealth Fund. Launcelot found Harkness a 'modest and delightful man', but felt it 'curious having a formal luncheon with nothing but iced water to swill it down with, and the absence of liquor made a considerable difference to the atmosphere of the meal'.

Once arrived at Yale, he decided to study glacial morphology. This had not been his original idea, but he was inspired by a lecture given by a dynamic young professor, Richard Foster Flint. He also felt drawn to the idea of geological exploration in remote parts of the world, and since one after-effect of his scarlet fever was the inability to sweat on one side of his body, he realized that he would have to explore ice-bound polar regions rather than the burning deserts of Arabia. His eventual thesis, on the glacial geomorphology of Long Island Sound, was considered very creditable at the time, although subsequent work with improved methods modified its conclusions.

Commonwealth Fellows were encouraged to see as much of America as possible, and the Fund helped towards the expenses of doing so. Launcelot bought a Model A Ford, which he used for his geological explorations and also for drives round the New England countryside, often with another Fellow, Jim Puxley, who remained a lifelong friend and recalled: 'While the rest of us expatriates were [moaning] because we weren't getting to know anybody, Launcelot somehow managed to pick up friends'. A group of Commonwealth Fellows spent a Christmas vacation learning to ski in New Hampshire, and on another occasion toured in the Appalachians.

During the summer vacation of 1930 Launcelot joined a group of ten Yale students – seven British, two American, and one Japanese naval officer – who went in four cars on a long trip that took them right down to the Mexican border, and up through the Rockies (where he saw the alarming 'Have you been saved?' notice that he later used in a sermon). They took in the Grand Canyon, Los Angeles, Hollywood, San Francisco, and Yellowstone Park, returning via Chicago, Detroit (where they went round the Ford works) and Niagara. As well as seeing America, they met a wide cross-section of its people; it was for all of them a mind-broadening experience.

All the time, the question of possible ordination was at the back of his mind.

It was in my second year [in America] that I felt more definitely drawn to ordination. I liked the American people I met enormously, but one thing I didn't like about the American way of life was that there seemed too much emphasis on the dollar, and I think it was a reaction against this that led me to ordination.

There was at Yale a good Episcopalian Chaplain, Grant Noble. Twelve years later the war brought a chance for Launcelot to preach in his church and attest that

Grant and Ruth Noble were such very good friends to me twelve years ago in Yale, and to preach from this pulpit has a special value to me inasmuch as your Rector played a bigger part than he probably realises in helping me sort out the perplexities of my mind and finding my calling.

George Chase also continued to keep in touch. It was partly because he was its Dean that B. K. Cunningham had suggested Trinity Hall as a suitable college for Launcelot; and Chase in his turn realized that Westcott House under 'B.K.' would be the best theological college for a hesitant potential ordinand like Launcelot. Since Launcelot's parents were friends of 'B.K.', who in concert with Chase steered him towards ordination and encouraged him to take the plunge, it can be said that it was indirectly through parental influence that Launcelot became a priest – as he told those Atlantic College students during his talk on Vocation, 'the Christian religion ran strongly in the family'. Launcelot knew that his parents would approve if he 'became a parson', but it would not be true to suppose that he did so *because* of their wishes. Although his mother was never reluctant to tell him what she thought he ought to do, she had the good sense (helped by her husband!) not to try herself to persuade him to take such an important step. Close observation of his relationship with his mother when he was Bishop of Portsmouth showed that whereas he almost always deferred to her wishes in small matters, he invariably resisted any pressure from her over matters of real importance.

So, the decision to be ordained was ultimately his own and no one else's; it is significant that he did not take it until he had put the Atlantic Ocean between himself and any blandishments from George Chase or B. K. Cuningham. Let this chapter end with words that Launcelot wrote, twenty-five years later, to a prospective ordinand:

You ask, 'Is the fact that I enjoy engineering a valid reason for reading it?' Most certainly Yes; and if Ordination should later seem the answer for your future job, I think you would find how extremely useful it was to have done a job like Engineering for your degree. This, perhaps, is a bit of auto-biography on my part, for I have certainly never regretted reading Science before going on to Theological College, thought it is true to say that when I was reading Science I had not the least idea that I would end up by being ordained.

3

Westcott House with
Northern Interludes

I am anxious that men ordained from this place, to whatever
school of thought they may belong, should above all else be
real in character and belief and worship.

*(Canon B. K. Cunningham on becoming Principal of
Westcott House)*

Bishop Westcott had founded a Clergy Training School in Cambridge in 1881. In 1919 Canon B. K. Cunningham became its
Principal, and under him Westcott House produced some very
fine priests. Critics complained that his anxiety to avoid producing stereotyped 'parsonical' clergymen, coupled with his conviction that the great glory of the Church of England was its
comprehensiveness, could result in Westcott men being woolly
in their theology and belief – gentlemen in holy orders rather
than a professional priesthood. There was some justice in this
criticism; 'B.K.' certainly did not hold with the Catholic idea of
'formation' of clergy, and too much emphasis on individuality
can obviously have drawbacks. Nonetheless, clergy who think
for themselves are as a rule more effective than regimented
clones – and certainly, any accusations of snobbery were wide
of the mark, for 'B.K.' was far too big a man for that.

When his two years at Yale were over, Launcelot had hankered after a few more months' travel before going to theological
college, and he 'had a very nice letter from B. K. saying he could
take me in January 1932. . . . He advised staying in one country
such as India for two or three months rather than travelling.'

But in the end Launcelot felt he had been abroad long enough, and he went to Wescott in October 1931 though he was still not sure about his vocation, and stipulated that acceptance of a place did not necessarily commit him to ordination. 'B.K.' was very wise; he gave Launcelot plenty of rein where others might have told him what he must do. (In later years Launcelot would seldom say 'You ought to do this' but would point out the pros and cons so as to help people work out the answer for themselves; perhaps he learned this technique from B. K. Cunningham.)

The normal course at theological colleges then was one year, but it was agreed that Launcelot should spend two years since he had not read theology at university and, unlike most ordinands, had not done sixth-form classics so that his Greek (necessary for any serious study of the New Testament) was rudimentary. Westcott House was near the middle of Cambridge, in Jesus Lane, so its students could attend university lectures and learn theology from first-class scholars such as Hoskyns and Burkitt. Launcelot never paraded his knowledge of theology, but in fact knew more than some who claimed to be theologians – his approachability and great gift for friendship often obscured the fact that he possessed a first-class academic mind. George Chase evidently felt confident that Trinity Hall would give him a Fellowship, combining the work of Chaplain with tutoring in geology. He had written in October 1930 to say:

I feel that at the back of your mind is the feeling that such a job would be too pleasant. . . . I believe on the other hand that that is clear guidance that it is the sort of job God wants you to do. For it is not a selfish job but a real bit of service. [quoted in Lindsay, *Friends for Life*, pp. 51–2].

Chase was not simply using a Fellowship as a lure to persuade Launcelot to be ordained; he really wanted him to come to the Hall as Chaplain.

Living in Cambridge at a theological college meant that

Launcelot felt pulled in two directions. Despite Chase's assurance that being ordained to a Fellowship rather than to a parish would not be an easy or non-sacrificial option, he found it difficult to reconcile his preparation for life as a priest, with its framework of prayer and worship, with coaching Hall boats on the river and enjoying dining rights in the College. The fact that he *did* feel uncomfortable shows that he took his vocation to the priesthood seriously, and did not suppose that the office and work of a priest consisted simply in being a 'gentleman in holy orders'. His ministry might, however, have run along very conventional lines – clerical don, leading perhaps to a public school headmastership or some senior ecclesiastical post – but for a chance encounter that led to an adventure that on the face of it side-tracked him from his vocation but in fact led to his fulfilling it far more richly. He described it all much later in a lecture light-heartedly entitled 'How I Went Astray'.

Early in the May term of 1932 V. E. Fuchs, a geologist of St John's College, stopped me in Sidney Street and said that a small expedition was planning to go to Iceland and they wanted a geologist. I was at Westcott House at the time but I was not keeping a long vac. term so it really seemed an interesting way of spending the summer vacation.

However I naturally wanted to gain the approval of my Principal, B. K. Cunningham. His interest and enthusiastic support did not at the time surprise me in the least, but looking back on it I've often wondered how many ecclesiastics would have taken the same line. I believe his reaction was symptomatic of his genius in the training of young men for the ordained ministry. It was certainly symptomatic of his anxiety to safeguard ordinands from the danger of becoming professionally separated off and departmentalised.

We sailed in a trawler from Hull. The voyage took five days. It was very rough. A really nauseating smell from the barrels in which the fishes' livers of the previous catch had been stored aggravated seasickness. But we enjoyed the skipper and ship's company of the *Lord Balfour of Burleigh* and

I think they enjoyed having us. A couple of lads in immaculate suits who took passage with us were even more seasick than we were. The skipper told us they were 'pleasurers', which seemed an exiguous description.

I remember our landfall as we approached the Iceland coast; wild black mountains half veiled by mist; and how they represented the beginning of an adventure of a completely novel kind for every member of the party. We had a tremendous amount of gear; an experimental seismograph which was a horrid awkward bulky affair; explosives; all our fuel. We had sledges, and a tent, and camping equipment. At Hohn we were met by the Icelander who was to guide us to the edge of the [Vatnajokull] ice cap. He collected a whole train of ponies. First we had to travel west thirty miles or so across the plains between the mountains and the coast, and this meant crossing innumerable rivers carrying the melt water from the glaciers, [over which] local farmers would guide us, for there was no pathway and the quicksands were constantly changing. The level at which your pony swam seemed an important factor in your choice of steed; a good many swam at a level at which the water flowed directly into your thigh-boots.

Once at the edge of the ice cap the guides and ponies left us and we were for the first time alone on a venture which we liked to think had some of the character of a polar expedition. We had sledges, man-hauling harnesses, cold weather clothing and food; and we were visiting little known territory. But we had not thought of polar exploration in terms of rain. Torrential rain started the evening we pitched camp and lasted five days, soaking all our equipment, and by the time the rain stopped the snow surface all round our tents had dropped a couple of feet.

Launcelot's diary, written in pencil at the time, adds that the seismograph broke down at this point: 'June 30. Worse luck, the seismograph was found to be unmendable. . . . It was a terrible blow, especially to Brian [Roberts] who had taken every precaution with [its] handling . . . We were all very fed up that evening.' But fifty years later, he added: 'The seismograph was heavy. Having lugged it to the edge of the ice-cap – it didn't work. So we fired the gelignite in one big bang. We took a seismograph later to Spitzbergen. It didn't work there either.'

Vatnajokull is about the size of Yorkshire. We sledged across, spent some days mapping and geologising and botanising on the northern edge, and returned by the same route to pick up the seismograph. We enjoyed it all immensely, not least because we got on very well together and everyone had some particular responsibility in the scientific and survey side of the expedition's programme. We were divided into two three-man sledge teams each pulling a Nansen sledge loaded with 1000 lbs of gear. For most of the time we were on skis, which on an uphill grade had to be fitted with skins to get a grip. Man-hauling is very hard work and is apt to make one mule-minded – with a sullen suspicion that you are the only member of your team who is really doing any work, until you discover that the others have exactly the same idea. The main constituent of our sledge rations was Pemmican. It is advertised on the tin as a meat extract rich in albumen, meat fibre and animal fat – which is exactly what it tastes like. You take it like a soup and it is more palatable with pea flour added. A plate full after pitching camp gives you the impression you've had a five course dinner; the great thing is to go to sleep before you discover you haven't – because sledge-rations are deficient in solid food and though one gets plenty of energy and vitamins, it is chiefly conveyed as liquid and the result is that one's inside is astonishingly empty.

When we got back to Hohn we learned that the trawler company were unable to fetch us back. This was a serious blow. But our guide's father was a Member of Parliament, and when he learned the news he said very helpfully 'I will telephone the Prime Minister'. Now, in Iceland all the telephones were on a party line; he who speaks loudest gets through. Thorliefson was an accomplished telephonist. He blew everyone else off the line, and presently announced that the Icelandic Navy couldn't help because a third of it was off the North Coast, a third in dock, and the other third – they didn't know where it was. Eventually we managed to hire a motor boat. The crew of four kissed the entire populace of Hohn before we set off – an ominous sign. We left in sunshine setting course for the Westermann Islands. At about 4 o'clock the skipper, who appeared to be alarmist by temperament, pointed to the horizon and said 'Storm'; and storm it jolly well was. The entire night there was a vicious wind and we were uncomfortably close to a lee shore. I passed through those two stages of seasickness – first of fearing that you are going to die and then of fearing that you won't. At dawn, the skipper was obviously lost; we followed in the wake of a trawler, but as trawlers trawl in a circle that didn't get us anywhere. Eventually one of our own party sighted the Westermann Islands. We sailed home in the mail steamer to Leith, which was the only prosaic part of the trip.

The haunting beauty of that Icelandic ice-cap made a lasting impression on Launcelot: 'the colours of the sky were unlike any I have seen elsewhere, and as the sun rose parts of the ice cap glowed with a rose colour while in the South the horizon was a deep indigo shade'. When there was a chance the following year to go on a similar expedition, he found it irresistible, even though it involved spending the weeks immediately before being made Deacon preparing equipment for sledging rather than preparing for ordination! A week after the Bishop of Ely ordained him, the expedition set off, as Launcelot described in 'How I Went Astray':

Iceland had given me an appetite for exploration; and another chance came the very next summer. I was ordained Deacon in Ely Cathedral on Trinity Sunday 1933, and sailed a week later to Spitzbergen – again with the approval and backing of B.K. [Cunningham]. This time it was an Oxford University Exploration Club expedition, but in fact half the party were

Cambridge. It was a more ambitious affair than the Iceland trip; we were about 25 strong and on reaching Spitzbergen we divided into five parties each engaged on a separate piece of research. The party of which I was a member [he led one of the two sledge teams] was landed at the Northern tip of Spitzbergen, just on the 80th parallel, and we sledged down the centre of the New Friesland ice cap and then, skirting the Stubendorff Mountain, arrived at the expedition's base hut at the end of the Ice Fjord. We again had a seismograph which wouldn't work, and again we travelled on skis man-hauling our sledges. We arrived home not long before term began, and I returned to Trinity Hall as Chaplain.

Launcelot had to procure everything that a four-man sledge party would need – fuel, tents, rations, sledges and sledge harness, compasses, etc. – and borrow items of scientific equipment from various university departments. When one reads the letters he wrote from Westcott House just before his ordination retreat and from Trinity Hall just afterwards, it seems extraordinary that the Principal of any theological college would have allowed, let along encouraged, such a distraction at such a time. But 'B.K.' can be seen with hindsight to have been right. Iceland was basically a holiday adventure; this expedition was a more serious affair. Its aim was to explore the largely unknown New Friesland ice-cap in the north of Spitzbergen – closer to a Pole than the British Graham Land Expedition was ever to get. It gave Launcelot much valuable experience that was useful not only in the field of polar exploration.

The leader was to have been James Martin, but at the last minute it became evident that he would not recover in time from frostbite contracted on a previous expedition, and A. R. (later Sir Alexander) Glen was appointed leader in his place. Glen was a good choice, but having to take over some two dozen men whom he had not chosen himself, and some of whom he did not know very well, made it much harder to weld them together as a harmonious team than had been the case with Brian Robert's much smaller Iceland expedition. On the voyage out, by mail boat to Tromso and then on a Norwegian seal boat (with a draught designed to withstand pack-ice, so that it rolled horribly), some of the more 'Hooray-Henry' members of the expedition took pot shots at gulls in the rigging until seasickness drove them below, and there is some evidence that not all the subsequent scientific observations were carried out accurately – as someone said in another context, 'If you find counting birds on rocks gets too boring, you can always make a good guess at their numbers.'

The two sledge parties, however, were landed not at the base hut but round on the north of the island, and were not botanists or zoologists but geologists and geographers. Launcelot's sledge team consisted of J. M. Edmonds, an Oxford research geologist, Carrington Smith, a Royal Engineer officer and Ordnance Survey expert, and A. S. Irvine whose brother had died on Everest with Mallory. As soon as they were put ashore at Treurenberg Bay they realized that they had been wildly over-optimistic in estimating the load that could be man-hauled on a sledge under the conditions they found. The July sun melted the surface snow, and before reaching the ice-cap they had to make the steep ascent of the Duner Glacier. Launcelot and the other team leader therefore set out (with Carrington Smith) hauling a load of some 1000 lbs (on two sledges lashed together, one in front of the other), to establish a food and fuel depot above the base hut where they were due to end up, leaving the rest of the sledge party to follow more slowly doing scientific work as they went.

Both sledge teams had a tougher and more hazardous time of it than 'How I Went Astray' suggests. The warm July sun made the snow so heavy that as they ascended the Duner glacier they could only manage one hundred yards in an hour, so they decided to travel by night and rest by day. 'The first two hours sledging went quickly enough,' wrote Launcelot, 'but at the end of each day, when the heavy loads began to tell, the last half hour dragged out into an eternity of effort', and they almost fell asleep over their supper (Launcelot did once doze off while smoking his pipe, and awoke with a start when he felt his shirt burning).

They established a depot above the Lomme Bay glacier (which led down to the base hut) by 22 July, and went back to rejoin the other sledge party. But this took longer than expected; sunshine had been followed by thick fog and snow which made the surface too soft for the sledge, and it was a full week before they were able to rejoin the others, who had managed to relay some 2500 lbs of food and equipment to an advanced base eight miles up the Duner Glacier. At last, on 30 July, Launcelot and his sledge team could start their original task, and set off to explore the ice-cap.

The next forty days taught Launcelot how vital it was for any polar expedition to allow good safety margins. For the first few days of August they were completely shut in by fog; they could not even look for rocks to geologize as swirling fog made it easy to lose any sense of direction while drifting snow quickly obliterated their tracks. When the fog lifted on 5 August, Smith and Irvine set out for an observation point with their surveying equipment, while Launcelot and Edmonds became so engrossed in finding rocks to geologize that they travelled seven miles from their tent before they realized that a storm was brewing and their tracks had been obliterated. More than once in the swirling, disorientating snow flurries they found they had gone round in a circle, and Launcelot was put in mind of Piglet's alarm when in A. A. Milne's *Winnie the Pooh* he mistook his companion's footprints for those of some large and alarming creature ('Where the Woozle Wasn't').

It took them five hours to regain their camp, and for the next two days the weather marooned them in their tent, anxiously hoping that Smith and Irvine would find them. Luckily they had brought reading matter (including Doughty's *Arabia Deserta* 'which Edmonds had brought as an antidote to the cold'), and to their great relief the survey party got back to the camp on 8 August. When two days later the weather relented and they could move on, it took them seven hours to disinter their stores and equipment that had been buried in snow.

They spent the next fortnight on the high ice, surveying and geologizing when the weather was fine and sledging when the visibility was bad. They had to find their food depot before the rations they were carrying ran out on 21 August. They were lucky; after three days of thick fog when they could not find the cairn they had made to mark the depot, the weather cleared just in time and all was well. All that remained was for them to sledge downhill to the base through the mountains and glaciers of Garwood Land, and on 10 September they reached it and found 'roast pheasant, letters, the weekly *Times* and dance music from Daventry'.

In 'How I Went Astray' it all sounds so simple, but in reality the descent was difficult and dangerous. One of those who went to Spitzbergen wrote after Launcelot's death,

> The obituaries . . . all miss what I think about him, as a Lancashire lad . . . that is, he really had guts and courage both mental and physical. To go into the Church after doing Geology takes some courage [at a time when the intellectual climate among scientists was dismissive of Christianity]. And his efforts with us showed him to be physically full of guts. But he had one weakness that I knew to my cost; he was prone to seasickness. He had a bunk above me as we rolled from side to side for three days from Tromso to Icefjord – I will say no more!

One of Launcelot's sledge party said later that it was thanks to Launcelot's good leadership that they came down safely, without disappearing into a crevasse or falling off a precipice; and when in 1949 Sir Alexander Glen congratulated Launcelot on being made a bishop, he wrote that he 'had no doubt that you were cast for important duties. This I remember feeling so clearly as your party was coming down Ebba valley after crossing the ice-cap.' 'Leadership qualities' are highly desirable (and sometimes lacking!) in bishops and even in priests. Spitzbergen helped to equip Launcelot in many ways for his future ministry; 'B.K.' and George Chase had been right, and wise, to allow and even encourage him to join the expedition.

4

Voyage to Antarctica

There are men who carry with them a dimension, of whom
one is conscious that they have had a glimpse of wonder and
have been touched ineffaceably by it, have been humbled by it.

(Lord Runcie)

Launcelot was back at Trinity Hall for the Michaelmas Term
of 1933. He had been elected to a Fellowship a few days before
being made Deacon in June, and in later years liked pointing
out that he had been ordained to 'serve his title' not to a parish
but to a Fellowship. He felt it underlined the fact that Trinity
Hall was (like other older colleges, as their names suggest) a
religious foundation, even though by the 1930s it was unusual
for anyone to be ordained to a Fellowship.

But anachronistic or not, this was certainly not a sinecure.
There were less than three hundred undergraduates, but a chaplain had to get to know them all if he was to be effective. George
Chase as Dean had the responsibility of training Launcelot, just
as a vicar would have to train a new curate; and he was a very
good mentor. The Master, Professor Harry Roy Dean ('Daddy'
Dean as he was known to generations of Trinity Hall undergraduates), was also very supportive; he considered that the
Master of a College had a pastoral responsibility towards its
undergraduates and his concern for their welfare and development meant that he understood the point of having a college
chaplain. As well as undergraduates, there were a dozen or so
Fellows who with the Master constituted the governing body,
and a large staff – maintenance men, gyps (responsible for the
rooms on their staircase), porters, etc.; almost all of them were

long-service employees who took genuine pride in being part of the college. Just as a hospital chaplain must have a good rapport with doctors and nurses in order to minister effectively to patients, so too the same principle applies for a college chaplain. And in addition to all this, Launcelot was a supervisor in geology and had to keep up his academic work in that field.

The secret of his success was that getting to know people was for him not a means to an end (as in 'a good officer must know his men') but something he *wanted* to do. Because he saw everyone as a potential friend, that was usually what they became; he would have cared about people at the Hall even if he had no pastoral responsibility towards them. He kept up with hundreds of Hall men long after they had gone down, as he did too with Langley, his old gyp, and his family. Most of the Fellows also became lifelong friends, and he started with the advantage of having already got to know them thanks to having enjoyed dining rights while at Westcott House. And he was devoted to the Master – he almost seems to have thought of him as a second father, and 'Daddy' Dean was for his part almost paternal towards Launcelot.

Not surprisingly, his Icelandic and Spitzbergen experiences gave the new chaplain a certain glamour among undergraduates fresh from (mainly public) school which helped him in his work. It was not therefore very surprising that when (as Launcelot recounted)

> John Rymill the leader of the British Graham Land Expedition visited my rooms and asked if I could go with him as Chaplain and Geologist, at first I thought the answer must be no; but on discussing it with the Master and Dean, and with B.K., and after further reflection about it myself, the college gave me leave of absence and I accepted.

The primary aim of the expedition was to explore the virtually unknown coastline of the south polar region lying south of Cape Horn, known as the Falkland Islands Dependency. Graham

Land, now known as the Antarctic Peninsula, was then thought to be an island while Alexander Island to its west was then thought to form part of the Antarctic continent. The expedition had been planned by Gino Watkins, but after his death in a kayak accident in Greenland John Rymill, who had been with Watkins in Greenland, took over the project.

The plan was to leave England in August 1934 so as to arrive in Graham Land by the beginning of the Antarctic spring – i.e. the northern hemisphere autumn – establish a base and spend the (Antarctic) summer surveying, geologizing and botanizing. The expedition would then spend the winter (i.e. April–October 1935) at the base writing up their field work and doing maintenance work, ready to set off on their main journeys of exploration in the (Antarctic) spring, returning to the base to re-embark in March 1936, before the sea froze, having been away for rather less than two years. That was the plan.

The British Graham Land Expedition was the last truly amateur polar expedition from these shores. It was sponsored by the Royal Geographical Society, and the Colonial Office gave some financial support. The Royal Navy seconded two Lieutenants, E. H. M. Millett as Chief Engineer and R. E. D. Ryder as Master of their ship, while Ryder's brother Lieut. L. C. D. Ryder and Lieut. I. F. Meiklejohn were seconded from the Army to act as Second Mate and wireless operator respectively, and the Admiralty also seconded Surgeon Lieutenant-Commander Ted Bingham to be the medical officer. Even so, most of the money required for the expedition had to be raised or contributed by its members themselves; consequently, it was done on a shoe-string.

John Rymill bought a three-masted topsail schooner, 192 foot long overall with a beam of 24 foot, which had originally been built in 1908 as a Breton fishing vessel, and after a spell as a training ship had been fitted out as a private yacht. Rymill re-christened her *Penola* after his Australian farmstead, and had her strengthened to withstand ice. A wooden ship was obviously less strong than a steel-hulled one, but it was believed that pressure from pack-ice would squeeze a wooden ship upwards where a heavier steel ship would simply be crushed.

The voyage out in *Penola* was more hazardous than most of the amateur crew realized at the time. Much later, Robert Ryder wrote:

> I was a keen young naval officer chosen out of some 200 applicants. What I found was an expedition crew composed mostly of university graduates. Most charming and delightful they were but to them the very idea of any discipline was anathema. On previous expeditions they had merely contracted some Norwegian sealer or other vessel to put them ashore and to re-embark them at a certain date. So none of them had any real experience or indeed understanding of ships and the problems surrounding them. We had a very rotten, defective and unhandy ship. This at once became apparent on our way from Southampton to St Katherine's Dock. It was a sobering experience and I felt that if we were to avoid disaster it would require the utmost vigilance and efficiency in all matters of seamanship. . . . As against all this, the expedition members who were to crew the ship approached the task as if it were in the nature of an enterprising yachting trip.

Ryder was not by nature timorous or alarmist – he did after all win a VC at St Nazaire – and was not exaggerating the danger.

However, as Rymill explained when giving an account of the Expedition to the Royal Geographical Society, 'As it was a question of taking an amateur crew or not going to the Antarctic at all, there was no alternative'; and few doubts or fears assailed *Penola*'s crew. Colin Bertram wrote ecstatically (though admittedly years later and safely on dry land) of 'the hugeness and emptiness of the Southern Ocean with its giant swells, down which *Penola* made her way at four knots', making it sound as if sailing through the roughest seas in the world with engines out of action was indeed just 'an enterprising yachting trip'. Ryder did have a professional Chief Officer (First Mate) on whom he could rely:

James Martin had been both to the Antarctic and the Arctic – far more experienced than I, but lacked any navigational or pilotage ability. . . . With his unfailing loyalty and good humour and with his wide ranging experience he was a tremendous asset and I don't think he ever really received his due. James in fact joined me on the outbreak of war in my Q ship and was sadly lost when we were sunk.

In addition, Ryder's soldier brother who was also on board was a keen yachtsman, and at least one of the expedition members, Verner Carse, was a very experienced sailor.

Launcelot described the voyage in 'How I Went Astray':

This was the first major Antarctic expedition to leave these shores since Scott's last expedition which had sailed in 1911 [Shackleton's expedition in fact sailed for Antarctica in 1914 but never reached the mainland]. The voyage out was an unusual experience because . . . the members of the party were the crew. It was less expensive that way. We had one paid hand – a cook. He was a nice chap but our leader when he interviewed him forgot to put the leading question as to whether he could cook. Only a minority of our party knew which rope to pull and this made the task of the Captain and two mates doubly anxious.

We ran into bad weather five days out when we got into the bay of Biscay. One incident will illustrate the kind of problem which faced our officers. The storm gathered force at night, and we had to shorten sail with all hands on deck. I was given a rope by the second mate. When he said to let go I paid out the rope round the belaying pin. He got a bit agitated and shouted Let go; so I took the rope off the pin and let it go. Up shot the rope into the inky skies and down came the top yard on the cross trees with an almighty crash. It then transpired that one of my shipmates was somewhere aloft in the vicinity of that yard . . . when he got back on deck he said a lot of things which were not at all proper for a parson to hear. . . . The sailor's terminology, however, often

lacks clarity; 'Vast heaving'; well, the first time we got that
order we gave a vast heave, and felt a bit hurt by the Mate's
pitying smile.

However, we got the way of it; 68 days to Montevideo;
about 20 more to Port Stanley the capital of the Falklands,
and another 16 or so to Graham Land; working watch to
watch. It was a good way to get our party settled down, and
once we were into the fair weather of the Trade Winds belt
it was most enjoyable for all of us except for one of our party
who was sick every day from England to Montevideo. The
Mate [James Martin], who was not a beastly man, took the
view that seasickness was caused by the imagination so always
sent him aloft when he was ill. We resented this as much as
he did; it was not the more obvious danger of his position
relative to our own, but the fact that he invariably used to
shed a marline spike or a knife as a sign that all was not well
with him. He was much better after Montevideo.

Launcelot felt a particular responsibility for the seasick victim;
Norman Gurney was a Trinity Hall undergraduate who had
been keen to come, and Launcelot had encouraged him. Gurney
did not really enjoy the experience; being younger and less academically qualified than the others made it hard for him to fit
in, and meant he had to do less of the interesting work and
more of the chores. Launcelot was very aware of this and did
what he could to make life happier, and it made him critical of
the over-strict (as he saw it) naval discipline imposed by Ryder.
He particularly disliked the way that Martin, as a professional
seaman, worked on the theory 'that fear is the dominant motive
in making people work. He has always dealt with people of less
intelligence than himself, and he has been trying to treat us (at
least afloat) in the way he treated them'. Launcelot quoted with
approval the words of one of those who saw the expedition off
from London: 'Canon Marshall, ex-naval commander, was most
explicit that he would rather have a crew of educated men,
whose heart was in it, even if amateurs, than ordinary sailors.
He says that one week will teach them everything.' Bob Ryder,

who knew he was 'responsible as master for the safety of the ship and those on board', was less insouciant, though looking back fifty years later he admitted that his impatience with colleagues who could not appreciate his difficulties could 'no doubt be attributed to the intolerance of youth':

It was my first contact with university graduates as working partners and it clearly came as a disappointment. It was of course a vintage which nurtured Philby, Maclean and Burgess and at a time when the Oxford Union voted against fighting for King and Country – coming as I did straight from Submarines I felt the difference.

I wish to add that since those days certainly three of those whom I so readily criticised have become friends of long standing whom I much admire. Launcelot Fleming (The Bish) is a valued friend, my daughter's godfather and my son's sponsoring bishop [for ordination], Steve [Alfred Stephenson] is a very good friend, and Colin Bertram restored my self-confidence by asking me to command his ship [on a planned return trip that never took place because war intervened].

Launcelot did in fact appreciate the problems facing *Penola*'s captain; but he also appreciated the feelings of those who had joined the Expedition in order to carry out scientific research and not to work as unpaid crew members. A reconciler seldom escapes criticism from either side, but after the event the expedition members all gave Launcelot credit for keeping everyone remarkably harmonious despite great frustrations. There is no doubt that *Penola* was not up to the job, but Launcelot was worried by Ryder's critical report to the Royal Geographical Society (1 November 1937) after the Expedition had returned, as he felt that despite Ryder's disclaimer it could be taken as a criticism of John Rymill for buying the ship. Bob Ryder said:

I was asked to prepare a few words about *Penola*, but I am afraid that I find it somewhat difficult to say anything very complimentary about the old ship. As a sailing vessel she was

not a good performer, and motoring was not exactly her
strong suit either. . . . In commenting on the ship I in no way
wish to reflect on Mr Rymill's organisation, nor on the ability
of Mr Meek who most nobly helped and advised us while
fitting out. Many of the limitations and decisions were unavoid-
ably influenced by the financial considerations, and the arrangements had my entire approval when we left England. . . .
The fact that the *Penola*'s engines were able to complete the
entire voyage was little short of miraculous, and Lieutenant-
Commander Millet [chief engineer] certainly deserves a very
great deal of credit.

The President of the Royal Geographical Society seems to have
taken offence at Ryder's remarks (another reason why Launcelot,
who disliked confrontation, was worried by them), and said,
'Many uncomplimentary remarks have been passed on the *Penola*, but in spite of her weaknesses, in spite of the fact that she
was merely an old, semi-retired Breton fishing boat to start with,
she did 30,000 miles . . .' But Ryder had not exaggerated; though
only much later did Launcelot realize quite how unsuitable *Penola* was. Verner Carse told him in 1985:

Under power and with a clean bottom (no barnacles) the ship
could make 5½ knots in a flat calm. She couldn't beat to
windward; a head-wind stopped her dead. You made your
landfall by eye – it was there when you actually saw it and
not before (no radar); if you hadn't had an astronomical fix
in two or three days you had to be very circumspect in your
approach. There were several occasions in the totally un-
charted waters off the west coast of Graham Land when we
grounded and had to kedge off. Bilge-pumps and anchor-
capstan apart, it was all muscle-power; halyards, topping-lifts,
derrick-winches, working the cargo, etc.

Carse did also reveal that *Penola* went aground on nine
occasions, though most of the crew were only aware of two of
them. On one occasion they managed to kedge her off an ice-

shelf just in time before the iceberg calved (i.e. part of it split off) so that several hundred tons of ice crashed down on the spot where they had been half an hour earlier.

The reason for dwelling on the shortcomings of *Penola* is that they explain the frustrating delay in establishing a southern base, and why the Expedition returned to England a year later than had been planned. Against that background of frustration it must have been difficult to avoid friction between ship's party and shore party, and keep everyone in good heart and on good terms with one another when it became difficult to reconcile the conflicting needs of scientific field work on the one hand and exploration and survey on the other. There were inevitable tensions and irritations, but the fact that there were no real breakdowns in personal relations even though things did not go according to plan was very largely due to Launcelot's influence. His role of chaplain on that polar expedition was as valuable as that of geologist.

5

Chaplain in Antarctica

His Grace is very glad to know that you are going with the
Expedition as Chaplain – a thing which, so far as he knows,
has never happened before in any previous expedition. He
sends his blessing on the Expedition.

(Letter from the Archbishop of Canterbury's chaplain)

Launcelot had been ordained priest on Trinity Sunday, 27 May
1934, having served his year's apprenticeship, as it were, as a
deacon. Not surprisingly, he stipulated that he could only join
John Rymill's expedition if he went as Chaplain as well as geologist. He started as he meant to go on; before *Penola* sailed
from St Katherine's Dock he arranged for a service of blessing
to take place on board, which was conducted by the Bishop of
Gibraltar whose diocese was held to include any part of the
world not covered by any other Anglican bishop (Launcelot had
tried the Archbishop first – he always believed in going to
the top). How much Bob Ryder appreciated having *Penola*'s
deck taken over by assorted clergy – including Launcelot's uncle
Prebendary Holland – and a congregation of friends, relations
and other well-wishers while he was trying to stow stores and
equipment and carry out last-minute checks, we shall not know
until his Polar Diary is opened for inspection in ten years' time;
but in general Ryder was supportive. Much later Launcelot
described how he set about his somewhat unusual chaplaincy.

Among the personal factors which the [Expedition] party was
obliged to accept was the presence of a chaplain, and I was
naturally a little anxious as to how they would take it,

although I knew some of the party personally before we sailed. So far as Church services went we had a Communion Service on Sundays and saints' days before breakfast, and on Sunday evenings a service which was followed by a glass of sherry or port, and then by supper. The post mortem of the sermon often lasted far into the night. The apparent responsiveness to religion on the part of the members of the party did not necessarily bear any obvious relationship to the labels by which they preferred to define their position in these matters. Two of the most regular and receptive members of the congregation declared themselves to be scientific agnostics; after three years I almost persuaded one of them that the definition he gave himself was not entirely accurate.

After Launcelot's death a Trinity Hall colleague who knew him well for over forty years remarked that he had never heard Launcelot say anything that was nonsense. Anyone regularly exposed to ecclesiastical dignitaries, or politicians, will recognize that as a rare accolade; probably those post-mortems on his sermons were a good training. Some of them are in fact more compelling than some of those that he preached when a bishop. This was partly because the inspiring majesty and awe of the Southern Ocean and Antarctica meant that, as the Psalmist put it, he 'saw the works of the Lord and his wonders in the deep'; partly because he had more time to prepare; but largely because he knew that he would have to defend what he said to friendly but critical colleagues afterwards. Also, his later sermons were almost invariably read aloud before being preached, either to his chaplain or anyone else who was handy – often, at Portsmouth, it was Mrs Nex the superb Scottish cook – after which, whether criticized or not, there were scratchings-out and alterations which could blunt the message. A chaplain once had to point out that 'God, and all that that term implies' was not a very inspiring phrase when coming from a bishop preaching in a parish church – but of course it would have been appropriate when trying to convey the meaning of 'Creator' to a group of largely agnostic scientists in a base hut in Antarctica. Launcelot's preaching carried conviction not through oratory but because his hearers could sense that here was an intelligent man saying what he sincerely believed, and being scrupulously honest in not making claims that he did not think could be substantiated.

Making *Penola* seaworthy for an Atlantic crossing had taken longer than expected and the expedition did not sail from England until 10 September. The voyage across the Atlantic to Montevideo and thence down to Port Stanley was desperately slow, with *Penola* travelling at what on dry land would literally have been a walking pace; from London to Montevideo took sixty-eight days, and from Montevideo to Port Stanley took another twenty days. Services were held regularly on board; Norman Gurney told Launcelot's mother that 'when it is fine we have Matins or sometimes Evensong on deck and it occasionally rains during the sermon, then we scuttle below and finish the service in the saloon'. One of the party, Quintin Riley, a meteorologist, was a devout Anglo-Catholic whose father Athelstan Riley had presented the expedition with copies of the *English Hymnal*; Quintin accompanied the singing on a piano accordion, and Launcelot recalled that 'the speed at which he played would have put even the slowest Presbyterian organist to shame'.

It was not until December that they reached Port Stanley, where three more of their party were waiting with the sledge-dogs they had collected from Greenland and Labrador, together with the bulk of the expedition's stores. Hampton and (Surgeon Lieutenant-Commander) 'Doc' Bingham embarked on *Discovery II*, which had been lent to carry the dogs and most of the expedition's stores – including the Tiger Fox aeroplane – to Port Lockroy, a harbour at the north of Graham Land used in summer by whalers. Launcelot stayed at the Deanery at Port Stanley, and was twice asked to preach in the Cathedral. Both sermons are here very much abbreviated, but their gist is clear. First, an Advent sermon on the kingdom of God ('Stanley Cathedral Dec. 16 1934 Evensong'):

Matthew 18: 3 'Verily I say unto you, except ye be converted and become as little children, ye shall in no wise enter the Kingdom of Heaven'.

The Kingdom of God was the phrase Christ used for the Gospel of good news which he laboured incessantly to make real to those among whom He lived. If they were to be true to their own selves they must not only *see* the Kingdom of God; they must also *be* it. Our acceptance of it is what brings peace of mind, purpose, true happiness; our refusal is what brings bewilderment, misery and discontent. And if we are to accept the Kingdom of God, we must recapture some quality which as children we enjoyed and which in growing up we lost. That quality is not childishness or ignorance, but humility.... Pride and self-sufficiency continually make us refuse to be aware of God; to pride yourself on your intelligence makes you refuse the effort to understand by which alone you can become intelligent; to pride yourself on your own goodness makes you unwilling to see and understand all that is highest.

What is it that keeps a child humble? Aristotle calls wonder the beginning of wisdom; and so long as we exercise this quickening sense of wonder there is hope for us.... Ordinarily we walk as in a narrow valley between steep hillsides, with our view limited by the barriers put up by our pride and self-sufficiency. What we need is to become like little children, full of the spirit of adventure and with new eagerness to climb out of the valley. And as we climb we see the opening out of a wider view of God's creation and His purpose than formerly we ever believed to exist.

On Christmas Day his sermon was again thoughtful, eschewing such anecdotes as 'When a storm blew up and we wondered if our ship would founder' which many preachers fresh from his adventurous voyage might have used to pad out a thin sermon. Launcelot always took the trouble to prepare a sermon properly (which was why, as a bishop, he preached less frequently than some people wanted him to). In his previous sermon his own sense of awe at 'the wonderful works of God' in nature comes through; his Christmas sermon reveals the powerful impression made on him by the example and self-sacrifice of Christ.

'And the shepherds said one to another "Let us go even unto Bethlehem and see this thing which is come to pass".' The shepherds were not content simply to listen to what had been told them; they must go and see. There is no substitute for first-hand religion; if we would find and serve God we must travel not as tourists in a bus but as mountaineers . . .

Christ's words have the ring of eternity; 'heaven and earth shall pass away'. And to add to this you have the compelling authority of his life; for once, a man who practised as he preached. No man lived as this man; if his words are inspiring, his life is compelling and carries full conviction. . . . He has revolutionised the world, for he has raised our values to a different and higher plane. Without him, you see Nature red in tooth and claw and man with his philosophy of the struggle for existence – devil take the hindermost. On the other, you see a child born in a manger and a man who was crucified for others on a Cross. That is why we keep Christmas Day as a day of joy; for like the shepherds we go and see, and so doing we begin to learn that at Bethlehem God stooped to men that men might be divine.

On 31 December *Penola* was sufficiently recovered from her Atlantic crossing to continue her voyage to the south, but alas it was a false start. In Rymill's own words (at the Royal Geographical Society's evening meeting, 1 November 1937):

On the first night at sea we had a serious misfortune which was to alter the whole course of the expedition . . . we met stormy weather with a heavy sea, and Millett discovered that the engines were running out of line. We immediately turned back to investigate the trouble, and on reaching harbour under sail alone Millett found that it had been caused by the engine beds, which had been made of unseasoned wood, warping while on the long, hot voyage through the tropics. The fastenings had come loose, allowing the engines a considerable amount of movement. We were now faced with two alternatives; either carrying out repairs in the Falkland Islands, which would mean . . . not getting south until the next summer, or disconnecting the engines and carrying on by sail alone . . . and then carrying out repairs ourselves during the first winter. I chose the latter course, and we sailed again on January 5.

The nine hundred miles from Port Stanley to Port Lockroy entirely under sail took them fifteen days. Rymill described the voyage as 'uneventful', and Colin Bertram recalled that the worst bit was not any storm – they were lucky there – but 'days of rare and unexpected windlessness south of the Horn. In the absence of wind upon our sails we rolled heavily 45° each way, and we felt we might ultimately shake ourselves to fragments.' They made a perfect landfall, which reflected great credit on *Penola*'s master, and found that Hampton and Bingham had arrived at Port Lockroy only just before them, having had to wait for a month on Deception Island, an abandoned whaling station 150 miles to the north, until the ice broke up. The Fox Moth was launched, and they found that there was no possible landing place on Graham Land itself but there was a good site for a base and a safe anchorage for *Penola* some forty miles south of Port Lockroy, on the Argentine Islands (just south of the 65th parallel).

The base hut was a two-storeyed wooden building measuring 22 ft by 14½ ft; the downstairs room was a combined workshop, kitchen, complete with Aga (which had to be assembled), and dining room, with a corner partitioned off for the wireless operator; upstairs was the living room with bunks around the walls. A man's bunk was his own private space; Launcelot's bunk, according to Colin Bertram, was in a permanent state of chaos with prayer books, geological hammers and specimen rocks, sermon notes and articles for the *Times* and *Glasgow Herald* (which had appointed him their Special Correspondent), all mixed up together. (In later life, too, no one who saw the litter

of papers on Launcelot's desk could understand how he managed to be the first-class administrator that he was.) Considering
that since leaving Port Stanley he had been constantly busy, first
as a member of the ship's crew and then in helping to build the
base hut, it is remarkable that he evidently managed to produce
a course of sermons on 'the relevance of Christianity at the
present day'. A sermon in almost worse than usual handwriting,
dated 'At the base, Argentine Islands, Quinquagesima March
3/35', ran as follows:

I chose this topic [*the relevance of Christianity*] because I
believe there are a good many people who regard Christianity
as at best a great tradition which scarcely applies any longer,
or even as a superstitious cult which is a fiction of men's
imaginations and fails to touch the real issues of men's
lives. . . . [But] the ultimate test of the relevance of Christianity
is whether Christ's teaching still stands or not. Some people
maintain that men's values are emerging and evolving. But if
what life is supposed to mean is itself in process of evolution,
then it is hard to maintain that it has any real meaning, for
the world will mean something different every morning. In
fact we know that goodness is never anything but good and
never can be, in time or in eternity. As we grow in understanding, our previous ideas of goodness will be seen in better
proportion, or may even be displaced. But it is not goodness
that is changing so much as our own insight.

In the Sermon on the Mount the Christian ideal of goodness
is set before us. . . . The Beatitudes are much deeper than rules
of conduct; no amount of good conduct can take the place
of goodwill; good conduct that springs from goodwill is of
infinitely greater value than good deeds done unwillingly or
with a bad grace. . . . No virtue that has not pleasure in it is
virtue at its highest. One of the most striking things about
the Beatitudes to my mind is that they carry with them a sense
of 'Blessed are the incomplete; damned are the self-sufficient'.
The person for whom there seems no hope is the self-sufficient
man, set in his ways, completely satisfied with the rut in which

he is stuck. Christ does not condemn the adulterous woman but the self-sufficient Pharisee. Under any test of attainment it would be monstrous to condemn a Pharisee and not a Publican; but the Pharisee was only aware of his achievement, the Publican knew his insufficiency.

The Christian character is the childlike character, whose humility is not that of a slave with downcast eyes but of the child who looks up trustingly. The disease Christ condemns is what in athletes you call staleness – unresponsiveness and inertia in place of childlike eagerness. Blessed are those who know their own insufficiency and, knowing this, look up and ahead to learn more of God and his will.

Clearly, by now Launcelot knew his congregation! He was not preaching to the converted, though those like Quintin Riley who were committed Christians found plenty of meat in his sermons, but his hearers were educated men who knew their Bible even if they did not believe what it contained – they knew what Pharisees or Publicans were, there was no culture-gap between preacher and congregation. This made preaching easier in some ways, but it also meant that the preacher could not get away with slipshod argument or second-hand ideas. The following Sunday's sermon developed the same theme of the relevance of Christianity, with the text 'Whose service is perfect freedom' and using the polar explorers Nansen and Edward Wilson to illustrate how one person's example can stir another to emulation. But three days later, 13 March, showed what the chaplain was up against; a house-warming party to celebrate the completion of the hut and John Rymill's birthday resulted in one or two men getting objectionably drunk. Rymill tried to convince Launcelot that an occasional binge was a good way for men living under difficult conditions to let off steam, but with just one combined living room and bedroom for everyone it was not possible for those who became the worse for wear to sleep it off where they wouldn't disturb everyone else.

Launcelot's position would probably have been impossible had he not insisted, before he agreed to go on the Expedition,

that he would be its official Chaplain. Having spent his first
year as a clergyman in a senior common room and not a clergy
house, he had learned to be extremely practical about such
things as conditions of employment; academics have a reputation for absent-mindedness and having minds above such sor-
did things as money, but there are few City institutions with a
keener eye than Oxbridge colleges for looking after their financial interests.*   Because he had a recognized position as Chaplain, Launcelot could stick to his guns; on Palm Sunday he gave
out his 'church notices' for Holy Week, which included Holy
Communion on Maundy Thursday and a simple Good Friday
service 'before breakfast or after supper according to how this
will fit in with the day's work'. He also urged them all 'whether
or not you are confirmed in the Anglican Church' to feel free
to receive Holy Communion, especially on Easter Day:

> After all, the Communion Service is the only one which was
> instituted by Christ himself and which we celebrate according
> to his express wish. There are many who feel uncomfortable
> about this service because they suspect it is in the nature of
> a magical rite. There is of course no belief in the material
> alteration of the bread and wine, but the meaning of the use
> of bread and wine may be compared to coinage; the silver in
> a half crown is not worth anything like two shillings and
> sixpence [*times have changed!*] but because the King says it
> is two and sixpence that gives it an effective purchasing power
> independent of its intrinsic worth. So in the sacrament the
> bread and wine though not materially changed are charged
> with a new meaning and a new value. You cannot fail to
> believe in sacraments when you've got a body; there is nothing
> magical in receiving the gifts of God through material means.

* One reason why Launcelot became such an effective bishop was that
he applied a hard-headed approach to diocesan appointments, as I learned
when being interviewed for the post of domestic chaplain; Launcelot said,
'You haven't asked what the pay is', and when I said that I had assumed
it would be no less than my pay as a curate, he rebuked me quite strongly
for not having found out definitely.

Launcelot's Graham Land sermons have mostly survived, often with almost indecipherable embellishments and alterations which, like battle scars, show how they were adapted and used again on different occasions long afterwards. Most of them present basic Christian teaching in a way that an intelligent agnostic could understand even if he were not convinced – and one or two were convinced.

This Expedition, unlike its predecessors, was in touch with what was going on in the world as the lengthening shadows of Hitler and Mussolini became steadily more obvious and more threatening. The year 1935 saw Mussolini's invasion of Abyssinia, and August 4, the anniversary of the outbreak of the Great War, fell on a Sunday. The evening service included Chesterton's hymn 'O God of earth and altar', with the lines 'Our earthly rulers falter, our people drift and die; the walls of gold entomb us, the swords of scorn divide. . . . From all that terror teaches, from lies of tongue and pen, from all the easy speeches that comfort cruel men . . . Deliver us Good Lord', and the sermon was on 'the Peace of God', which

> does not mean a sort of lethargic state of vacuum, but the presence of God in men's hearts – and this can only be attained through conflict with evil. . . . Christ said 'I come not to bring peace but a sword'. The peace which he *did* come to bring was one which can only be won through a continuous persevering struggle. The world is a wonderful place, but frequently it is far from pleasant. But ultimately it is not the circumstances that matter, but the way a man meets them; and in this his faith is put to the test.

Just as these sermons reveal the beliefs that formed Launcelot's character, so also having to write those sermons probably helped him formulate those beliefs. Having to preach to the same small group that were his only and constant companions for two and a half years meant not only that his words had to stand up to critical judgment, but also that he had to try and live up to them; no amount of pulpit eloquence would have cut any ice in such a tight-knit community unless the preacher practised what he preached. This could not have been easy in those conditions; as he later put it:

Perhaps the feature that distinguishes expedition life is that it enforces the doctrine of acceptance. You just have to put up with the stores you've got, it's no good complaining about what you've left behind; you have to put up with the limitations imposed on your plans by the weather; but above all you have to put up with your companions, and they with you – because there's no escaping them for the next one, two, or three years. On the whole we got on extraordinarily well with one another, but I remember one incident near the end of the expedition when a member of the party was annoyed – and it illustrates this matter of acceptance. He was annoyed with the leader – who I should say was a good leader – and he lost control of himself to the extent of taking the barometer off its shelf and smashing it to the ground – and then dramatically sweeping out of the hut and banging the door. But – you see the point. He couldn't stay out; he couldn't apply for another job elsewhere. He had to come back, and to his credit he did so with extraordinary composure and dignity, apologised to the leader, and the incident was forgotten.

Although Launcelot prefaced those words by saying 'The personal side of expedition life . . . depends on the people you are with; and in that respect I was extremely fortunate', that did not mean that he always found it easy to get on with them all. Most members of the Expedition kept private diaries because, as Launcelot said, 'it's very relieving to one's feelings, when one is a bit pent up, to loose off steam by writing it down in one's diary'. His own diary contains no startling comments and is remarkably restrained; indeed it really says nothing that cannot be gleaned from his letters home and his reports as Special Correspondent to *The Times*. Quite rightly, though, everyone agreed that their private diaries should be embargoed until there was no one who could conceivably be hurt by comments made in the heat of the moment.

Just as Bob Ryder admitted that he felt exasperated at times with Launcelot and the other scientists but later came to respect their point of view, so too Launcelot at the time criticized Ryder for trying to impose strict naval discipline but later came to appreciate the need for efficiency if *Penola* was to get to Antarctica and back in one piece. In any case, not finding it easy to get on with someone was never, for Launcelot, a reason for failing to do so – it was said by one of the party that by the end of the expedition Launcelot was the only man to be on speaking terms with everyone else. There were moments when the shore party and the ship's party were being very critical of each other, and Ryder recalled that Launcelot 'really more than anyone else acted as a moderating influence and prevented criticisms from becoming acrimonious'. He had always been good at seeing things from the other person's point of view, and Graham Land gave plenty of scope for honing that skill.

One thing that Launcelot found difficult to cope with was the swearing and bawdy talk most of his companions indulged in. When, years later, he re-read his diary, he commented, 'I get the impression that I really was a pretty insufferable prig in Graham Land with so much emphasis on a dislike for bad language and getting drunk at a party.' But the others do not seem to have thought he was a prig; after all, they would as a rule have moderated their language in the presence of a priest, and although that inhibition broke down when they were in Launcelot's company all the time, they would not have expected Launcelot to approve of bad language. Indeed, Ryder thought that he 'stood up to our ribald jokes with the greatest good humour. I was the first person to nickname him "The Bish", and The Bish he remained.' (Ryder's life in the Royal Navy would doubtless have ripened his language – Launcelot recalled that 'Doc' Bingham too used language 'hardly suited to the drawing room', but at least it 'had a certain style, largely because he did not repeat himself'. All good training for Launcelot when he became a naval chaplain during the war.)

'Doc' Bingham himself records one incident that shows Launcelot's influence for good. In August 1936 he and Launcelot were each driving a dog team on a journey to try and retrieve a food depot that had been abandoned on the ice in Marguerite Bay. Reloading the sledges and harnessing the huskies each morning was a tricky and time-consuming business, and it was a relief to get going at last. One morning Bingham's sledge caught the end of a guy-rope as he moved off; the result was a welter of dogs and traces, an overturned sledge, a torn tent, and the whole morning wasted. Launcelot's only reaction was, 'What very bad luck.' That made a bigger impression than any amount of sermons could ever have done.

Reading about Launcelot's time in the Antarctic, and knowing the golden opinions that he won, can give the impression that being Chaplain was quite easy and pleasant. It was not. In the words of Donald Lindsay (*Friends for Life*, p. 91), 'Never before had he been brought so starkly face to face with the task of dealing with men to whom Christianity meant little or nothing'; and as Launcelot himself said:

> It is desperately difficult to preach Christ to those who have had opportunities to learn of Him and have been left relatively indifferent in their attitude to His way of life. Even if one has seen a vision dimly . . . it is bewildering to live with others who care little for the 'music' of that vision.

And as he told his mother at the time:

> As you can imagine my job as Chaplain is not an easy one. The outlook of the party is so very mixed in things religious I find it difficult to know where to begin! Every Sunday we have Holy Communion before breakfast. We use the work bench as an altar. Quintin Riley made a scarlet frontal . . . and we use the Communion set which Chase gave me and the Cross you gave me. Generally only two come to this, though at intervals one or two others come and at Easter

time we had ten. Most of the party at the base come to the evening service and some from the ship – there are generally nine or ten. . . . My chief difficulty is to find a form of service which will meet the spiritual needs of a very staunch and argumentative Anglo-Catholic, a keen Wesleyan, a Presbyterian, a Christian Scientist by upbringing and one or two others who do not quite know whether they would call themselves Christians or not. . . .

There were times when it all felt very depressing; and times, too, when in the midst of his companions he felt very lonely. But looking back, he saw that it

made me realise, sometimes with almost painful yearnings, the truth of all that Christianity involves and the very great need for living in communion with God and by His Power. . . . I do seem to have found my neighbour and myself as they are; we have little in the way of artificial disguises and we are free from the dangers of trying to win popular credit or pandering to public opinion. A man sees himself here as he really is and not as he wants other people to believe him to be.

That seems to sum up the experience of being Chaplain to the Expedition.

6

Geologist in Antarctica

I am very pleased to hear the excellent account of the work done by the Graham Land Expedition, and Mr Fleming's description of the geology. I look forward to the more detailed examination of over a thousand specimens of rocks which he has collected.

(W. Campbell Smith at the Royal Geographical Society meeting)

Before the Expedition had sailed, Professor Debenham, who had been on Scott's last expedition and as a Fellow of St John's College was known to Launcelot, wrote to him from the Department of Geography (July 1934):

As I have already told you, I look upon you as chief of the scientific staff, though just as in our own much bigger expedition the title meant much less than the man who held it. John Rymill, with all his good qualities, is of course not a scientist and requires conversion.... One cannot *hammer* such notions into one's leader. On the other hand, with the long winter evenings together it ought to be possible to get the non-scientific members to see the interest in what you and the others are doing. Thanks to Scott's own interest our party spent lots of time over purely scientific problems, and.... I am perfectly certain that every one of them with the possible exception of Meares ended by being as keen in general as the scientists themselves. They still smiled at the *methods* which they did not understand, but were hot on the *problems* themselves. I would not think of quoting the Scott expedition to you if it were not that in one or two other expeditions, notably

those of Shackleton and Mawson, there was a rather serious
rift between the two parties; impatience on the part of the
non-scientists and something approaching rancour on the part
of the scientists. This could hardly happen with John's show,
but the merest suspicion of it should be avoided.

Yours very sincerely, Deb.

After establishing their base in the Argentine Islands in March,
for the next three months Stephenson ('Steve') with Quintin
Riley's help carried out local surveys by motor-boat, Bertram
and Roberts carried out marine and ornithological biology, and
Rymill piloted by Hampton made air reconnaisances. Launcelot
found the Argentine Islands geologically interesting; the huge
mass of snow on each island, coupled with snow-free areas near
the shore lines suggested that the ice must have been receding
– on a very much smaller scale the same effect can be seen on
stones or branches of trees after a heavy snowfall has been
followed by a thaw.

Besides the scientific work, there were plenty of chores to
keep them all busy – Launcelot had brought out a copy of *War
and Peace* to help him get through the long winter evenings,
but the book returned from the Antarctic unopened. It is difficult
for us to realize how different conditions were before the age of
satellites and high-tech means of communication and transport.
They had a Fox Moth aeroplane, but its range was only 150
miles and launching it either with skis or with floats was hard
work; they had a small air-cooled Bristol tractor (given by
Launcelot's father) which proved robust enough to survive four
months' total immersion, but was only suitable for short-term
hauling and had to be abandoned on breaking sea-ice when
taken on a longer journey.

Sledges were pulled by huskies – forty-five dogs came to
Graham Land and Bingham managed to breed over fifty puppies
during that first year; and dogs had to be fed. Seal-meat was
the only fresh food available; no one liked killing what Launcelot
described as 'attractive creatures with very large childlike eyes,
[which] lie on their backs in the snow and look at you with

most benign expressions'. But at least the need to kill them for food enabled Colin Bertram to 'make a collection of over 100 skulls, innumerable ovaries and much else besides [and] the resultant thesis on comparative behaviour with an evolutionary theme was in a way the forerunner of some of the new biology of decades later'. A total of 367 Weddell seals, 177 Crabeaters and 14 Leopard seals were killed, and although many today would condemn such killing as cruel, it is certainly arguable that energy-intensive methods that enable scientists, and tourists, in Antarctica to live more comfortably cause more death and suffering than anything that men in the 1930s did. The difference is that we don't as a rule see the mayhem caused by pollution, whereas when seals are shot we can see it happening.

The ship's party, composed of non-scientists, had a very hard time of it. They had to repair *Penola*'s engine beds by making a concrete base in the bowels of the ship with cement brought from Port Stanley – Launcelot felt particularly sorry for Norman Gurney for whom the expedition had so far brought little more than seasickness and hard labour. The scientists' work was more interesting, and when winter snow and darkness reduced the scope for ornithology, surveying and geologizing, they learned the art of driving a dog-team. Launcelot described it in a speech at the Norwich Union Boat Club Dinner in 1968:

Driving a dog team had strong affinities with coaching a crew. There are days when nothing goes right and the dogs (or the crew) look up at you with ill-concealed scorn. Then there are the other days, the halcyon days, when everything seems to click. I suspect that coaching is about 85% psychology and 15% knowledge. Some dogs are immensely conscientious and no trouble at all, some sly and only working when the driver is looking; some with a hearty and boundless energy frequently misapplied, some languid and apparently self-pitying. You can of course turn their susceptibilities to good account. If Ginger hates Hero, and Hero is afraid of Ginger, then put Hero immediately in front of Ginger and you have two dogs pulling their best.

But these husky dogs are almost without exception affectionate and loyal, and one gets extremely attached to one's
own team even if they can be exasperating. Two of their most
tiresome habits are fighting and gnawing. They fight with such
a will that immediate action is necessary to prevent them from
doing serious damage. As for gnawing, that too can be serious
because if they get half a chance they will chew almost any
part of the equipment, and that means that on a sledge journey
you have to go asleep with one ear awake. But all in all sledge
hauling with dogs is infinitely preferable to man-hauling.

Skill was needed as well as psychology; to start with Launcelot
often 'succeeded in whipping most parts of my anatomy, [or]
got the whip entangled round itself, like one does when trying
to cast too long a fishing line'.

To start with, Launcelot found it difficult to get through to
John Rymill, and found him a 'queerly lonely person'. He was
by nature uncommunicative, a man of actions not words, but
proved himself an inspiring leader. Ryder described him as

> a most charming person [who] was, in my view, essentially a
> leader of sledging expeditions. In this capacity I found him to
> be both inspiring and impressively competent. . . . I felt quietly
> honoured when he proposed that I should accompany him on
> one of the long journeys. . . . I felt prepared to follow him to
> the end of the world.

Launcelot was to be Rymill's other companion; the conversation
between the three of them took place as they sat by the Aga
after the Midwinter party on 21 June 1935, and Launcelot,
like Ryder, felt honoured though it was a 'rather awe-inspiring'
invitation. The journey was to take place the following year,
but in the event it never happened.

However, on 1 September 1935 Rymill took Launcelot and
Stephenson on a surveying journey which Rymill described later
to the Geographical Society:

> We worked slowly south, being hindered by rotten and young
> ice, which made travelling difficult but interesting. . . .

Stephenson determined astronomical positions at frequent intervals, and from these positions took both vertical and horizontal angles with the theodolite. . . . We finally met Bingham and Ryder [who had gone ahead to find a landing-ground to which the aeroplane could take supplies] on September 11, and both parties returned to the base four days later with the survey completed.

'Interesting' that sledge-journey over rotten sea-ice certainly must have been. Rymill was utterly fearless, but as he was also extremely competent they got away with it.

The Expedition did however have at least one very close shave. In June of the following year, 1936, air reconnaissance showed that the ice in Marguerite Bay 'all looked good and solid, with none of the grey patches which are a sign of thin ice', so:

Bingham, Stephenson, Riley, Bertram and myself [i.e. Rymill] with the dog teams and Hampton with the tractor [set out]. All went well at first. . . . The night of June 16, after five days' travelling, found us about 40 miles from base. The wind got up soon after we went to bed and blew an off-shore gale for thirty-six hours; the ice started to break up and a quick move to endeavour to reach some islands about 4 miles away had to be made. The tractor could not be moved from the camp and, together with the greater part of our depot, had to be left behind. After nine hours of hard travelling over loose ice-pans and high pressure ridges, we at last reached the islands where we had to wait for a week before the leads froze sufficiently to allow us to make an attempt to return to the base. These islands we called Terra Firma.

They were lucky, as well as brave and skilful, to get away with it; had the leads between the ice-floes become very slightly wider they would have been marooned on their melting ice-floe as it drifted out to sea. Launcelot's diary records the acute anxiety the rest of the party felt when the six men failed to return on time, and he may have felt relieved that his dog-team had not been well enough trained for him to go with them.

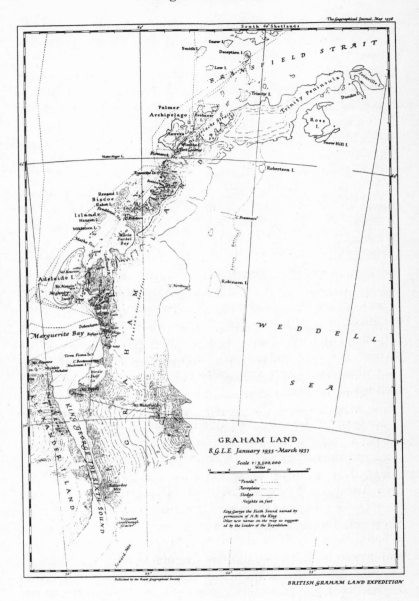

GRAHAM LAND

B.G.L.E. January 1935 - March 1937

Scale 1 : 3,500,000

"Penola" . . . .
Aeroplane _ _ _ _ _
Sledge _ . _ . _ .
Heights in feet

King George the Sixth Sound named by
permission of H.M. the King.
Other new names on the map as suggested by the Leader of the Expedition.

However, that was in the future. For the whole of 1935 the Expedition remained based in the Argentine Islands. Local surveying from the motor-boat continued, but as Rymill put it 'there was little else we could do until the ice opened up enough to allow the *Penola* to work south and we could establish a new base'. Not until 3 January 1936 was the ship able to leave the anchorage, and then only by several days' sawing through the ice that held her in. First, she had to sail north to Deception Island to collect timbers and other material to build a new hut from a disused whaling station, returning on the 27th. On 16 February the whole party, with a very full deck-cargo now supplemented by nearly a hundred huskies, set off south. Air reconnaissance gave them a course round the west (the outside) of Adelaide Island and they found a good anchorage and site for a base on the coast of Marguerite Bay, some 180 miles south of the Argentine Islands. The new base was also close to a group of six islands, which they christened Debenham Islands in honour of the six children of the Cambridge Professor of Geography.

Launcelot was not entirely happy at this time about the way the Expedition was shaping. From the scientists' point of view, they had certainly not 'found little else' to do, for the Argentine Islands were a productive area for their work. Roberts considered himself

> lucky at the Argentine Islands in having quite close to our base a small colony of Wilson's petrels; little birds which migrate every year to the North Atlantic, but of whose breeding habits practically nothing was known . . . the comings and goings of one pair were automatically recorded by means of a thermograph, and every bird in the colony was marked with a small numbered aluminium ring.

Besides petrels, Roberts could observe blue-eyed shags, Dominican gulls, brown skuas, antarctic terns, and several other species, whereas two hundred miles further south penguins would be virtually the only birds on offer. Stephenson had set up his weather station, with a Stevenson screen, thermometers, hygrograph and hygroscope, sunshine recorder, Besson nephoscope, wind direction recorder and Lownes anemometer on the hill behind their camp, and although 'this entailed a three-minute walk and a steep climb up each time we did the observations' it provided 'a splendid view all round' and proved a more informative weather station than Marguerite Bay where the winds were deflected by nearby mountains. As for geology, the Argentine Islands provided Launcelot with 'many interesting rocks' and he was able to make 'detailed readings of the rate of growth and decay of the sea-ice above and below the original ice surfaces' and collect samples of ice from different depths to find 'the variation in salinity and detect any change in the proportion of sulphates to chlorides'. It was against that background that Launcelot wrote on 6 February 1936 to Professor Debenham:

My mother and father told me that you would be writing to me about the scientific work and in particular of what you wanted in the way of mentioning our scientific findings to the *Times*. I find it difficult to persuade John to let me write all that I would like in that way but I shall do my best.

So far the scientific work has been perhaps too subordinate in the general plans. The repeated alterations in the plans which have been forced on us [by *Penola*'s limitations] ... have in some cases been a handicap in planning our scientific programme ... many more results might be produced if journeys were planned with more objects in view than long distances and reconnaissance mapping. . . . It is of course difficult to hold the balance, but if circumstances prevent long distances being covered, as has been the case this past year, one is liable to suffer from having put all one's eggs into one basket ...

John's letter will presumably have explained how the condition of *Penola* has affected our movements. Except for short dashes (only the word is scarcely appropriate as *Penola* is slow as a tortoise) such as this moving of our base, she cannot be used in these waters. . . . In her present condition without a paid crew it has been a full time job for the ship's party to keep *Penola* in fit condition. . . . If they had not been so conscientious it is extremely doubtful if we would ever have been able to go further south. . . . The ship's party have not had an easy time; they have had the lion's share of the dirty work which they have done uncomplainingly. From your own experience [with Scott's expedition] you will realise the tension that is apt to arise from the difference between civilian and naval outlook . . .

Perhaps (but I hope it is otherwise) all this may sound depressing. It is certainly not meant to be so, but it is as well to give you some notion of difficulties which have affected our plans and work. But fortunately despite these we live together as a very friendly and cheerful party, and some of the party have shown endless resources of tact which makes things run smoothly . . . we have had no rows and I see little chance of these taking place in the future. For my own part I am more grateful than I could tell you for having been asked to come, and have had opportunities which as a parson I particularly value . . .

I regard the enlistment of John's understanding in things scientific as one of my principal jobs. As you yourself prophesied it is not an easy undertaking, but by no means an impossible one! He is beginning to be interested in survey, meteorology and some branches of glaciology, regards geology as a sane pursuit, and is beginning to feel that biology is not so insane as he was at first led to suppose. So I have hopes that we may be able to carry out a complete conversion!

That particular hope may not have been entirely realized, but Launcelot's fears about the scientific work proved groundless. Brian Roberts had developed a grumbling appendix, and Bingham ruled that he must be taken to the Falkland Islands for an operation rather than risk peritonitis. Although this was desperately frustrating for him, the resultant absence of *Penola* did not prove as much of a handicap as it might have done since bad sea-ice coupled with inhospitably mountainous coasts would have made it impossible to use the ship to ferry sledge parties across Marguerite Bay, while air reconnaissance proved more effective than anything *Penola* could have done.

In the event, the scientists had far more scope from their new base than they could ever have had if they had stayed in the Argentine Islands. The rock formations and fossils of Alexander I Land were major geological finds. Doubtless those discoveries would in any case have been made before very long by some other expedition, but that does not diminish the achievement; and almost more important in the long run, perhaps, was that Launcelot's glaciological observations and Stephenson's meteorological observations in the Debenham Islands compared with those taken in the Argentine Islands enabled them to conclude that the ice had 'recently' (meaning decades or centuries rather than millennia) receded considerably. To have made that discovery before the days of man-made global warming has proved very valuable.

Geology involved long hours of writing up notes and labelling specimens, whether in Cambridge or in Antarctica. But the term 'field work' took on a new dimension. Launcelot's first sledge journey from the southern base camp was undertaken in company with Stephenson and Riley, its purpose mainly 'to explore the complicated fjord system which lies to the north-east of Marguerite Bay'. They left on 20 July 1936 and covered some 200 miles. Launcelot found Stephenson a very congenial leader; he was a trained scientist who wanted to make accurate geographical surveys and not simply press on to explore as far as possible. While Stephenson and Riley did their surveys Launcelot looked for rocks. They had two tents between the three of them, taking it in turns to have the single tent, and one evening Launcelot was surprised as he was returning to the tent he was sharing with Riley to hear voices coming from it. The explanation was that Riley was 'having an argument with a Roman Catholic nun, and I was winning'. Riley was always ready to engage Launcelot, too, in theological argument; but it was a joy to have a companion to join in saying the daily offices of Matins and Evensong.

7

King George the Sixth Sound

His Majesty the King, our Royal Patron, has graciously consented to his name being given to this geographical feature which will be known henceforth as King George the Sixth sound.

(Announcement by Professor Henry Balfour to the Royal Geographical Society, 21 February 1938)

Six years before the Expedition sailed, Sir Hubert Wilkins had flown down the west (Graham Land) coast of the Weddell Sea. He reported that there were channels running through from the east to the west coast of Graham Land; in other words, that Graham Land was an archipelago, a series of islands leading down towards a part of Antarctica that he called Hearst Land. In 1935 Wilkins was again in the south polar region, this time on a ship, the *Wyatt Earp*, which was used as a base for an American attempt to fly right across Antarctica from the Weddell Sea to Little America. Wilkins, who was in wireless contact with the pilot, Lincoln Ellsworth, radioed to Rymill at the Argentine Islands base: 'For your expedition and private information only. Ellsworth on November 21st passed ... over Stefansson Strait which he saw running about thirty miles to westward....' Stefansson Strait was the name Wilkins had given to the main sea channel he thought he had seen cutting through Graham Land; both he and Ellsworth also reported seeing the Lurabee and Casey 'channels', all of which indicated that there were good sea-level routes for Rymill's planned sledge journey across Graham Land eastwards from Marguerite Bay.

The other major sledge journey Rymill had wanted to do from the Marguerite Bay base was round the western side of Alexander I Land, but reconnaissance in the Fox Moth showed that the ice in that direction was very bad. Nor could they see the Stefansson Strait or any other channel through Graham Land. What they did see, however, was 'what appeared to be a great channel running away to the south for as far as we could see' between Alexander I Land and Graham Land. Accordingly, Rymill decided to send a sledge party in that direction, composed of Launcelot the geologist, Colin Bertram the biologist, and Alfred ('Steve') Stephenson, the most experienced polar traveller, as leader.

Their journey was described by Stephenson and Launcelot at a meeting of the Royal Geographical Society on 21 February 1938. Launcelot as their newspaper correspondent had sent back reports to *The Times*, but these had to be brief and covered all their activities and not just his own; they were also edited by John Rymill who was understandably reluctant to publicize any mishaps or problems. Those limitations, coupled with the fashion for understatement in 1930s *Times* reporting (it was the age of 'Small Earthquake in Chile: Not Many Dead') meant that Launcelot's accounts were laconic in the extreme. A friend pointedly sent him an extract from the *Bystander* which read:

The despatches of the Times Special Correspondent with the British Graham Land Expedition are models of their kind; plain, forthright, unemotional Nordic prose devoid of fla-fla. Nothing exciting has happened as yet, but if the whole expedition went up in smoke that boy wouldn't show any more emotion than a Red Indian. He'd cable something like:

'Bodger, Willis and Griggs fell off an iceberg today. M'Whaup and Jake have been eaten by bears. The sea, which has been stormy of late, inclines to be worse. The sledges and stores disappeared on Sept 8 in a blizzard, and the ice is breaking up.... The weather which has been remarkably changeable now tends to be colder with hurricanes and snowstorms; the curious formation of clouds in the north-west . . .' etc., etc.

This is what is called the Waterloo School of English prose, betraying no surprise nor exaltation, divorced alike from anguish and joy, a level grey expanse where no birds sing; so named from Victor Hugo's majestic line: 'Waterloo, Waterloo, Waterloo, morne plaine!'

Launcelot's private diary is also restrained, but does reveal more feeling. He copied out some extracts for his family and friends which reveal something of what those three men felt, and some of the actual events that lie behind their report to the Royal Geographical Society, which opened with Stephenson's account:

In September [1936] two sledge parties set out together to cross the col [at the southern end of the Wordie Ice Shelf – see map on page 55] into the 'great channel leading away to the south' which had been spotted from the air. Rymill and Bingham planned then to travel westwards across Alexander I Land while Stephenson, Bertram and Fleming were to continue south and turn east should they find a channel [Stefansson Strait or Casey Channel] into the Weddell Sea. But the col proved far harder to cross than had appeared from the air, and also they were held up for eight days by bad weather with visibility nil. Accordingly, it was decided that Rymill and Bingham should return to base, and then fly in stores to a forward depot, thus reinforcing the supplies of the Southern party so that despite the delay they would still have a full eight weeks' rations.

The steepest part of the rise to the col was the first 700 feet, and we got all the loads up to this height before the others left us. Again we had bad visibility, but by making a fresh trail each time we were able to relay our half-loads slowly to the top of the col. October 1 had a blue and cloudless sky and we raced down slopes of wind-driven snow, doing 25 miles that day. As October 2 was fine we made it a 'survey day'. This meant that Fleming went off geologising while Stephenson, with Bertram's help, did an astronomical fix and rounds of angles to outstanding points. From this camp of October 1 and 2 which was about 1200 feet above the sea we got down to the shelf-ice of the Sound without too much difficulty; most of the crevasses were well bridged, but on one occasion we nearly lost a sledge. Once clear of the rifts we did between 20 and 25 miles a day. We had two tents between the three of us, and took it in turns for one man to be in a tent by himself. With a tent to oneself there is more room for drying wet moccasins and blanket shoes; one can sleep in the middle of the tent so that one can turn over without sending showers of hoarfrost into the top of the sleeping-bag. The daily ration for one man was: biscuits 2.7 oz, cocoa 0.8, oats 2.0, chocolate 2.4, pemmican 5.6, sugar 3.2, yeast 0.4, milk powder 1.6, margarine 5.6, pea flour 1.6, making a total of 25.9 oz., with one tablespoon of concentrated orange juice and one Adexolin capsule (halibut oil). The paraffin ration was 1 gallon for 1 tent for 10 days. This sounds luxurious, but we found it paid, for when lying up we were sufficiently comfortable to write up and think about our scientific notes. Each morning when we turned out with dry footwear and dry gloves we could get down to work with a speed impossible had we been forced to put on stiff and frozen gloves.

Our routine was to get up at six [*Launcelot would generally get up first to 'light the primus and put the pots on, since I like to have time to read my Office and say my prayers'*], and usually we had had breakfast, struck camp, loaded the sledges and harnessed the dogs by 8.15 or 8.30. We then travelled for two to two and a half hours before stopping to disentangle the traces and give the dogs a rest, after which we would go on until one o'clock when we took an hour off for lunch. We had to stop sledging at 5pm. When we had finished supper and written our personal diaries we still had plenty to do. Fleming always had to write up the glaciology and geomorphology.

By October 16 we had reached latitude 70° 30' and at last

saw something new. No longer did the east shore continue just as far as the next promontory; instead it changed into broad sweeping glaciers, with only isolated mountains here and there; and, biggest change of all, it began to curve round in front of us. On the 19th we went on to latitude 72° and as we were already two days beyond our scheduled time for turning back we very reluctantly decided to stop. The Graham Land coast ran for some 50 miles slightly west of south before disappearing from sight.

At this point Launcelot took up the narrative:

On the opposite side of the Sound, the coast of Alexander I Land could be seen almost as clearly as that of the mainland, although it was more distant. The air was so clear that we could have seen any high land in this direction if any such existed within 50 or perhaps 60 miles; it is thus probable that Alexander I Land is an island, but an island some 300 miles long instead of only 50.

We had pitched our tents with the doors facing the setting sun. The view we got must be as clearly impressed on our memories as any we saw in the course of the expedition; for while we cooked and ate our supper we left the sleeve doors of our tents rolled up and looked into the distance, wishing that we need not turn for home, but not without a sense of satisfaction that we had had the good fortune to see where the Sound was leading.

A return journey has never the same exhilaration as the outward one, but for us it was not in every sense an anti-climax; there were still the stratified rocks on the western [Alexander I Land] side of the Sound to be examined. The temperature had fallen to −22° fahrenheit [= −30° celsius] and was still several degrees below zero when we started off.*

* Colin Bertram told me that King George V asked a previous polar explorer who had experienced even lower temperatures how he had coped when having to spend a penny. 'Scissors, your Majesty,' was the answer.

In another two days we landed on Alexander I Land; we were the first to land on this island, although it had been discovered over 100 years before by Bellinghausen who named his discovery after the then reigning Tsar. Next morning we were off on a fossil hunt, armed with hammers. We chipped at the dark shales but could see nothing resembling a fossil. Then a slab of rock was broken in which there was a vague and faint impression which, with the aid of some imagination, might be a shell impression. On the other side was a nearly complete cast of a shell about which there could be no question, also a few plant remains which indicate that the beds in Alexander I Land are Middle Jurassic. It was by far the most interesting day's geological work since the Expedition had left home.

Next day brought us new discoveries of a different kind; a bowl-shaped basin, nearly a mile across, bordered by ice-cliffs 100 feet high. In the bottom of the depression were several mounds of angular ice-blocks piled up to a height of 30 or 40 feet; the appearance was not unlike a miniature in ice of the ruins of a volcanic mountain whose centre has collapsed and fallen inwards to form a caldera. Soon we came to a level place to land where we could camp; we pitched our tents on hard glazed ice without even enough snow to pile on to the skirts of the tents for anchorage. This surprising amount of thaw is due to the black specks lying everywhere on the ice. The adjacent rocks are broken up by frost action into a fine dust which absorbs the sun's rays to cause excessive melting. We named this camping place Ablation Camp. It was a geologist's paradise; to spend only a single day there was tantalising, even though it was obvious we could afford no longer.

By next morning it was far too stormy to travel, and we had an extra day to geologise, but it is not easy to look for fossils in a blizzard and we added only a few specimens to our collection. There was no question but that we must leave Alexander I Land for good and make the best pace we could for home. We had 22 days' food left on the basis of making a ration box last twelve days in place of ten and we had to cover a distance which had taken 32 days on the way out.

Our first obstacle was the rifted part of the ice-shelf. Bertram had to stop his sledge for the ground was beginning to fall away in front of him; he and Stephenson went ahead to prospect, while Fleming stayed to look after the dogs. They were ski-ing down what they thought was the drifted side of a rift, and were convinced they had reached the foot. The next moment they fell 30 feet and landed luckily in a soft bank of snow. This incident gave us an added respect for poor light. [*Launcelot later said that this was his worst moment during the whole expedition; it looked to him as if the two men had fallen to their deaths down a crevasse, leaving him with little hope of reaching base on his own.*]

Bad weather was not our only enemy, for with the days becoming warmer the hard-crusted surface of the shelf-ice had given place to a deep soft snow. Our skis would not slide and became caked with clinging snow . . . The dogs were having a really hard time of it. We still had crevasses to cross on both sides of the Col, then there was still ahead of us the climb itself to the top of the Col (and if the surface did not improve that would take several days) and finally we had to negotiate 50 miles of sea-ice [the Wordie ice-shelf], the state of which we could only conjecture. Now we had ten days' food left on reduced rations to take us to Terra Firma Islands, and on the outward route this distance had taken us more than twice that time . . .

The weather was really becoming desperate; when we camped beyond the crevasses we had covered only four miles. It was therefore a welcome surprise to wake next morning [11 November] and find a cloudless sky. Shortly after midday we were at the top of the Col enjoying the view, our last good view of King George VI Sound. Just as we were ready to be on the move once more we saw two black specks moving in the distance, which resolved themselves into Rymill and Bingham with two sledges and dog teams. The meeting had been opportune.

Launcelot's account that he sent home to his parents, based on his personal diary, is not written in quite that 'Waterloo style of unemotional Nordic prose':

Oct. 29th. The sledge wheel which is tied to the back of my sledge is causing me some anxiety. I hope I can keep it in order for the remainder of the trip since it is essential for the coming part of the journey to know our position – we depend on it for our dead reckoning . . .

Nov 1st. A day of lying up but it cleared this afternoon. Steve and Colin efficiently despatched those dogs which we have had to part with – Silver, Whisky, Jim, Cyclops, Pie and Rosie. It's horrid to lose them but thank God the deed is done. They also fed the dogs and I prepared tea for the three of us. Then we had a short All Saints Day service; a Psalm, two lessons and some prayers. We now have 20 days dog-food and 19¼ days man-food to take us to Terra Firma Island where John has promised that there will be a depot for us . . .

Nov 4th. This is a bad place to be held up and we may yet be hard put to it to make rations last to get to Terra Firma Islands, and thereafter who knows but that the sea-ice may be breaking up. However sufficient unto the day is the evil thereof, and one must trust to God's good providence. Meanwhile we spend our time lying up in idleness whiling away the hours as best we may – and we are in very good spirits I'm glad to say . . .

Nov. 7th. A wretched day of snow and so we have been forced to lie up and open our last 3 boxes of food. We are likely to reach Terra Firma very hungry and having to sacrifice more of our dogs. However there is no use fretting and we must needs learn to accept the conditions which come and there is no saying but that we may have a change of conditions to help us on our way . . .

Twenty-five years earlier on the last British Antarctic sledging expedition Scott and his companions had been held up by similar weather conditions when only a few miles from their food depot, with fatal results. There was a period of ten days or so when Launcelot and his companions realized that they might meet a similar fate. However, after 11 November the weather turned in their favour:

> In the good light crevasses were easily negotiated. Two days of travelling took us to the Terra Firma islands . . . and could enjoy an orgy of porridge, margarine and chocolate. From there home, the journey was uneventful. The dogs raced the last part of the way home, for instinct told them what was in store. They revelled in blubber for the next week, ate it all day and slept in it at night, and their nice clean shaggy coats were soon a mass of matted hair. They must have been thankful for a rest, and full well they deserved it. They had been our constant companions for ten weeks, and many of these dogs were known to us from the day they were born. Why or how it is that dogs will consent to sledge on for mile after mile when they can sense little of the thrills of new discovery, when they have to sleep out in all weathers, licking the snow for drink and having to be content with one meal a day that takes less than a minute to consume; how they do all this is difficult to understand. But they do it.

How they must have hated having to kill those six dogs in order to reduce the consumption of dog-meat and at the same time use their carcasses to eke out the rations for the dogs that remained. But if they had not done so all of them, dogs and humans, would probably have perished; it was a close-run thing. The three men who had to live on those reduced rations could never again eat a large amount at a sitting; their stomachs had shrunk. Each year the three of them dined together, and the food was carefully chosen and delicious, but never too filling.

One anecdote that Launcelot told later drives home how difficult conditions were then as compared with now. Starting off one morning, he looked round to make sure he had not left something behind; and then found the clothing round his neck had frozen solid; he could not turn his head and had to sledge for the next two hours with his head on one side. He always averred that that the biggest single improvement in polar travel was the invention of nylon clothing that kept out moisture and did not freeze.

That journey of exploration certainly marked those three men for life.

8

Postscript to Antarctica

Almighty Father, Ruler of the elements and Maker of the universe in its tremendous majesty . . . Grant us a fuller realization of the wonder of thy presence, which is in all, and through all, and in all; through Jesus Christ our Lord.
(Prayer written for the British Graham Land Expedition by
Canon B. K. Cunningham)

Archbishop Robert Runcie was to have given the address at the memorial service to Launcelot in St George's Chapel, Windsor. He was unable to do so as he had to go into hospital for an operation, but this excerpt from the address he had written describes the formative influence that Antarctica had on Launcelot.

Launcelot Fleming was unique. As a young man, only just made priest, an experience was given him which has been given to few, and will not ever come again to others.

Into what other Bishop's study would you go, and see quietly there on its walls those pictures of another world to the one that most of us will ever see – the world of the Antarctic? Launcelot was away for three years; away in the 112 foot three-masted *Penola* for three summers and two dark winters – one of sixteen men who were to prove by their dog-sledge journeys on the sea-ice that the supposed Antarctic Archipelago was in fact the Antarctic Peninsula. Here was probably the last discovery of unknown territory on the earth's surface. Three men of that company, of whom Launcelot was one, penetrated the great ice-filled structures now known on the atlases as King George VI Sound.

He was with the Expedition as its Geologist and Chaplain. *Penola*'s Captain, Robert Ryder, was to win a VC at St Nazaire. Their Biologist, Dr Colin Bertram, was to say of those years that for him, in his own life, they were the formative ones: 'to see new land, great glaciers and mountain ranges never before beheld by the eyes of men, and to travel that land with good companions and teams of well-trained dogs – one cannot ask for better'.

The same writer has described 'the wind-crusted ice; ahead stretches the white plain, with pinnacles of ice dancing in the low mirage. To the left the mountain cliffs are in shadow. On the right, all in glittering brilliance, red-rock summits divided by great glaciers; the crevasses and ice-faces gleam with ocean blues and green, and above rides the full moon, clear with yellow light. The sun moves a little to the west of north, and slides behind a distant berg with a parting flash of brilliance and green.' And of the Chaplain: 'In Launcelot Fleming we had a man who exerted a great influence for good. He was, technically, parish priest for the largest parish in the world, five and a half million square miles, containing just himself and fifteen companions as the entire flock – sixteen men in the two contrasted states, the completest solitude, and (on board and in the hut) the greatest overcrowding.'

There are men who carry with them a dimension which makes one conscious that their eyes have seen something; that they have had a glimpse of wonder and have been touched ineffaceably by it, have been humbled by it. 'Where wast thou,' says God to Job out of the whirlwind, 'when I laid the foundations of the earth? Declare it if thou hast understanding. Who laid the measures thereof, if thou knowest? Where are the foundations thereof fastened? Or who laid the cornerstones thereof, when the morning stars sang together, and all the sons of God shouted for joy?'

We know that Launcelot had shared that exhilaration because we have known him as the man he was. It never left him. The pictures hanging in his study bore their quiet witness to the dimension in which the work of a busy bishop or dean, practical man, administrator, pastor, was done. And there had been also the close fellowship of that mixed company; something that he somehow carried with him into every room into which he went; always the same Launcelot, unpretentious, real, in whatever company he was – that of old friends, or with the young who responded to that outgoing interest, that taking of them seriously.

His freshness of vision and his lightness of step were qualities of a man who, taking the measure of himself and of others, had not lost the wonder. Behind the professionalism that was Launcelot lay the professionalism of the trained geologist who had seen God's wonder; who had commanded the affection of his fellow men in that remarkable first curacy both by being himself and by being ready to be got at and in that sense shaped by them. He had the professionalism that combined vision with a just assessment of what was practicable.

He was a man among men – and by his total lack of condescension loved also among women – and he was, indelibly, and with all the lightness of his step, a man of God. And these things were of a piece, as he was. You could not, nor did he, see them separately.

Colin Bertram, who gave that description of the awesome beauty of King George VI Sound, wrote a short memoir, 'Launcelot is doing my anchor-watch for me tonight':

Launcelot Fleming has to have been the only bishop to have stood anchor-watch aboard a three-masted topsail schooner in the Antarctic – and quite possibly the only geologist ever to share his bunk with books, seaboots and his 'rocks', and still get a good night's sleep.

He was unquestionably the only member of the Expedition who was always welcome, whenever, wherever, whoever. Launcelot treated me to my first cigar; he acquainted me with Axel Munthe; he employed me as labourer-with-the-ice-chisel to chip out samples of sea-ice, a job that got me away from the mock service discipline of the ship. Launcelot's contribution to the morale of the Expedition was incalculable; he upheld and comforted and counselled, he kept the peace while trenchantly arguing Christian dogma and ritual with Quintin Riley; he helped maintain standards of civilised behaviour just by being himself.

We used to refer to our Chaplain as 'the Bish', a term of affectionate respect not-to-be-taken-too-seriously-but-just-*maybe*-prophetic; and also we weren't above tongue-in-cheek asking him to intercede, which would explain a comment in my diary for Sunday, 23 February [1936, while sailing from the Argentine Islands to establish their new base in Marguerite Bay]: 'Our Bishop has again made a good job of his blessing. All day we have made our four knots in a flat calm with a small swell and are now hove to just south of Adelaide Island . . . the wind is negligible, the sky very nearly cloudless and the sea all but flat.'

I like to think that Launcelot, who was much loved, had a hand in our good fortune; I wouldn't have put it past him, even then, to have made himself heard in the right quarters.

It was nearly three months after all the sledge parties had returned before *Penola*, having had to go into dock in South Georgia for engine repairs, could reach Marguerite Bay to take them home. Launcelot, in addition to being Chaplain, Geologist, and Special Correspondent, was also the Expedition's photographer and went up in the Fox Moth to film *Penola*'s return. They embarked on 12 May – 'This morning they closed up the Base,' wrote Launcelot; 'oddly enough I do not much regret leaving; in fact I am so heartily looking forward to home and Cambridge that the parting was in no way a sorry business.'

A month later they reached South Georgia. It had been arranged for the shore party – the scientists – to take passage back to England on a Norwegian whaling-ship (an experience which Launcelot made use of twenty years later when he made his maiden speech, on 'Whales', in the House of Lords). So in May 1937, two years and eight months after sailing from St Katherine's Dock, Launcelot was back in England.

9

Dean of Trinity Hall

Places of education, religion, learning and research . . .
(Definition of the purpose of colleges in the university)

While the Graham Land Expedition was in Antarctica, George Chase had left Trinity Hall to become Bishop of Ripon. It was a remarkable tribute to Launcelot that the Master and Fellows elected him Dean *in absentia* in Chase's place, although he had only been in residence as a Fellow for one year and was not due to return to England for another two years. But the Governing Body knew what it was about; Launcelot had already shown that he had a way with undergraduates and was a useful and congenial member of the Senior Combination Room, and – essential qualification in donnish eyes – was 'academically respectable'. Moreover, George Chase had warmly recommended him.

Trinity Hall in the 1930s had far fewer Fellows than it does today. This could have resulted in a somewhat acerbic Senior Common Room (as portrayed in C. P. Snow's novel *The Masters*) but in fact it was remarkably friendly. The Fellows were by no means a homogeneous collection. Louis Clarke (later head of the Anthropology and Archaeology Department of the university) was a member of the Royal Geographical Society and had been one of the sponsors of Rymill's expedition; a friend of Augustus John, he was a discriminating art connoisseur and collector. Shaun Wylie the mathematician was to spend the war deciphering Enigma codes, while Owen Wansbrough Jones the scientist achieved the distinction during the war of being promoted straight from Captain to Brigadier in one day (to give him equal status with his American opposite number). The brilliant though reclusive classicist Franklin Angus, who had been a Baptist minister, was Senior Tutor, to be succeeded by the historian Charles Crawley; and there were the law dons for which the Hall was famous. The Master, H. R. Dean, who was Professor of Pathology, looked on Launcelot (as we have seen) with an almost paternal affection; although at best an infrequent communicant he always attended Sunday Evensong. His affection for the college and pastoral concern for all its members were a strong influence on the atmosphere of the Hall. Virtually all these Fellows became Launcelot's personal friends.

A verbal assessment from a post-war Trinity Hall colleague rated Launcelot's intelligence higher than he himself would have done. At Fellows' meetings, and in general, his views were listened to with respect; they were persuasively put and usually won acceptance. Launcelot was emphatically not considered a lightweight by his academic fellows.

Before the new academic year started in October 1937 there was a great deal for the new Dean to do. During the first few weeks after his return to England he was laid low by a bad dose of 'flu, almost inevitable after nearly three years in a germ-free environment, and when he recovered he had to sort and classify a thousand or so of his 'rocks', and write up his geological and glaciological notes in time for the Royal Geographical Society's meeting on 1 November. (In fact, Launcelot was never able to do full justice to his Antarctic findings, because to start with he felt he must throw himself wholeheartedly into the life of the college, and then the war intervened.) A letter from Brian Roberts, the ornithologist who had to return home early because of appendicitis, gives us some idea of the work involved:

Scott Polar Research Institute, Cambridge 21st August 1937. Without your returning your list we could not deal with your cases as we should have liked at Portsmouth [where *Penola* had just docked]. I had two sent up here which looked hopeful (both left by you unlabelled at Winter Island and labelled by me). One of these turned out to be old boots and clothes, the other water samples and geological specimens. These are here waiting for you to remove them. This would I am sure be appreciated by Betty at the earliest date possible as they smell strongly.

I have nearly been to jail over one of your cases. Rashly (perhaps) I certified that not one of [them] contained anything except scientific specimens. A customs official came along and said 'Well, I'd just like to look into that one' – pointing at one of yours. I opened it and right on top was a large box of South American cigars! And my shame was increased when I then took out about 15 pairs of *very* old footgear, all saturated with mildew. . . . However, he was kind . . .

Religion in the university in the 1930s was at a low ebb; Christianity was out of fashion, and most of the college chapels were moribund. Bishop Ross Hook, who was at that time an undergraduate at Peterhouse, recalled that Trinity Hall was about the only college chapel that was alive and well attended, and that people put this down to its young Dean. Launcelot's polar experience gave him a certain glamour, and his scientific background made people more ready to listen to him because in an age when science was felt to have discredited religion here was a scientist who was an avowed Christian. But perhaps the most important factor was Launcelot's remarkable gift for making friends; it is difficult to describe this without sounding mawkish, but it was a combination of a sense of humour, an ability to read people's characters, and being genuinely interested in them. People mattered; he really cared for them; and this came through.

Trinity Hall chapel is quite small. There are two rows of seats facing inwards that hold about eighty people, and before long an extra front row, retractable when not in use, had to be added. Only a faithful few normally attended chapel on weekday mornings before breakfast – a shortened form of matins, or on Thursdays and Saints' Days Holy Communion – but a shortened form of Evensong between first and second hall (in those days undergraduates had to dine in hall four or five days a week) soon attracted some forty or fifty undergraduates and two or three dons. On Sundays Holy Communion was followed by a breakfast in the Eden Room for anyone who wanted, and people soon learned that 'Christian fellowship' need not mean heartiness, but can mean reading the Sunday papers interspersed with desultory conversation. Sunday Evensong usually saw a full house – often uncomfortably so as people were encouraged to bring relatives and friends. The service was not strictly according to the *Book of Common Prayer*, since (as in Antarctica) Launcelot wanted members of the community of 'other denominations' to feel comfortable about worshipping in their college chapel – and he also understood the value of brevity. He was mortified when he heard this service called 'Flemingsong', but although he was no liturgical expert he was in fact anticipating the general shift towards greater simplicity and flexibility in liturgy that came about in the 1960s and 70s.

His first sermon as Dean, at the start of the Michaelmas Term of 1937, reveals his own underlying beliefs, and how he saw his job:

What is the reason why this place exists and why are you and I in it? In the time-honoured phrase, colleges are 'places of education, religion, learning and research'; the vast and essential business of coming to terms with the Universe, of discovering a purpose in life, that the University exists to foster.

During one's time here there is a singular opportunity to make friends with people who differ in the work they do, the character of their homes and backgrounds. At school or at home, public opinion is often strong enough to dictate conventions and opinions; here, there is a wider toleration of the opinions one can hold.

You are free to choose what time you get up, how much work you do, what books you read, how much and how often you drink. You are free to sow your wild oats. You are free to make your contribution to the college; you are free not to. You are free to come to chapel; you are free not to come to chapel. Such freedom is one of the best and most bewildering privileges of Cambridge. Don't be misled by it. Ultimately, we are only free to make good or bad use of our opportunities; more or less worthy of what St Paul called 'the glorious liberty of the children of God'.

A story is told of a young French nobleman who came to a priest and said 'Father, I have lost my religion'. The priest replied 'Thank God'. 'But,' said the young man, 'I said I have *lost* my religion'. 'And I said "Thank God," said the priest, 'because you have never had a religion of your own. You have had your Father's and Mother's religion, but you have never learned to practise your own. Now, go and ask the Holy Spirit to make your religion your own.' You will question and repudiate much of what you accepted without thinking; you will become more certain of what you don't know than of what you do. There are many who for a time become agnostics and atheists out of common honesty.

But don't throw out the baby with the bath water. When you've doubts and difficulties, the obvious man to approach is the chaplain – after all, it is his job. It is not for the chaplain to recommend himself, but this much allow me to say – the chaplain is never shocked and regards your confidence as a privilege and not a bore. We are groping for a religion in which we can believe without evasions, without dishonest ambiguities, without self-deception, without superstition. But we shall never find it in isolated searching. Friendship, fellowship, the Church – call it what you will – is vitally important.

The Christian religion began with friendship. And what may not that man become who daily holds company with Christ?

Launcelot knew the value of taking enough exercise to keep fit both mentally and physically, and in doing so he usually killed two birds with one stone. Playing a game of squash was a good way of getting to know people better; even when he was a bishop, he looked for opponents whom he wanted to get to know better, clergy or laity within the diocese, undergraduates, naval officers; when he went to preach at a school he usually asked the head beforehand to produce some boy or master who might be particularly worth getting to know. Later in life tennis fulfilled the same function, but while at Cambridge he considered tennis less useful then squash on the grounds that although tennis could involve three other people and not just one, a set of tennis took longer than a game of squash – and time was precious. And in the summer especially, rowing had to take precedence.

Rowing was Launcelot's main love. He waxed lyrical about it when he wrote the Preface to *A History of the Trinity Hall Boat Club*:

Rowing combines all the physical effort of which you are capable, with a gentle finesse of balance and control, a precision of timing and coordination and a sense of rhythm. Rowing is not only a sport; it is an art. Furthermore . . . members of a crew are more closely knit than perhaps in any other sport; the boat is a single unit [and] any fault, lack of balance or easing off affects the others and upsets the run of the boat. On the other hand when, even if only for a few strokes, things go right and the rhythm, timing, balance and power are properly coordinated, it is as if the crew were taken over. The boat moves forward mysteriously and without struggle . . .

I was fortunate enough in my time as an undergraduate that my tutor was happy enough that I should row and the Professor of Geology, no oarsman himself, positively encouraged me to do so. I did; and I owe much to my mentors and to Frank Carr [Captain of Boats in 1926] who talked me into it. . . . Later as Chaplain I frequently found myself encouraging freshmen to join the Boat Club.

To the end of his life he was convinced, and would cite statistics in support of his belief, that there was a clear correlation between a college's success on the river and its academic prowess. He also had a theory, which not all dons supported, that time spent on the river was not time wasted from an academic point of view but time well spent, on the grounds that the best academic work is always done under pressure (witness the way that war produces great scientific and technological advances), so that an undergraduate who has to get some work done before going down to the river will do better than one who has the whole afternoon to do it in.

More than most men, Launcelot hated hypocrisy – his time in Antarctica had taught him that it is what people really are that matters, and not what they set up to be – as a college sermon on penitence (it was during the Lent Term of 1938) shows.

At the beginning of our services we say the General Confession, and confess ourselves in no uncertain terms to be sinners. And then, with unfailing regularity, the parson pronounces the Absolution.

I read of a child's impressions when taken to church. The thing that struck him most was to find a respectable congregation declaring themselves to be miserable sinners, without showing the least sign that they really thought so. But that of course is the difficulty. The reason why diseases of the soul are so hard to cure is that men are unconscious of their existence – for the power that sin has over us is not only in its attractiveness, but its power to deceive us as to its own nature. There is little doubt that when a former Master of this college had two of the Fellows burned for heresy, he thought that this was for the greater glory of God. If we simply ask ourselves what evil we have done, we are unlikely to effect much, for so many habits are habitually condoned and excused that they take on the appearance of duties, and the hypocrisy is increased by the sanction of others.

This hypocrisy exists in the most unexpected places; when a libertine boasts 'At least I'm no hypocrite', is he really facing up to the consequences of his own actions or merely trying to throw dust in his own eyes?.... The most blinding of all hypocrisies is the amazing illusion that privilege, abilities, position and success are grounds for self-esteem, and not, as is really the case, responsibilities and grounds for humility.

As I understand it the real power of Christ as Saviour and Redeemer is the power he has to make people sincere about themselves. . . . [His teaching shows] an overturning of conventional morality with all its shallow casuistry; the self-satisfied Pharisee 'praying with himself', the self-righteous crowd accusing the woman of adultery; Jesus saw them all and touched on the quick the self-deception that had been their shield. Yet his touch was not hard and callous, but was like a purifying fire – it hurt that it might heal.

By the time Launcelot's second Michaelmas Term started, war was looming. That September of 1938 had just seen Hitler invading Czechoslovakia, and Chamberlain's return from Munich where he had met Hitler; war was averted for the time being but few believed the Prime Minister's claim that the piece of paper he brought back with him meant 'peace in our time'. As was his custom Launcelot preached on the first Sunday of term.

Not many days ago it seemed as if it would not have been possible for us to be here. As we adapt our minds to getting back to normal living we wonder, with varying degrees of uneasiness, will future generations be able to say that the last week of September 1938 proved a turning point in the civilised world – that we learned a lesson enabling a fresh start to be made; or will they have to say that not even the bitter anxiety of such a crisis proved strong enough to save us from falling into worse confusion and ruin?

We feel more and more like puppets in a drama over which we have no control. Yet responsibility for the future does in some real measure lie in the hands of ordinary people like ourselves. What is most needed is a re-dedication of the lives of individual men and women to the elementary virtues of honesty, courage, unselfishness and love. Christian people have sometimes felt it is a matter for regret that there are no clear answers in the New Testament to social or political problems. Apparently Christ regarded such problems as symptoms of the health or disease of the individuals who make up a community; to seek to cure the symptoms without attacking the root cause is the way not of the physician but of the quack . . .

The social and political problems thrown up by the threat of war could not, however, be ignored. Like many undergraduates of his generation Launcelot inclined towards pacifism – in 1930 while in America he saw the film *All Quiet on the Western Front* and Felix Greene noticed what a strong impression it made on him, all the more because when they adjourned to a café after the film their waiter happened to be a German who had had to fight in the German army opposite his Canadian father. In 1939 Father Denis Marsh of the Society of St Francis, and the priest and scientist Canon Charles Raven of Christ's College, both of whom Launcelot admired, reinforced his feelings that pacifism was the right line for a Christian to take. When conscription was introduced early in 1939 there is little doubt that had he been eligible for call-up he would have registered as a conscientious objector. (Much later, in a speech in the House of Lords on 16 March 1967, he told how 'I myself attended several tribunals as a witness in the early months of the war, and was immensely impressed. . . . The attitude of respect and fairness shown by the judge in itself helped to discriminate between the hypocrite and the man of genuine conviction.') Nine days after war was declared on 3 September 1939 a letter written to Alfred Stephenson (about someone who was trying to avoid paying royalties on their Antarctic photographs) reveals what Launcelot felt about the war:

Many thanks for your letter. [The errant publisher's] suggestion that his offer is a generous one is of course all Bla. . . . The difficulty is to know what he is really thinking, whether in the event of our holding out he would be obstinate, or climb down. It is just like the political wrangling with Hitler

and helps to endorse my conviction that the ultimate cause
of this war is the business mind and outlook and big business
interests.

Launcelot usually filed his sermons away in case they might live
to fight another day (and in emergencies was not above
borrowing someone else's – Owen Chadwick at the Windsor
memorial service recalled affectionately how 'he would come
up to you, blushing pink but not more ashamed than pink, and
say "I've got to preach a sermon on St John the Baptist. You
don't happen to keep one in your file?"'). But the real value of
his sermons during the first nine months of the war lies in what
they reveal of his own state of mind. He preached in the college
chapel, and in several schools including a series of Holy Week
addresses at Rugby (Easter was very early in 1940). He clearly
took trouble over them; they are typed out neatly, and are all
good, solid stuff – a course on the Lord's Prayer, on Judgment,
Heaven and Hell, on Faith. But they are stilted, and even when
preaching on our Lord's Passion are dull and lifeless. Take, for
example, a sermon in Trinity Hall chapel on Trinity Sunday
1940:

> There may be many of us who suspect that the doctrine of
> the Trinity is a tortuous and incomprehensible formula. . . .
> It is said that the Athanasian Creed is the only accurate state-
> ment of the doctrine and that it achieves this by virtue of
> following every assertion by its formal contradiction. Surely,
> at all events in the stress of times like these, we may leave
> this matter to those with a mind for speculative metaphysics
> and aim to follow Jesus simply with the vivid picture we get
> of him in the Gospels. But ultimately the dogmas and the
> doctrines of the Church were designed to help men to under-
> stand about God.

The whole sermon would have taken a good fifteen minutes to
deliver, and can only be described as platitudinous. It suggests
a preacher who is trying to block out something; he is not really

engaging with the world as it is but is taking refuge in repeating doctrines that he knows of old – except for just one passage where it comes alive because it comes from the heart:

> We have behaved as discourteous guests in God's world; taken His scenery and filled it with slag heaps, slashed the countryside with trenches and craters in pursuit of our wealth and our hatreds; taken God's cities and defaced them with slums; and if that were not enough, we and other nations glibly talk of our country, our possessions, our empire. . . . We need reminding that the earth is not British or German or French or American; the earth is the Lord's and all that therein is.

It is clear (later reminiscences bear this out) that Launcelot was being pulled in two directions. Denis Marsh and Charles Raven had persuaded him that intellectually the pacifist argument was unanswerable; at the same time Launcelot's whole upbringing had taught him that 'doing my duty to the King' as the catechism enjoined must not be shirked. During peacetime, and during the 'phoney war' period through the winter of 1939–40, there was no conflict between the two ideals of pacifism and patriotism – as we saw, he regarded the war as having been caused by the business mind and outlook and big business interests – but by May 1940 the German panzers had broken through in France and threatened the very existence of Great Britain; pacifism had become difficult to reconcile with patriotic duty. As Launcelot preached in Trinity Hall chapel on that Sunday evening of 17 May 1940 he must have been aware that the British Expeditionary Force in France was facing destruction, and that it would have included men who a year or two earlier had worshipped in the same building in which he was now preaching. Yet there was nothing, apart from a passing reference to 'the stress of times like these', to suggest that as he spoke the fate of Britain and France hung in the balance.

The following Sunday, 24 May, was a Day of National Prayer.

Launcelot in his introduction to the special Service of Intercession was clearly agonizing over his dilemma:

> There may be some who look to a Day of National Prayer as a form of spiritual Blitzkrieg aimed to storm the citadels of heaven and win God to our side. If we pray as followers of Christ we shall be safe from this danger. Christ taught us to pray that God's will might be done. With this in mind, can we honestly pray for victory? Surely the answer must be that we *must* pray for victory – the victory of truth and freedom, for all that we have learnt to regard as best in God's gifts to men. In such prayer, Christians will never be divided against one another. There is no splitting of the Church into Pacifist and Non-Pacifist. We may or may not regard war as such an evil thing in itself that to take any part in it is worse even than submission to the most terrible and widespread Nazi tyranny. Whatever our judgment of such matters – and of course we must judge – the important matter is that we should submit our hopes and actions and, if need be, revise them according to the will of God.

By the following Sunday, 3 June 1940, Launcelot's own judgment had brought him to the conviction that submission to Nazi tyranny would be more wrong than agreeing to fight it. He spoke with a fire and conviction that for the previous nine months had been lacking, and there is a poignancy in the fact that this was the end of the term and of the academic year and that many, if not most, of those present would be unlikely to return to Cambridge for several years, if at all:

> There is so much in flux that the sanest, most level-headed man might be excused if he feels in danger of losing his sense of proportion. Such uncertainty makes one susceptible to a feeling of futility, as if the bottom had fallen out of a world that had looked stable. . . . But the Gospel starts with faith; and we are thrown back to search into our foundations, unto the rock whence we are hewn. And this Gospel is not a private

matter between you or me and God. God was in Christ reconciling the world to himself. He admits us and summons us to
share in his world-wide and age-long redeeming action, to be
active agents in his redeeming purpose. God gives us the power
to work for a purpose which is eternal, against which the
Gates of Hell cannot prevail; and it is a small matter that
we should be shifted out of the pleasant ways of a normal
Englishman's life.

Be sober, be vigilant, for your adversary the devil as a
roaring lion walketh about, seeking whom he may devour;
whom resist, steadfast in the faith. And the God of all grace,
who hath called you into his eternal glory in Christ Jesus,
after that ye have suffered a little while, make you perfect,
stablish, strengthen, settle you. To him be glory and dominion
for ever and ever.

By the end of June Launcelot had decided what he should do.
A letter to the editor of the *Geographical Journal* dated 2 July
1940 seems symbolically to pull down the shutters on pre-war
Cambridge:

Dear Mr Myers, I really am sorry for being so dilatory about
that review. Honestly, the fates have been against me, and it
has been incredibly difficult to find a moment of time, the
more so as just lately I have decided to accept a Chaplaincy
in the Navy and start on next Tuesday at the R.N. Barracks,
Portsmouth. I can't promise the review before I leave, and if
it is not finished I shall just have to send the book back to
you, with much shame on my part. But I do hope to get Oliver
Gatty's obituary written, and I also hope to submit to Mr
Hinks a short paper on Graham Land Glaciation which I very
much hope you may be able to publish, despite the haste in
which it has been written.

By way of postscript, let it be recorded that Launcelot's 'Relic
Glacial Forms on the Western Seaboard on Graham Land' was
duly published in the August 1940 *Journal*, supplementing his

'Structure and Flow of Glacier Ice: A Review' published in the November 1938 number. (And thirty-five years later Launcelot was thrilled to be told that the Fleming Glacier was currently thought to be the fastest-moving glacier in the world!)

Wartime Naval Chaplain

[The Chaplain] is inferior and superior to no one, and a friend to all on board.

(Admiralty Instructions)

Launcelot spent just a week at Portsmouth being initiated into the ways of the Royal Navy before being posted towards the end of July to HMS *King Alfred*. This was a shore establishment at Hove for training Volunteer Reserve officers – men of similar background to Trinity Hall undergraduates, but engaged in a life very different from a university, and with very little time for people to get to know one another before they were posted to their respective ships.

Almost the first sermon Launcelot preached at HMS *King Alfred* was on 'Courage'. After the war, a revised version formed part of a widely acclaimed talk to a group of school teachers and university dons called Dons and Beaks, entitled 'Humility, Compassion and Courage'; but the original version is more striking, and understandably so since those budding naval officers knew their courage would soon be put to the test at sea where the odds at that time were against them:

In many respects the world has become extraordinarily cynical, and delights in debunking. There is, thank God, one quality which has survived this process and at which few have thrown mud; that is, fortitude or courage. I feel it is rather an impertinence for me to talk to you about it, but courage is a quality which in these times is so necessary for all of us that it is worth giving thought to what it is and what is its source.

There are various kinds of courage.

First, there is the 'dutch' variety, which comes out of a bottle.

Secondly, there is the dramatic variety; you know, sticking out your chin, grinding your teeth, and eyeing the world with a glassy stare.

Then there is ignorance, or lack of imagination. There is a story of a new recruit who saw his sergeant looking singularly green. 'Why, Sergeant,' he said, 'I believe you are afraid.' 'Yes, I am; and if you were half as afraid as I am you'd run away.'

I can't help reminding you of a delightful incident in the story of Winnie the Pooh. Pooh and Piglet were tracking the Woozle. They didn't know much about the size or muscularity of Woozles, which made it all rather alarming. And suddenly they saw a double set of tracks; and Piglet jumped; and then, to show he hadn't jumped from fright, jumped up and down again 'in an exercising sort of way'. Piglet, gifted with a very vivid imagination, was also exceedingly brave. I wonder if a man can be really brave who is not also afraid? Real courage, physical or moral, means being fully aware of the dangers involved and yet not letting them prevent our doing what we know we ought to do.

Or again, and this is particularly needed just now, courage means not losing our sense of values; not ceasing to be kind and tolerant where others are cruel or intolerant, or thinking nothing is worth while because everything is in danger. Surely such courage is a religious quality – or is it? Religion may become a refuge from the harsher sides of life, and God be looked upon as a personified air-raid shelter. Stage curates are sometimes portrayed as a cross between a pussy-cat and a goose, rather soft and contemptible. But even his enemies did not think Jesus soft or contemptible. He fairly took the breath away from staid respectable people, drove a coach and horses through convention, drove the money-changers from the temple, and at the same time had the audacity to claim he could forgive sins. To speak of 'Gentle Jesus meek and mild' may seem an easy way to keep children from making too much noise, but it leaves them with a singularly unfortunate and untrue picture of the strong Son of God.

In his disciples Jesus looked for active courage. They must not be frightened of trading with their talents in a world where banks go bankrupt, but must have the courage and initiative to see and meet the needs of the world despite the risks. And this courage came from a confidence in God. Courage is not bombastic heroics, but an imperturbable serenity based on confidence. Those who recognise that the Lord God omnipotent reigneth have no cause to fear; they know that God knows what he is doing, and has not lost control of this crazy world; that he loves us even when he slays; that he makes all things work together for good to those that love him.

In November Launcelot was posted to the battleship *Queen Elizabeth* at Rosyth. For the first time in his ministry, most of his 1,200 'parishioners' were products of elementary schools that they had left at the age of fourteen. There was no TV then to widen people's knowledge, and there was a yawning educational and culture gap between those who had left school at fourteen and grammar and public school boys and girls who had stayed on until they were eighteen, so for someone like Launcelot who had spent his life among highly educated university graduates the culture-gap was enormous. The sailors on the lower deck simply did not speak his language, nor he theirs. To make things worse, he was by nature rather shy – the hesitant language of his sermons denotes diffidence as well as a desire for strict accuracy. Those first few weeks as Chaplain in HMS *Queen Elizabeth* were probably the most difficult time of his life.

Another Cambridge don, Meredith Dewey, later Dean of Pembroke, also became a wartime naval chaplain and his biography tells how 'the appearance of the chaplain on the stokers' mess deck would give rise to audible comments of a highly unflattering nature expressed in crudely nautical language.

Ultimately the visit had to be made or nothing could be accomplished.' Dewey persevered, and his diary a few months later records 'Visited Stoker _____ who badly damaged his arm, compound fractures, in the battle; v. interesting talk with survivors.' In much the same way, it was after being in action that Launcelot broke through the culture-barrier; though in his case, his polar experience gave him an advantage since although his Antarctic companions had been educated men like himself, he had learned how to rough it and had doubtless gained some experience of naval language from Ryder and Martin. On the rare occasions when he wore a uniform, moreover, the Polar Medal which Rymill's team all received from the King early in 1940 earned him respect.

But it was his gift for friendship combined with a thoroughly professional approach to the job that really made Launcelot a good naval chaplain. Among his papers was a foolscap HMSO notebook that contains the names and addresses of over 1,200 men, together with any relevant personal details. Also the notebook painstakingly records a list of letters written; some to his own friends and family, but also a great number to the families and fiancées of crew members (he claimed to have written a successful proposal of marriage on behalf of one of them). He wrote more than fifty letters a month even during the hectic weeks of 1941.

A Leading Seaman who joined the *Queen Elizabeth* in Alexandria wrote, some forty years later, about Launcelot:

I first met him when I was morale-wise at my lowest! We had just been torpedoed on a convoy to Malta. . . . I was really 'chocker-block' – and along came the Padre! He was marvellous. His tiny little cabin below the bridge crammed with us 'lower-deck' types eating up all his biscuits and drinking his cocoa. He was always squatted on the deck holding forth, and listening to us. Mostly listening to our beefs and making the odd comment and generally cheering us up.

Launcelot's sermons tried to bridge the communication gap
between a clerical don and the lower deck. His actual words
may not have got home to many of them, but what did get
across was that he was genuinely concerned for each and every
one of them; it was obvious that they were not just pew-fodder
but that he really cared for each individual. Even the sermons
themselves remain a moving testimony to a faith that has stood
the test. Sunday 26 February 1941 saw the *Queen Elizabeth* in
company with the ill-fated HMS *Hood* steaming south to inter-
cept the German pocket battleships *Scharnhorst* and *Gneisenau*;
Launcelot always remembered how their Captain, Claud Barry,
had found exactly the right words to steady everyone's nerves.
That was the background to this sermon for that First Sunday
in Lent:

Nothing can be quite so annoying as waste. Under certain
conditions customs officials are bound to throw away contra-
band, and I've always hated to think of a member of that
august body pouring a cask of rum or a bottle of precious
scent into the sea. It does hurt to hear about waste, even if
you haven't a chance to benefit from the things that are being
wasted. Before the war it was terrible to think of vast stocks
of corn or rubber being destroyed, to keep up the price, when
there were plenty of people who could have done with those
things.

If you come to think of it, war is a curious mixture of
carefulness and extravagance. Whether you call something
wasteful depends on whether you think the object it is spent
on is worth the price. You are only wasteful if you use something for a wrong purpose. And the most tragic form of waste
is when people are wasted.

Lent is a time when Christians are reminded to have a good
look at themselves and see in what ways they might be less
extravagant. It should be kept as a time of fasting – doing
without things in which one is being wasteful. And it's a time
of prayer and almsgiving – being more extravagant of oneself
towards God, and other people. One evening when Our Lord

was having dinner with some friends – it was not long before his Crucifixion – a woman who had an alabaster box of ointment, very precious, broke the box and poured the ointment on Our Lord's head. Some of his disciples thought this was too much of a good thing; 'to what purpose is this waste?' they said; surely the money would have been better spent in helping the poor. But Jesus said, 'The poor you have always with you, but me you have not always'.

To what purpose is this waste? Some have said, or felt, that about devotion to Our Lord. But just apply this thought of waste and extravagance to the Christian duties of Lent; prayer, fasting, almsgiving. You cut down on waste in things like food, drink, the satisfaction of the flesh, and can be a great deal more extravagant in prayer and worship and in kindness and consideration for others. 'For the Kingdom of Heaven is like a man . . . who, when he had found one pearl of great price, went and sold all that he had and bought it.'

So 'Be not anxious for your life, what ye shall eat, nor for the body what ye shall put on . . . but rather seek the Kingdom of God, and all these things shall be added unto you.'

Those last words 'be not anxious for your life' were very apposite. As the official history (Roskill, *War at Sea*, Vol. 1, p. 378 footnote) tells us:

> Neither of the newly joined ships [*Hood* and *Queen Elizabeth*] was in proper operational condition at the time, but the urgency was considered such as to justify the employment of ships which were unlikely to develop their full fighting capacity if an action were to take place.

In other words, their guns were not calibrated, and (to use Launcelot's own words much later) 'We knew we were for Davy Jones's locker if we did meet up with them.' Luckily, unknown to the Admiralty, the German ships had already reached Brest.

The next occasion when it was possible to have a full church parade of the whole ship's company was 27 April, and Launcelot preached on 'The Kingship of Christ'. At the time they were returning from escorting a convoy to Freetown and were on their way to join Admiral Somerville's 'Force H' at Gibraltar. They knew what might lie ahead, but at least the ship was now in a proper state of readiness.

'I saw heaven opened, and behold a white horse; and he that sat upon it is called Faithful and True, and in righteousness doth he make war. His eyes – a flame of fire! On his head – many crowns! And on his vesture is written "King of Kings and Lord of Lords"' (Revelation 19:11–16).

Men, even Christian men, have too much forgotten the authentic majesty, the awe-striking authority and the power of Jesus. To ignore or even to minimise the Kingship of Christ is to reduce the religion He founded to the level of a voluntary imitation of a good man; and that is to misunderstand what it is that has made Jesus a moving force in history. . . . [What made] sane human beings suffer and die gladly for Christ's sake was [that] they were fired by a King of a Kingdom which cannot be destroyed, whose Kingdom is 'not of this world' – that is to say it exists not by virtue of human consent but because of an eternal authority and validity.

Today too many people think that Jesus the King has been defeated. No important activity in this year of grace 1941, they say, is Christianly controlled; if Christ were once King, He is King no longer; there are not enough people behind Him. But Christ rules not in proportion to the degree that mankind happens to honour and approve of Him; He rules because as God He must rule. When He stood before Pilate, it was as one wholly rejected but still King. It does not rest with us whether or not Christ shall rule; what does rest with us is whether or not Christ shall rule in the hearts of men on earth today. . . .

Men and nations are at present being judged according to God's law. The end of Godlessness – of putting men in the place that belongs to God – is and always has been the cry of the mob in the street, riot and ruin, blood and starvation and great woe. But once we turn to Christ the King and acknowledge the Kingship which is His, then we see Him not as a stern, cold, distant Monarch but a God who, in sheer compassion, has come among us and shares our woes and lays His strong hand upon us with the gifts of courage and hope and the secret of that life and reality which is eternal.

'Art thou a King, then?' asked Pilate in surprise. 'I am,' answered Jesus, 'And you shall see Me sitting on the right hand of power and coming in the clouds of heaven.'

Nine days later they were steaming past Gibraltar with a convoy carrying much-needed tanks to the Eighth Army by the direct route through the Mediterranean. We now know that 'the Admiralty expressed grave doubts regarding the success of the experiment now that the Luftwaffe was established in strength in Sicily, but once the decision had been taken [they] used the opportunity to send substantial reinforcements to Admiral Cunningham' (Roskill, *War at Sea*, Vol. 1, p. 437). The *Queen Elizabeth* was one of those reinforcements. Launcelot, for one, never forgot the sight of enemy aircraft approaching, apparently unstoppably, when the entire armament of the battleship was fired off at once to produce a protective curtain of metal. The convoy did get through, with only one of the five merchant ships sunk and another damaged, and the *Queen Elizabeth* joined the Mediterranean fleet at Alexandria.

For the next eight months they were constantly in action. In September HMS *Warspite* was damaged and Admiral Cunningham moved his flag to the *Queen Elizabeth*. On 25 November Launcelot witnessed an event that he described at the first service he took, for college servants, in Trinity Hall chapel after the war as 'the experience which made the strongest impression on me during my time in the Navy':

[The battleship] *Barham* was a sister ship of ours; she had been in company with us for several months, so all of us had a good many friends in her. Then one glorious sunny afternoon when we were at sea, the *Barham* was torpedoed. I won't go into details but she sank in 4½ minutes and blew up as she sank.

That evening we heard that over 500 survivors [out of 1200] had been picked up and a little later we had prayers broadcast throughout the ship over the loudspeaker so that men in every part of the ship should be able to take part – in the boiler rooms, engine rooms, the magazines, the galleys, the turrets and the messdecks – and together see behind this disaster to the Lord of all life and eternity. One of the prayers we used was 'that while we pass through the changing things of time we should not lose the things eternal'. It's always hard to convey the atmosphere of an experience like that, and I wish I could describe to you the difference those prayers made; but I can tell you this for certain; every man jack in that ship knew himself to be united with his shipmates and with the ship's company of the *Barham* in a bond which had brought him into touch with the Living God.

Did this last? Well, I don't know; I suppose in many cases preoccupations and indifference threw that time of prayer into the background; in others it may have meant a really new perspective to their lives. But it's a rather appalling thought that it needs a major disaster to bump us into a realisation of the Presence of the God and Father of us all.

On 19 December the Mediterranean Fleet's two remaining battleships, *Valiant* and *Queen Elizabeth*, were torpedoed by Italian midget submarines in Alexandria Harbour. The *Queen Elizabeth* came to rest on the bottom and was raised by a floating dock; for the next five months her crew were uncomfortably aware that during the frequent air raids on the harbour the ship's masts were the only objects that stuck up above the smoke screen. One of her crew wrote many years later to Launcelot:

During an Air Raid on Alexandria . . . we were all wondering, if the Floating Dock got hit, would the Q.E. float off safely or turn over? A sick bay attendant and myself were allocated to you as messengers. He and I were scared stiff as there were

a lot of bangs going on all around us. You kept cool, calm
and collected, which was very reassuring to us. [Launcelot
replied 'Yes, I remember the bombing in Alex, although I can
assure you that if I looked cool that is not what I felt'.]

However, life went on; in December the Anglican Bishop of
Egypt and the Sudan held a confirmation for Launcelot's candidates; and shore leave gave the ship's company a glimpse of
what life in the Middle East was like. Launcelot was one of
those who managed a brief visit to the Holy Land, and in his
Good Friday sermon in 1942 was able to make the scenes of
the first Holy Week come more vividly alive:

As the road swings over the brow of the Mount of Olives you
get an impressive view of the City of Jerusalem; the temple,
streets and pinnacles all easy to distinguish in the hot glare
of the Mediterranean sun. Eastern people are of course a good
deal more emotional than the British. You only have to see
the tradesmen in the streets of Alexandria or Cairo to realise
how that crowd on the Mount of Olives was in a ferment
when they had come to see Jesus as their King.

Yet the central figure hardly paid any attention, but looked
beyond the crowd to the city which he was soon to enter. 'If
thou hadst known the things which belong to thy peace. But
now they are hid from thine eyes.' Terrible words of judgment.
One wonders whether those same words might not apply with
equal force to the world we live in today. . . . We sometimes
call ourselves a Christian land. I wonder if we really are.

Well, you may say, what are you going to do about it? As
Jesus stood and wept over Jerusalem he almost admitted that
there was nothing you could do to shake Jerusalem out of its
worldly attitudes; any attempt was doomed to failure. And
yet, he set his face and went down to Jerusalem. Was this just
foolhardy?

Well, there's one thing certain; neither you nor I will ever
see why it is of any use to follow the Lord unless we are
willing to take that first step of faith down that dusty path

right into the turmoil of the world. Let us pray that we may give ourselves in obedience to travel that path with Christ.

It was not until May 1942 that the *Queen Elizabeth* was made sufficiently seaworthy to risk the long journey round the Cape and limp across the Atlantic to the United States, where she could be properly repaired with no interruptions by air raids. Years later, when Launcelot dedicated a memorial plaque to Admiral Cunningham, he said:

> It is wholly fitting that this plaque should be dedicated at this annual Trafalgar Day Service [21 October 1979]. For the service which Andrew Cunningham rendered to this country in the last war was comparable to that of Nelson in his victory over Villeneuve's fleet. It is probably no exaggeration to say that without Nelson, Napoleon could so easily have overrun this country, and that without Cunningham, we could so easily have lost the Hitler war.
>
> It was very largely because of Andrew Cunningham's resolution that Britain held the Mediterranean on her own; held it when Malta was close to collapse and the Mediterranean Fleet had been severely battered. And in both cases, the defence of freedom was at stake. 'Stick it out' was the message he made to his ships in the Battle of Crete; and this, patently, he did himself – and because he did, those under his command were better able to do.

He added a personal reminiscence of Cunningham: 'a staunch Presbyterian, when he left the *Queen Elizabeth* he shook hands warmly and, looking at me with his penetrating eyes, said with a cheerful smile, "Padre, I've always wanted to have a good theological argument with you." I was rather relieved that the opportunity had not presented itself!'

The *Queen Elizabeth* remained in the US naval dockyard at Norfolk, Virginia, for thirteen months. Launcelot set himself to make sure that each and every member of the crew should be able to spend shore leave with American hosts. He was always

ruthlessly unscrupulous in using personal contacts and friendships to further any good cause, and during those months in
America he put to very good use the contacts he had made
during his time at Yale. One ordinary crew member who had
hesitantly mentioned that he was fond of horses found himself
spending a week in Kentucky with a millionaire who had a
string of polo ponies, another 'went to Washington with
[Launcelot] and had tea with Lord Halifax [the British Ambassa-
dor]. We spent one day visiting the National Press Club and
had a sing-song with all the prominent War Correspondents
and Newsmen, among them Walter Cronkite.'

And so it went on. The administrative burden of arranging
holidays for over a thousand men – for that is what Launcelot
did – must have been a nightmare, but he managed it (just as
later on he managed to keep up-to-date files not only of all the
clergy and ordinands of his diocese, but also of some five hundred potential future recruits in what was labelled 'Patronage
File'). It was a notable achievement, and among his papers were
a great many letters showing how very much his efforts were
appreciated by all on board.

By the time the *Queen Elizabeth* returned to England in July
1943, the ministry that Launcelot had embarked on with such
trepidation two and a half years earlier had developed into something infinitely fulfilling. His gift for friendship coupled with
hard work, unfailing prayer, and highly professional efficiency
had done much; but perhaps what had finally broken down the
culture-barrier that had existed was their shared dangers. His
voice over the tannoy whenever they were in action, giving a
running commentary to those, especially those below the water-
line, who could only hear the bangs and could not see what was
happening, had become familiar – and those broadcast prayers
after the *Barham* went down had struck a chord even with those
who had felt they had no time for religion. When Launcelot
retired some thirty years after the war's end he was invited to
spend five weeks on HMS *Kent* as honorary chaplain – a great
compliment, since even on a peacetime summer cruise the presence on board of a 71-year-old who could not walk without a

stick might have been quite a liability. The temporary appointment was a great success, however, and he found that being a
chaplain in a Guided Missile Destroyer commissioned in 1963
was much the same as it had been in a battleship commissioned
in 1912. He wrote an article entitled 'The Naval Padre's Job,
as Seen by Our Own Padre the Rt Rev. Launcelot Fleming' in
the ship's magazine:

The Chaplain of a naval ship is in much the same position as
the Vicar of any parish on shore; the ship's company is his
parish and the job is basically much the same as that of any
other parson. There are three sides to it:

First, he is appointed to be their Pastor. My own approach
to this is first to get to know as many of the Ship's Company
as possible; and it's really quite a job to find ways of meeting
500 people spread round a ship of this size, and to invade the
innumerable places where men are living and working without
being a nuisance. Then somehow or other I want to make it
known that if there are any people who have problems and
they would like to talk about them, I am at their service.

Then secondly the Padre is responsible for arranging and
conducting services. It takes a lot of time to get ready for the
Sunday services – to think about the choice of hymns, lessons
and prayers, and prepare an address. Incidentally I find it
takes more time to prepare a short sermon than a long one –
and I'm sure sermons should be short. Obviously it is encouraging when a number of people want to come to the Church
Services, but it's absurd to imagine that your religion consists
primarily in going to church. Christianity is concerned with
how your life is seen by you and the way you live it, and
Church services should have some bearing on this.

Then thirdly the Padre has the job of endeavouring to com-
municate and interpret the Christian religion. You can't push
this sort of thing down people's throats, but I've found time
and again that people are often glad to have the chance of
talking about these matters.

Some Padres may seem rather aloof and stand-offish, and

others too matey; some a bit serious, others rather hearty. For my part I feel I can only go about things in my own way and try to be myself. All Padres however are expected to be men of God and to practise what they preach. This is getting near the bone and I couldn't make any comment; but it's worth recalling that the requirement 'to be what you profess' applies to every man, and no one can really get away from this by saying 'I don't profess any belief', for no man worth his salt does not have values and ideals by which he is endeavouring to live.

A Padre in the Navy has the advantage of being given a status appropriate to his job. He wears no badges of rank. [Throughout his wartime service Launcelot almost invariably wore civilian clothes (including an Anthony Eden hat because he had to be able to take his hat off to salute the quarter-deck)]; he is defined in Admiralty Instructions as 'superior and inferior to no one and a friend to all on board'. That is to say he is on the same footing as the person he is with, be he an Admiral or a Junior Seaman. Sometimes I find myself called 'Padre', sometimes 'Sir', sometimes 'The Bish', sometimes 'Launcelot' and sometimes 'Bill'. Take your pick; I answer to them all.

I have been asked whether I find the job of Padre difficult. Well, yes, I think it is; but I need to remind myself that the resources are infinite.

Admiral Jock Slater, who was commanding HMS *Kent* at the time, wrote:

I will never forget the weeks he spent with me in HMS *Kent* in 1977. . . . Despite the difficulty he experienced in getting about the ship at sea, he did just that and there wasn't a single sailor who didn't know – and love – the 'Bish' after only a few days. . . . When Launcelot asked me if I thought the sailors might like to hear about the Graham Land Expedition and see some of his slides, I immediately agreed but was concerned that not many would turn up. Little did I know! The dining room was packed to bursting.

Launcelot's last wartime naval posting, in 1943, was to HMS *Ganges*. Like his first posting at Hove, this was a shore training establishment, this time near Ipswich, with 4,000 men. It was a ten-week course so each week 400 new eighteen-year-olds arrived. He alluded to his experience in *Ganges* in a sermon a few years later:

> The other padres and myself used to see all the new entries who bore the label C of E. The vast majority ... had very little education in the sense of schooling. But what did surprise and shake one was to find how small a proportion of them had ever seemed to ask whether there was any purpose in their lives or in the world in which they lived. The very suggestion of a purpose in life struck them as something quite new and original, and not unnaturally was something that usually aroused their interest.

Launcelot had only just over a year at *Ganges*. In December 1944 he was appointed Director of Service Ordination Candidates and his service in the Royal Navy came to an end.

11

Post-War Cambridge

> He was one of those not so rare scientists for whom the
> search for the truth about God and the search for the truth
> of this physical realm were not two separate endeavours, but
> a single quest.
>
> *(Dr Owen Chadwick)*

When Launcelot returned to civilian life in December 1944 he
shared a flat in Kensington with Kenneth Carey, the other secretary of the Central Advisory Council for Training for the Ministry (CACTM). Launcelot dealt with ex-Service ordinands and
Ken Carey (later Principal of Westcott House) with the rest.
London by that stage of the war had suffered much, and was
still suffering from V2 rockets; fuel was short, the black-out still
in operation. Despite uncomfortable journeys on crowded and
often late trains, Launcelot was glad to get down to Cambridge
for weekends at Trinity Hall. But although London life was far
from luxurious, Launcelot and Ken Carey were old friends, got
on well together, and managed to entertain a certain amount
and have a reasonable social life.

CACTM had been set up by Archbishop William Temple so
that instead of each individual bishop deciding whether a man
should be ordained or not, there could be a co-ordinated system.
War service had weakened the links that potential ordinands
had with their own dioceses, and a vocation was more likely to
have come through some chaplain than through a man's vicar;
so CACTM selection boards for potential ordinands were set
up, based on the War Office selection boards for potential
officers. The secretaries' job was mainly administrative, and

Launcelot was a very good administrator who loathed bureaucracy and constantly reminded himself and those around him
that the coming of the kingdom of Heaven must not be confused
with achieving an empty in-tray. He was also a very shrewd
judge of character, and had the knack of getting people to ana-
lyse their own motives, strengths and weaknesses; Fr Denis
Marsh always said Launcelot had an 'uncanny' ability to judge
a man's vocation, and Peter Brooke, with considerable experience in politics and as a government minister, said at his funeral
that Launcelot was 'brilliant at one-to-ones'.

There was very little in Launcelot's papers about his time
at CACTM, and what there was were notes and letters of a
confidential nature that needed to be destroyed after a cursory
glance. The few occasions when he mistook a goose for a swan
seem usually to have been with men from a working-class background, probably for two reasons. First, Launcelot's wartime
experiences, especially at HMS *Ganges*, had opened his eyes to
the the fact that alarmingly few of those who had left school at
fourteen had any real understanding of Christianity, so that any
potential ordinand from such a background was particularly
welcome; secondly, although Launcelot could very quickly judge
the suitability of someone from a similar background to his
own, it took a little longer when a culture-gap had to be bridged
– and in his job a single interview was usually all that was
possible. The fact remains, however, that he was uncannily good
at discerning anyone's vocation, and not only vocations to the
ministry. In Owen Chadwick's words at Launcelot's memorial
service at Windsor:

He liked the human race very much. Ken Carey used to tell
him 'If you say about any more people, I like him *enormously*,
I shall bang you on the head.' Launcelot took a more charitable view of men and women than the facts warranted. But
the strange thing was, this did not make him a bad judge of
character. On the contrary, he knew within a minute or two
in an interview whether somebody was suitable for a job. It
was said of the great Archbishop William Temple that he

liked everyone so much that he could not distinguish between good and bad. Launcelot liked everyone just as much, but knew perfectly, instinctively, how to distinguish.

His spell as Director of Service Ordination Candidates proved a help after he had become a bishop, as it had enabled him to get to know clergy whom he could try and lure into his diocese. It also gave him an insight into the way CACTM worked; but so far as one can tell he had little influence on church policy over the selection and training of clergy. He did his CACTM job well, but his heart was in Cambridge.

Sermons he preached during the immediate post-war years remind one how ethical issues that seemed to be at the time, and indeed really were, important got quickly buried by even more momentous events. A sermon in Trinity Hall chapel in July 1945 shows how appalled people were by the discovery of the German concentration camps, because up to then no one had thought that such barbarity was possible; but although that came as an enormous shock, a few weeks later the atom bombs on Hiroshima and Nagasaki would drive everything else from people's minds.

> What should our reaction be as Christians to the German people in the face of such evidence [at Buchenwald and Dachau]? Whatever view we hold about war crimes trials, this is an exceedingly perplexing problem. Just as it can fairly be claimed that the German people as a whole and not some Nazi minority are to some extent responsible for concentration camps, so must each of us admit responsibility for whatever measures are taken in the treatment of the conquered countries.
>
> The trouble is that whilst I know what my Christian attitude ought to be towards Tom Smith who commandeers my bicycle just as I want it, it's a very different matter when I try to apply the same principle to the German people – partly because the nature of the evil is infinitely greater, and partly

because the harm has not been done to *me*, but to Poles, Jews, French, Norwegians. It would be nonsense to say 'If I ought to forgive Tom Smith, therefore I ought to treat the Germans in exactly the same way.' But we can narrow down the question by ruling out two attitudes that seem contradictory yet strangely enough are often held by the same people.

The first is Vengeance, the desire to get even – 'exterminate the rats'. If you were really to set about this you would qualify for extermination yourself by having acquired the same mentality that you were seeking to destroy.

Equally unChristian, but often found masquerading as the Christian attitude, is the soft man who speaks in sentimental terms of being nice to all the Germans. We should get it clear once and for all that the Christian law of love is not being nice and kind and soft. When parents spoil a child in the mistaken idea that they are being kind, they haven't taken the trouble to seek its proper welfare.

What then should be our attitude? First; to get clear the distinction between enemies and sinners. Christ said about enemies, 'Do good to them that hate you.' If your enemy also happens to be a sinner, your attitude to him must be determined by the nature of the sin, not by his being your enemy. The word 'love' in the Christian sense is not what you feel towards someone, but what you desire for them. We may not feel loving towards the Germans; that's not the point. We must desire their welfare. . . . Fortunately God does not despair of us as quickly as we despair of one another – 'God commendeth his love towards us in that while we were yet sinners Christ died for us.'

A year later, Launcelot told an audience of schoolboys and their parents (7 July 1946 at Wellington) how bleak the outlook for humanity seemed to be:

Dean Inge remarked of those who spoke of living in an interesting age, 'No doubt the Gadarene swine found the first part of their journey interesting.' There is much to support his contention that Western civilisation is on a similar descent to that of the Gadarene swine; the atom bomb, the crowded divorce courts, the disunity of the allied nations, it isn't a cheerful picture, and I suppose most of us have at the back of our minds the feeling that there could break upon us a worse catastrophe [i.e. nuclear war] than that of the war just ended; and it's hard to see a remedy.

Some people say that what you need is vision; others, faith. This is true; but more than that I believe we need the quality which springs from both of these – namely, fortitude or courage. . . . And your relationship with Christ will mark you . . . with something of his fortitude. . . . He may lead you along dangerous ways and through difficult going; he may at times seem distant and unreal; but he will never leave you or forsake you; 'When I go up to Heaven thou art there; when I go down to Hell, thou art there also.'

Cambridge in 1945 was a very different place from Cambridge pre-war. Post-war austerity ruled out the kind of *Brideshead Revisited* social life that had followed the first war, and for the first time the great majority of undergraduates had their fees paid by government grants and did not have to have parents who could afford the expense. They were older and much more mature than their predecessors, and having seen the effects of National Socialism and then become aware of the challenge of Marxism most of them saw the need to explore the underlying meaning and purpose of life. Christianity was no longer thought irrelevant or out of date; and in Cambridge there were several clergy of Launcelot's generation, such as Eric Heaton, Edward Wynn and Charlie Moule, of very high calibre and well able to expound and commend their faith effectively. Not all the dons were sympathetic to religion, but at Trinity Hall the Master was very supportive of the work of a chaplain and the Senior Tutor (Charles Crawley) was a committed Anglican Christian. Probably the only don who would have definitely called himself an atheist was Cecil Turner, a brilliant lecturer in criminal law who was also Bursar; and since that office tended to put him in opposition to the other dons, who wished to spend money while the Bursar wished to balance the books, his influence on general Senior Combination Room opinion was limited. (Cecil Turner lived to give away his daughter in marriage to a future Archbishop of Canterbury.)

It was hardly necessary as it had been in 1937 to advise freshmen how to use their new-found freedom wisely; most of them had come not from school but from holding responsible rank in the armed services. Nor was there any need to urge men who longed to establish themselves in civilian life not to fritter away the opportunities for learning – on the contrary, Launcelot had to plead that they should not think of a university degree 'in terms of a sound investment leading to the higher-paid jobs in one or other of the professions', but remember the true aims of a university (exactly the same as they had been in 1937). After all they had gone through in the six years of war, coming to Trinity Hall was 'an event to which we have been looking forward for a long time'. Launcelot recalled how in the bleakest days of 1942,

> when the outlook was thoroughly depressing, I received a letter from the Master concerning a proposed election for an honorary Fellowship. It was a wonderfully refreshing letter to receive, hinting at the future continuity of a kind of life which seemed infinitely remote. . . . In Chapel this evening, our first thought will be one of profound gratitude.

These excerpts from sermons need a word of caution. The present writer confesses that he must have heard two or three of Launcelot's sermons in Trinity Hall chapel during the 1948–9 academic year, including one given below, but cannot remember a single word of any of them – not even reading them forty years later sparked any recollection of their content. What did make an unforgettable impression on each generation of undergraduates was that by the end of the first term the Chaplain clearly knew you and was interested in your welfare. It was the personal touch, not the sermons, that counted; the value of the sermons was (as someone who heard Launcelot preach at St Thomas's Church in New York testified many years later) that you knew you were hearing a highly intelligent man of utter integrity who really cared that you should be able to share his own Christian conviction. That impression did get through to his hearers, even though the actual words might pass one by. The main interest in reading any of Launcelot's sermons today is that they show how his thoughts developed as time went by, and remind us of the background, very different from today, against which they were preached. The true verdict on Launcelot as a preacher was given in a sermon by Dr Owen Chadwick, who was Assistant Tutor and Librarian at Trinity Hall in 1948 and succeeded Launcelot as Dean the following year:

His sermons – how he worried about them, what crossings out. The text had lines leading everywhere and looked like the inside of a television set. He was a good preacher. But he was not a great preacher, because he was not a dogmatist, and he sometimes stumbled for words and he was too real to be a performer. But this was part of the mind that drew us; more than drew us, it fascinated us. Those crossings out; his was a questioning mind, looking for truth, feeling after truth, inarticulate in part but always hunting for words, not telling you what the truth is from on high, but in a search, so that his hearers wanted to try to go along with him and see what they could find in his company.

One reason his mind was magnetic was the extreme modesty – 'I don't see much myself,' he seemed to say, 'but these are the lines along which I am sure we ought to look if we are to find a way into the mystery of God.'

These sermons do not make easy reading, but they always make good sense. He knew what he was talking about when, for instance, he told people not to let scientific doubts lead them to abandon belief or the quest for the knowledge of God:

To wait for the light to break before making any venture of belief is a complete inversion of all experience. A scientist does not carry through his research knowing the answers in advance; light is thown on the object of his investigations as he carries them out. So with the ways of God. . . .

God's appeal to man is always more on the side of sense than of sentiment. For most of us it means, to put it in cruder terms, giving ourselves a spiritual kick in the pants.

My time is up, and I will not say more. But I hope you will make full use of this Chapel; think of it as a window opening out into the eternal world through which the power and the love of God may shine in on those who worship here.

This was the period when the novelist C. P. Snow, who was a Cambridge don, could write of 'the two cultures', Arts and Science, and almost all clergy were products of the Arts culture; Launcelot was not typical. A visit in May 1949 from his uncle Sir Henry Holland, who had performed miracles while an eye surgeon in India as a CMS medical missionary, resulted in a sermon on the meaning of Miracles.

Our pre-scientific forefathers had less difficulty than we do in believing in miracles and in having a simple reliance in the power of God to do mighty works. Much that [used to] seem inexplicable and so was attributed to the direct and special intervention of God can now be explained in terms of natural laws.

And yet the one place where the impossible may turn out to be true, and the incredible a fact, is in the field of science. In all the annals of the ancient world which record miracles of healing, there is nothing to compare with the cures of whole populations from plagues or diseases though discoveries in the medical sciences. The essential meaning of 'miracle' in the original Bible sense of 'the marvellous' or 'the amazing' has migrated from the realm of religion to the realm of science. Miracle does not have to mean a broken law of nature. When Cowper wrote 'God moves in a mysterious way, His wonders to perform', he may have thought of God as suspending or breaking natural law; but if instead we think of God using his law-abiding processes to do for us things incredible, then those words are just as true.

To take a single example; the Exodus from Egypt. Natural explanations for the drying up of the Red Sea have since been advanced; but they in no way invalidate the real miracle, that an enslaved and humiliated people became one of the most creative nations in all history. And the key to this transformation was a faith in God. Jesus threw all the weight of his authority to dispel the fascination of superstition and sensationalism to which men have always been susceptible; he did not want to be known as a miracle worker, but he continually insisted on the possibility that in anyone who really put their trust in God, the inner miracle of personal transformation could be brought about.

I remember in the Navy seeing the hopelessness of a sailor serving a first sentence in the cells; he knew he was a marked man, and would almost inevitably keep on returning. The attitude of the service to that man, and his own attitude to himself, is one that too often prevails in ordinary life; but as Christians we ought to know better. It is a faithless betrayal *ever* to regard ourselves or other people as incorrigible.

On Thursday the Church celebrates Our Lord's Ascension. Do not let us examine his Ascension in terms of whether the law of gravity was suspended. The reason it is so firmly established in Christian doctrine is that the Risen and Ascended Lord has shown himself able to raise any who put their faith in him to share his spirit and so transform their lives. We know our limitations; but with God all things are possible.

Far more influential than his sermons were the informal weekday evening gatherings in Launcelot's rooms which took place perhaps half a dozen times a term. There was usually an outside speaker and always a specific topic, and anyone was welcome. One memory is of some fifty undergraduates, mostly sitting tightly packed on the floor, still at eleven o'clock in vigorous debate with Alan Ecclestone, a priest whose extreme left-wing views were admittedly calculated to spark off a stronger reaction from that post-war generation than most speakers – but the numbers present were not exceptional. People came initially because they liked Launcelot, and came again because they found it worthwhile; and good speakers came because they liked Launcelot and he was very persuasive.

An old Trinity Hall man who had introduced his wife (a trained psychologist) to Launcelot asked her what she thought of him; she replied, 'He is a very ambitious man.' That seems an extraordinary verdict at first sight; but it was based on his unscrupulous use of what is now called networking. Exploiting useful contacts on the scale that Launcelot did is as a rule done in order to serve personal ambition, but Launcelot did it not to forward his career but to help the causes he had espoused. Whether it was obtaining good speakers and preachers for 'his' undergraduates, getting sponsorship for some polar expedition, raising money for VSO, Atlantic College, or some diocesan need – whatever was needed in that line, Launcelot used his wide circle of acquaintances unscrupulously and with unerring aim. What was remarkable was that this moral blackmail (as some victims good-humouredly described it) did not harm friendships, but strengthened them. At an everyday level, too, he was an unscrupulous delegator; who could resist a unwelcome request when prefaced by 'your kindness is only exceeded by your inesti-mable good looks and the inimitability of your personal charm'?

In 1947 at the age of forty Launcelot was appointed Director of the Scott Polar Research Institute in Cambridge. This was an important post in the academic world of science, and the appointment reflected his high reputation as a geologist despite the fact that the war had made him put his Antarctic research on one side. (In May 1940 at a meeting of the Royal Geographi-cal Society Launcelot and Colin Bertram's contributions to the mystery of Sir Hubert Wilkins's non-existent 'Stefansson Strait dividing Graham Land from the mainland' do not seem to have been very serious; they both seem to have felt there were more important things to think about just then. Bertram said that when they had 'told [Wilkins] we were thinking that some of his conclusions were not quite sound, he seemed more interested then in how to build a submarine', while Launcelot must surely have had his tongue in his cheek when he said, 'Mr Stephenson has very convincingly disposed of Stefansson Strait, and evidently with great personal satisfaction. I can regard it only as a calamity. If the . . . mountain chain in Graham Land had ended southwards in a few small islands, it would have been of great geological interest.')

Not everyone could have combined being Director of SPRI with being Dean and Chaplain of Trinity Hall satisfactorily, but Launcelot did manage a much heavier workload than most people could cope with. An appreciation in *The Polar Record* for January 1950 noted:

> Fleming's directorship of the Institute coincided with a very substantial increase in its staff, its funds and its responsibilities. His common sense and encouragement have been available to all who asked. . . . He also served on the Council of the Royal Geographical Society, on the Falkland Islands Dependencies Scientific Committee, and on the organising committees of the Norwegian–British-Swedish Antarctic Expedition.

Owen Chadwick described it all thus:

> This was a phase of his life when the people whom you met at his table were wiry, muscular, and shaggy. This side of his life mattered to him academically, but also in two other ways. He cared about the environment long before most of us knew there was an environment. Many people know how far he saw ahead about the political tensions which could arise unless the natural resources which lay under the sea-bed or under the deserts were placed under some sort of international umbrella and were not diverted to nationalist ends.

He was a scientist for whom the sense of God was that which fostered the sensitivity to see the beauty and the grandeur of our natural world.

Learning to fit in his work at the Scott Polar Research Institute with his college responsibilities was probably a good preparation for the work of a bishop. At least the process of getting to know members of the college could often be combined with getting exercise, either on the squash court or tennis court or on the river or towpath. Launcelot was never a first-class oar, but he was an outstanding coach and was twice asked to coach the University Boat for a spell – a hurried note to the CUBC President asking if the time of an outing could be slightly changed to allow him to fit in other commitments shows that he seldom wasted a minute.

A don's life did however allow time for proper holidays; when he went to Innerhadden he often invited quite large parties of undergraduates to stay and sometimes imported some of the college staff to cope with them, including George Langley and his wife and occasionally the superb Trinity Hall chef, Slootz – they had no need to come and it is a tribute to Launcelot that they enjoyed doing so. His private means made all this possible; he was very generous and, since his board and lodging in college was free, spent little on himself.

But Launcelot's life in Cambridge, so completely fulfilling, and enabling him to 'combine the job of a chaplain with that of a geologist' more completely even than George Chase had expected when suggesting ordination, was coming to an end. On 9 July 1949 he received a letter from the Prime Minister asking if he would be willing for his name to go forward for nomination to the bishopric of Portsmouth.

1. Launcelot and Archie with their mother at 10 Chester Street Edinburgh (see p. 2).

2. Launcelot aged seven; the portrait by Paul Croeber (see p. 5).

3. Iceland 1932 (note the Trinity Hall Boat Club scarf): 'the level at which your pony swam seemed an important factor in your choice of steed' (see p. 20).

4. Launcelot outside his tent in Antarctica (taken by Alfred Stephenson). Probably July 1936 (see p. 59).

5. *Penola* in her winter quarters, see p. 55 (*both 4. and 5. by kind permission of the Scott Polar Research Institute*).

6. Newly ordained Fellow and Chaplain of Trinity Hall (*by kind permission of the Master and Fellows*)

7. The *Queen Elizabeth's* 15" guns were cleaned by pulling a man through them and Launcelot felt that as Chaplain he ought to show willing.

8. Some – by no means all – of those who accepted an open invitation to a *Q.E.* reunion, in the big dining room at Bishopswood (see p. 119).

9. After his consecration as Bishop by Archbishop Fisher, 18th October 1949.

10. Playing for his own Bishop of Portsmouth's Hockey Team. (This photo caused him some embarrassment, see p. 154).

11. Royal visit of the Queen to Portsmouth

12. Commissioning HMS *Protector* at Portsmouth (Launcelot was then flown by helicopter to Lambeth Palace for a Bishops' Meeting; when Lord Mountbatten heard, he was cross as he had recently been refused a helicopter).

13. Processing to Norwich Cathedral for the enthronement, followed by Robert Runcie, then Dean of Trinity Hall, and Eric Staples a former chaplain.

14. Talking to Princess Margaret outside the West Door of the Cathedral after the enthronement. L to R: Sir Edmund Bacon, ? , Princess Margaret, Canon Waring, Launcelot, Norman Hook (Dean), Virger, ? .

15. The Missions to Seamen chaplain arranged
for Launcelot to visit the Gorleston lightship.

16. Industrial visits were important; the Norwich diocese
was not entirely rural and agricultural.

17. Inspecting the first issue of the Norwich Churchman with a picture of the Enthronement service. On Launcelot's right is Richard Gurney. On his left William Young, General Manager of the Norfolk News Company who printed the *Norwich Churchman*.

18. At the annual open-air service at St Benet's Abbey, on the Broads; the abbey is in ruins, but the Bishop of Norwich is still the Abbot.

19. Jane Fleming, shortly before her engagement to Launcelot, who kept this photograph on his desk.

20. With the Norwich Rowing Club.

21. Leaving St George's Windsor after the service on
Easter Day, the Queen and the Dean followed by
members of the Royal Family and the Canons
(Launcelot has a walking stick in his left hand,
which cannot be seen).

22. After he became lame Launcelot was less able to get about and spent more time at his desk.

23. Determination. Latterly swimming was the only strenuous exercise Launcelot could take, as well as being the best form of therapy.

12

Bishop of Portsmouth

He had the professionalism that combined vision with a just assessment of what was practicable.

(Lord Runcie on Launcelot)

Launcelot's name was first suggested for a bishopric by the Master of Trinity Hall, Professor Dean, who was a friend of Cyril Garbett, the Archbishop of York. The Archbishop's chaplain, who had been at Trinity Hall, recalled that

> when Cyril asked me about Launcelot and I said he was a lovely man, that cut no ice; but when I told him that Launcelot besides being Dean had been awarded a fellowship on the strength of his geology, then Cyril sat up and began to take notice.

Professor Dean's letter said:

> I cannot believe that any college in Oxford or Cambridge can have Fleming's equal as a dean and chaplain. His charm and youthfulness, and far more his interest and enthusiasm in all their hopes, ambitions and undertakings make Fleming outstanding to young men, and older men too. . . . He is not a scholar in any ordinary sense of the word. . . . I should not expect a critical or sophisticated congregation to think much of his sermons, but the boys love them and listen to him with a close attention, perhaps because they are so fond of him. I cannot honestly say that he has the gifts that make a good

administrator, but he has improved in these respects since the
war. . . .

Accordingly, Garbett wrote to the Archbishop of Canterbury to
say, 'I am inclined to think that Launcelot Fleming might do
very well at Portsmouth.' Archbishop Fisher was not easily convinced, and indeed never really recognized Launcelot's intellectual calibre – perhaps he had misunderstood the phrase 'not a
scholar in any ordinary sense of the word' to mean 'not really
very brilliant'. (In 1956 Owen Chadwick, asked if he thought
Launcelot would be acceptable as Edward Wynn's successor at
Ely, said yes, and Fisher replied, 'Oh, so Cambridge does not
want an intellectual as Bishop of Ely then.' Chadwick was
shocked that Fisher knew so little about the intellectual calibre
of a man who had been one of his bishops for seven years.)
    However, Fisher found that those bishops who knew
Launcelot thought that he 'might do well at Portsmouth'. Bishop
Bell of Chichester (who, it is thought, would have been made
Archbishop in 1945 had he not annoyed Churchill by condemn-
ing the Allied bombing of Dresden) gave 'an unhesitating Yes'
when asked if he thought Launcelot was 'episcopal material'.
George Chase's comment is interesting; he thought that Launcelot in his first year as chaplain had been 'too inclined to take
people at their own valuation and see them through rosy spec-
tacles'. That had of course been before the Graham Land
Expedition; indeed Chase added 'he has probably developed a
good deal' since then, and he had indeed. Antarctica had been
a formative experience; Launcelot had learned to see people
for what they really were. When the Archbishop submitted the
customary three names for the Prime Minister to lay before the
Queen, Launcelot's name was third on the list; however, one
of those ahead of him, Henry Montgomery-Campbell (later to
become Bishop of London), was appointed to Guildford instead,
so Launcelot's name went up to second place.
    Given the agreed 'job-specification' – that the new bishop
should have naval connections, and because the diocese was so
small should have outside interests – the Archbishop's hesitations

about him seem strange, since he alone fitted the bill. It seems that Fisher saw episcopal appointments rather like moves on a chessboard; Portsmouth gave an opening either to promote a worthy but limited senior cleric who could cope with a small diocese until he reached retirement, or else to put in a young high-flyer to give him experience in a small diocese to prepare him for higher things. Launcelot, as an unknown piece on the chessboard, would thus have been safer left alone until more was known about him. However, Sir Anthony Bevir, the Patronage Secretary in 10 Downing Street, had taken his own soundings and unhesitatingly recommended Launcelot's name for Portsmouth.

He hated the idea of leaving Cambridge, and the Prime Minister's letter came at a particularly unwelcome moment as he had just been invited to visit the polar research stations in Arctic Canada, all expenses paid, which he would have loved. Also, since his mother had been widowed the previous year she had come to lean on Launcelot, her unmarried child, and if he became a bishop he would not be able to visit her so often. Since he was about to go up to Scotland to see her, he was able to sound her out – and if he secretly hoped that she might implore him to say no and stay in Cambridge, he was disappointed. Needless to say he also consulted a great number of friends and colleagues, and although he wasn't free to say what job he had been offered (he asked one undergraduate if he thought it would be right for him to go and become Head Master of Rugby!), the clergy he asked had a pretty shrewd idea what was in the wind. All those he asked thought he should accept the offer, with the sole exception of Ken Carey who was probably swayed by wanting Launcelot to stay in Cambridge.

So, a fortnight after receiving that letter Launcelot went to see the Archbishop still feeling hesitant. He was not sure if he ought to become a bishop because he could not bring himself to say an unequivocal yes if he were ever asked 'Do you believe in our Lord's physical resurrection?' (Years later, when asked that question privately, he replied that before he could answer he needed to know precisely what chemical and biological changes were thought to have taken place; as his sermon on Miracles suggests, he was trained as a scientist before the days of nuclear physics, when it was thought that the known laws of nature were immutable.) He also confessed a similar difficulty over the virgin birth; but if he secretly hoped that the Archbishop would say that these doubts meant he should stay at Cambridge after all, he was again disappointed. Fisher ended the interview by producing his diary and asking Launcelot about possible dates for his consecration as bishop.

His friends were delighted. Fr Denis Marsh wrote from Cerne Abbas: 'I am so thankful that you feel the certainty of the rightness of it all together with the most gloriously liberating sense of the absurdity of it all! Would that all bishops held these two certainties together.' Letters of congratulation, often mingled with regret that he was leaving Cambridge, ponderous advice from older men such as his uncle Bishop William Holland, light-hearted advice from undergraduates, poured in, together with wise advice that he treasured. Eric Abbot, Dean of King's College London (later Dean of Westminster) summed up what many felt:

Dear Launcelot, *do not* let 'them' turn you aside from the primary function of a Bishop. Anyone can do administration ... people are longing for Fathers-in-God. I am sure your great capacity for exceeding friendliness will be the material for a most loving and patient episcopate.

His consecration took place in Southwark Cathedral on St Luke's Day, 18 October 1949; the preacher was Canon Charles Raven, the Master of Christ's and at that time Vice-Chancellor of Cambridge University. The next three weeks were hectic. His new house, Bishopswood, on the outskirts of Fareham, stood in about three acres of grounds – kitchen garden, lawn and a grass tennis court, flower borders, a strip of woodland and a small paddock. The house was attractive but not imposing, built in the *cottage ornée* style with a thatched roof. Downstairs were a large drawing room, dining room, study, chapel and secretary's office, together with the kitchen quarters and a staff flat. There were about nine bedrooms, some quite small and rather spartan, and also a large dining room used on special occasions. Even in the 1950s the Church Commissioners thought the house too big, but Launcelot invited their representative to inspect it together with various local representatives – all of whom, from a churchwarden who was a trade union stalwart to the Duke of Wellington who was Lord Lieutenant of Hampshire, were adamant that they wanted Bishopswood kept. They realized that as well as being a very nice house for its occupant, it was also an asset to the diocese.

Furnishing so large a house was difficult to start with, but Launcelot made full use of its space. Ordinands could stay there for pre-ordination retreats, the Rural Deans could all have lunch in that vast dining room (whose radiators could be turned off when not in use), annual garden parties could accommodate all who needed to be asked, and the house itself would hold some 150 people for a party. Informal entertainment was equally valuable – being able to invite some curate for a game of tennis was a good way of finding out how things were going with him (and helped keep Launcelot fit – when the brother-in-law of Christopher Pepys, Vicar of St Mark's, Portsmouth, was staying with him Launcelot would 'invite him to a game of tennis, after which over tea Mrs Fleming would say "Thank you so much for exercising Launcelot").'

Launcelot in fact made full use of Bishopswood and his attitude towards it epitomizes his general approach to clergy pay and housing. The guiding principle must be 'What does a man need to enable him to do his job effectively?' and not 'What salary level does he deserve?', which was irrelevant since clergy pay could never match that for a comparable secular career, and also introduced the concept of status, which Launcelot abhorred. He argued strongly against a proposal for bishops and other dignitaries to have bigger pensions than ordinary clergy (but he agreed not to vote against it when reminded that a married bishop without private means was in a very different case from himself), and he never on principle travelled first-class

in a train although the Church Commissioners expected him
to. (He once broke his rule when he had even more work
than usual to do while going up to London from Norwich,
only to find all the first-class compartments full because of the
Smithfield Show; and once Lord Albermarle insisted on giving
him tea in the restaurant car with the result that he had to pay
the difference between cheap day return and full first class fare.
These experiences confirmed his resolve to eschew first-class
travel.)

Except for his time in Graham Land when everyone had to
take a share in the chores, Launcelot had never had to be concerned with domestic arrangements; at home, at school, at university and in the Navy, everyday needs such as meals, cleaning,
laundry, had just happened – indeed, for most of his life he had
never even had to lay out his own clothes except on holiday.
Now, he had to run not only a diocese but also his own household. He inherited from his predecessor a cook and a gardener,
and was told of a very efficient married couple, the Adamsons,
who came and in effect ran the house for him. To his great relief
his Trinity Hall secretary Joan Hopkins agreed to stay with him
for his first few months at Bishopswood; when she left, Ernle
Drax became his secretary until he left Portsmouth; an Admiral's
daughter, she could cope with being a social secretary (who
ought to be invited to lunch, garden parties, etc.) and was
already familiar with many of Launcelot's outside interests such
as polar exploration.

Launcelot did not feel justified in appointing a chaplain –
Portsmouth was a very small diocese – but asked Alastair Gold
to come as a part-time Lay Assistant. Alastair had been ADC
to the Governor of Tasmania and had then spent a year at a
theological college but had to leave on health grounds – he had
been badly wounded in the war. After two years Alastair felt
he was well enough to go off and do a full-time job (he was
eventually ordained), and thereafter Launcelot always had a
chaplain. He had found that clergy were reluctant to discuss
even the most mundane ecclesiastical matters, such as whether
the bishop should wear a cope and mitre, with a layman. At

Portsmouth, the chaplain was also a part-time curate in the local parish; at Norwich the chaplaincy became a full-time job.

Being made a bishop also meant that episcopal clothes had to be bought. Archbishop Geoffrey Fisher had been a Headmaster and treated his bishops like school prefects; gaiters *had* to be worn on all formal occasions. (Launcelot hated wearing gaiters and when driving to some engagement where they were *de rigueur* would often stop and change into them behind a hedge shortly before he got there; once he was changing in a wood when he heard the sound of a horn, and the whipper-in watching that side of the wood was startled to see a be-gaitered bishop, rather than a fox, break cover.) Full evening dress was also needed in those days – a splendid purple outfit which, as irreverent junior clergy told him, made Launcelot look like a Ruritanian cavalry officer. What stuck in his gullet worst of all was being expected to receive an honorary Lambeth Doctorate of Divinity. Not only did that mean wearing an Oxford hood which went against the grain, but it also cost £50. That was just too much for an economical Scot who disliked the idea anyway, so he declined the honour. Alas, a wealthy layman then offered to pay the £50 so that his Bishop could be called 'Dr' Fleming, so Launcelot agreed to accept the degree, only to find that the man never stumped up so he had to pay the fee himself.

Launcelot had just three weeks after his consecration in October 1949 to organize his household and his episcopal wardrobe. The enthronement in Portsmouth Cathedral was a magnificent affair. There was a Bishop's Company of fifteen representatives, chosen on the basis of a 'This Is Your Life' programme: the Head Master of Rugby, the Master of Trinity Hall, Vice-Admiral Sir Claud Barry who had been Captain of the *Queen Elizabeth*, together with less exalted folk such as Roddy MacLean the Innerhadden shepherd and a Petty Officer from the *Queen Elizabeth*. As the *History of the Trinity Hall Boat Club* tells us (p. 21), Launcelot 'characteristically chose a Bishop's Company of varied experience, including the Head Porter and his own gyp [George Langley], who were taken by at least one member of the congregation to be the two peers who would introduce him to the House of Lords'.

Looking back after ten years at Portsmouth, Launcelot once said he thought he ought not to have been made a bishop at the age of forty-three. In theory he was probably right; he had no parochial experience either as curate or incumbent, and did not even know what a Parochial Church Council was, let alone a Pastoral Committee, Board of Patronage, or Advisory Committee. But in practice, because he was quick to learn and humble enough to listen, such ignorance proved bliss. There was much that was cumbersome and obviously inefficient in the way the Church of England was run, but most clergy by the time they became bishops were so familiar with the system that they had come to accept it. Launcelot, coming to it fresh, saw the weaknesses clearly. Curing them took longer, and was sometimes unachievable, but (in Lord Runcie's words) by

> deploying the fact of his inexperience (for example, his professed total ignorance when appointed Diocesan Bishop of what 'Dilapidations' meant) he could draw out of others their contribution, their glimpse of a possible ministry to him, and thus a new sense of a Diocese as a family of God. And behind it all was the vision; the glimpse of a kingdom; a kingdom of beauty; the kingdom of a Creator who became also Redeemer.

Fortunately Portsmouth was a small diocese, relatively easy to manage. It had been carved out of the Winchester diocese in 1927 and consisted of the Isle of Wight, Portsmouth and Southsea, and a mainly rural hinterland stretching up the Meon Valley. Portsmouth was an industrial city centred round the Admiralty dockyard, containing large parishes with several curates, so there was a good mix between urban and small rural parishes. Launcelot's naval experience stood him in good stead, as in addition to the naval bases there were many ex-Royal Navy men living in the area. He had two Archdeacons, one of whom, Ted Roberts, the Archdeacon of the Isle of Wight (who later became Archdeacon of Portsmouth and was eventually

Bishop of Ely), was the same age as Launcelot and could share his ideas more easily than some of the more senior clergy. Ted Roberts had been a vicar in Southsea throughout the war and the blitz, so knew the diocese well and was an invaluable aide; he became a close personal friend (and before long found himself on the list for coaching Trinity Hall boats).

The diocese as a whole quickly reciprocated its new bishop's friendliness. Because it was a small diocese there was a real sense of belonging, and the Diocesan Conference was a genuinely useful forum. The main item at Launcelot's first Conference was a scheme for pastoral reorganization, and he made it clear at the outset that he would never lose sight of the wood for the trees:

> Before we address ourselves to plans for reorganisation we should again ask ourselves the prior question – what purpose are these plans designed to serve? ... The one chance of restoring sanity and health to our world is to keep clearly in view the true nature of all mankind and the source from which that nature derives. That is what worship is for; the sanctification of secular life. Therefore:
>
> First; the parson has got to be fed to a far greater extent by the layman's experience of working life; secondly, there needs to be post-Confirmation training and systematic teaching of the faith; thirdly, there needs to be a deeper knowledge and understanding of the Sacrament of Holy Communion and its liturgy. . . .

He consistently argued that policy decisions must be dictated by actual needs on the ground and not by administrative convenience. That applied not only within the Diocese but in Church Assembly matters as well. In 1957, for instance, he made 'an appeal against the new set-up in Church Assembly':

> The Report speaks of the various Boards and Councils as 'having been determined largely by the accident of history', and it is clear from the context that they consider this to be

unfortunate. I should have thought it would be more accurate
to say that most of the Boards and Councils have come into
being not by the 'accident of history' but to *meet particular
needs*. This, surely, is the right reason for the origin of a
Central Board of Finance. . . . I submit that the structures now
proposed have the appearance of being 'bureaucratic', in that
the different needs which call for central bodies are being
made subordinate to administrative tidiness. I therefore hope
this resolution will not be passed.

Launcelot found Church Assembly meetings tedious, and usually
time-wasting. Under Archbishop Fisher's leadership most of the
1950s were taken up by debating the reform of Canon Law,
which lent itself to interminable discussion of trivialities – could
clergy wear light grey suits or must they be dark grey? Launcelot
was uneasily aware that Canon Law revision was irrelevant to
the real challenges facing the Church. He was clear in his own
mind that his priority must be the welfare and effectiveness of
the clergy, because they were the main agents for furthering the
Church's mission. After being in the diocese for only a year, he
warned that this would cost money:

Every parish should attempt to relieve its incumbent by paying
in full for the Rates and Dilapidations of the Parsonage. . . .
Everyone knows we are terribly short staffed and the clergy
are hard pressed. The laity can help, as indeed so many do, by
recognising that every Christian is commissioned to bring the
Gospel to those who are indifferent or hostile or ignorant. The
laity can lift from the shoulders of the clergy responsibilities for
some parish organisations, for administration and for finance.
The clergy must really be prepared to hand over specific
responsibilities to laymen and leave them to get on with it.

And again, in 1953:

There is still far too big a gap between what the parson needs
to do his work effectively and what he receives. The extent

of this gap is not always realised for the simple reason that many clergy succeed in disguising their difficulties and anxieties. There is still much clerical poverty and it is a very real obstacle to the spiritual effectiveness of the Church as a whole. . . . The principle in the matter of clergy stipends is not 'How much can we afford?' but 'How much is needed if the work of a parish priest is to be adequately done?'

Both in Portsmouth and later in Norwich, Launcelot managed to get the diocesan minimum stipend up to well above average. Never having been short of money himself, and accustomed as he was to institutions where the need for an adequate expenses allowance was accepted as a matter of course, he was shocked by the poverty he found in some vicarages. In the days before synodical government and the hyper-inflation of the 1970s it was obvious that it was up to parishioners to pay for bringing the ancient endowment income of their benefice up to an acceptable level. Whether or not this happened depended mainly on the lead given by the bishop. Portsmouth, and subsequently Norwich, were far more successful than most dioceses in raising stipends, not only because Launcelot could be very persuasive but also because, never having had to get used to living on an inadequate vicar's stipend himself, he realized just how inadequate most of them were.

His fellow-bishops often accused him of having more than his fair share of curates, and he had to see off an attempt by the bishops of Birmingham and Sheffield to impose a scheme of rationing so that northern industrial dioceses would have more curates and wealthier ones in the south would have fewer. Launcelot forebore to point out that if other bishops tried a bit harder to improve the housing and pay of their clergy and boost their morale, then some industrial northern dioceses might fare better. But he did emphasize that because Portsmouth was better staffed than most dioceses, it *produced* far more ordinands than it employed; far from being a drain on clerical man-power, it was a net producer of clergy. (Much later, the General Synod did adopt a scheme for rationing curates, the Sheffield Report, which Launcelot was convinced had largely contributed to the Church of England's decline.)

In 1952 Mrs Fleming came to live at Bishopswood; she had not been well and could no longer live on her own. Domestically, this was a mixed blessing; she took over the housekeeping, but that made the Adamsons redundant; they had been brilliant, and never again did Launcelot enjoy so trouble-free a domestic regime until he married. But having his mother living with him, though difficult in some ways, was undoubtedly a source of great support to Launcelot. If he was away for more than one night he always wrote to her, and when he was at home he always went up to say goodnight and talk over the day's events; and since his mother brought some of her furniture with her Bishopswood was no longer sparsely furnished. Launcelot missed no longer being able to invite people to Innerhadden, but a cottage on the estate was left to him and was in constant use both for his own holidays (and usually rather more guests than there was really room for!) and for lending to clergy families who could not easily afford a holiday.

Because Mrs Fleming was a strong and outspoken character it is not surprising that some people believed she was the power behind the throne, but anyone living in the house soon realized that although Launcelot very seldom contradicted her, he was not swayed by her advice and was never deflected by her from doing what he had already decided. He was wonderfully patient, too, when his mother regaled the company with something that he had said or done as a child, or when she treated him as a little boy. And in small things, and most domestic matters, Launcelot did do as his mother wanted.

The post-war years were a period of growth for the Church of England. The horrors of war had made people aware of the need to counter the dark side of human nature, and the Christian message of penitence and forgiveness, sin and redemption, struck a chord in many minds. Soon after Launcelot arrived, the city clergy pressed for a Mission to Portsmouth. It took considerable persuasion before Launcelot agreed, but it went

ahead in 1952, and he commended the Mission in a radio broadcast on the West of England Home Service:

> The object [of the Mission] is to show as frankly and clearly
> as possible what the Christian faith is and what it stands for;
> and to demonstrate its truth in a way which ordinary people
> can understand. Today a great many people go through life
> with practically no conscious contact with or knowledge of
> the Christian faith at all.
>   Some complain that if the world is in its present state after
> 1900 years of Christianity, it cannot be a very good religion.
> But no Christian would claim that Christianity can succeed
> in controlling the world without first being accepted. Christ
> himself did not reform the society of his day; he was rejected
> and put to death. But if accepted, Christianity succeeds in
> changing people ... it does something to and for human
> nature which human nature cannot do for itself.
>   Well, you may say, are we asking people to swallow that?
> No, that is precisely what we are not doing. What we are
> doing is to ask people to take it seriously.

The Mission took place in 1952, with each parish inviting
a Missioner from outside and with Cuthbert Bardsley (later
Bishop of Coventry) as Chief Missioner. It culminated in a week
of intensive evangelism throughout the city. Television would
soon put an end to this kind of mission, but although it did not
produce mass conversions it did strengthen the commitment of
existing church members and was felt to have been well worth
while.

It seemed only common sense to Launcelot that the success
or failure of the Church's mission hinged on the clergy. He
listened to – and used – the laity far more than most bishops,
but as he went about the diocese he couldn't help noticing how
closely the spiritual life of a parish, good or bad, almost invariably reflected the quality of the parish priest. Accordingly,
he took immense trouble over appointments, keeping an enormous 'Patronage File' of clergy who might fill vacancies (divided

into 'Vulnerable', i.e. ready for a move, and 'Non-Vulnerable', i.e. they ought to stay where they were for a bit longer). When a vacancy occurred, those within the diocese were considered first, but if none seemed quite right then the Patronage File was brought into play. The invariable principle was to find the best possible man for the job, and not to think in terms of 'prefer-ment' (does so-and-so deserve the job?). If a priest needed a move then every effort was made to find him one, but it must be something genuinely suitable; if there was nothing quite right for him within the diocese, infinite trouble was taking in writing to commend him to other bishops. Only once did Launcelot make an appointment for the sake of the man and not for the parish; the result was disastrous, and Launcelot said it taught him a lesson he never forgot. The filing cabinet also contained a capacious file of Ordinands – not just those from his own diocese, but anyone he came across and liked the look of; on his return from a trip to London or to a school or university, he would thrust near-illegible notes on scraps of paper at his chaplain, with a name, address, age, career plans, and a brief character-sketch, to be typed out and put in the files.

Launcelot soon became convinced the diocese needed some non-parochial clergy. He wanted industrial chaplains in Ports-mouth and in Cowes shipyard, but his main priority was a youth chaplain. A thriving urban parish might have curates to run youth clubs etc., but most clergy were too taken up with looking after their existing middle-aged congregations and the needs of the elderly to devote much attention to young people. He also instituted the Canford Summer School for under-25s; it took place during the summer holidays at Canford School (of which he was a governor), an ideal site, with all the leisure facilities of a well-equipped school.

But probably Launcelot's most important innovation was to have Archdeacons who were not also beneficed parish priests. This was initially made possible by a bequest 'to the Bishop of Portsmouth for the time being for the advancement of the King-dom of Heaven', which was used to buy a house for the Arch-deacon of the Isle of Wight. Launcelot then set out one evening on a begging mission of intensive visits to wealthy people in the diocese. That produced enough to buy a house for the Archdeacon of Portsmouth, and thus armed he persuaded the Diocesan Board of Finance to provide the Archdeacons' pay and expenses. It was another instance of a bishop who, having never encountered the Barchester-like world of diocesan administration before, saw the need for Archdeacons who could inspire and encourage parish clergy and instil new ideas, without being bogged down by having a parish of their own. That meant that Archdeacons had to be men of inspiration; when Ted Roberts left to become Bishop of Malmesbury, Michael Peck (later Dean of Lincoln) succeeded him.

This list of some of the things Launcelot achieved might simply give the impression of a worthy diocesan bishop who was a good administrator. But what made it all work was a light-heartedness that infected all that he did and said. Under his chairmanship, staff meetings (as Bill Llewellyn later found at Norwich) were fun; and they were waffle-free (if a prospective incumbent was described by his bishop as 'a sound man, but would not set the Thames on fire', Launcelot would say 'I bet that means he'd put it out'). Then the constant stream of visitors to Bishopswood – would-be explorers planning expeditions, undergraduates uncertain about their career, VSO volunteers, couples whom he was going to marry, all kinds of people not concerned with diocesan business – helped keep Launcelot young. The young probably went away thinking what a pleasant life a bishop had; if he had to leave them and work at his desk he managed to convey the impression that this was a rather tiresome and unusual interruption – and off they were sent to do some forestry work in the copse ('it's the ideal training for rowing/hockey/javelin-throwing') or in the garden until he rejoined them at a meal.

Life on Launcelot's staff was never dull – least of all was it dull being driven in a car by him (luckily there was only one brush with the law, a contretemps at a pedestrian crossing that gave rise to a headline in an evening paper 'Bishop innocent; woman to blame' which several friends cut out and sent him).

The most lively period at Bishopswood was while Dusky the Husky, a sledge dog who needed a home, was in residence. The yard by the back door looked like a charnel house, with large bones scattered round, and exercising Dusky kept Eric Staples, the current chaplain, very fit. Alas, her extravagant habits led to eventual banishment; she liked having something to get her teeth into, and when what looked like snowflakes but was in fact the contents of Launcelot's pillows and mattress floated down past the drawing-room window one afternoon Mrs Fleming put her foot down, and Dusky had to go.

Underlying all this was an unobtrusive but disciplined prayer life. Morning Prayer, preceded by twenty minutes of meditation, was said daily in the chapel before breakfast (Holy Communion was celebrated on Thursdays and saints' days), and Evening Prayer was always said if there was no evening engagement such as a confirmation or institution – which, if on the Isle of Wight, meant leaving the house at tea time and not returning until about eleven o'clock, though the Pursers on the ferry always let Launcelot use their cabin so that he could get on with some work. Although outwardly he might seem the most unclerical of clergymen Launcelot never forgot that first and foremost he was an ordained servant of Christ and his Church. It was symptomatic that although even as a bishop he seldom wore a dog-collar when not obviously on duty, he always wore his pectoral cross except when it was clearly impractical (as on the squash court!).

He was concerned that, after a post-war mini-boom, a shortage of vocations, and of money to pay clergy adequately, threatened to be an increasing problem. Shortly after becoming a bishop he wrote to Owen Chadwick:

I believe that a discussion on the possibility of ordaining persons to the Ministry who are already in secular occupations would be desirable. One result of such a conference might in any case be more vigorous development of the 'Order of Readers'.... But without anticipating the results of such a conference I certainly think it would be a good plan and hope you might include at least one senior representative of CACTM and at least one active and experienced layman.

Many years later, when Non-Stipendiary Ministers were an established feature, Launcelot seemed to have drawn back from that position. But his objection was not to non-stipendiary ministry itself, but to the fact that it was developing in a way that removed any sacrificial element in priestly vocation. Perhaps the best way of concluding this chapter on how he tried to carry out 'the office and work of a bishop' is by quoting his Charge to those he was about to ordain to serve in his diocese, delivered in his private chapel the evening before the Ordination Service:

... You can look back to the days when first the idea of ordination began to stir. The doubts you had about your vocation, doubts now largely or wholly resolved; the doubts about your fitness, stronger than ever – 'who is sufficient for these things?' Your ideas, of course, have changed a lot. You're perhaps less critical of the Church; but I hope there's left in you the kind of impatience which will arm your ministry for the task of interpreting the eternal things of God to a changing world. 'O Lord, give us the readiness to accept what we cannot change, the courage to change what we can, and the wisdom to know the difference.'

One thing about your vocation has remained the same. You know that tomorrow you will be committing yourself. You really are abandoning your life wholly for God to use – 'to take, bless and use'. There is much to give up – but the process of surrender has to go on all the time. And there is much to give – and the offering has to be continuous. And you will have given to you in return a growth in stature and grace and freedom; 'what I had I lost, what I spent I had, what I gave I have'.

Commit to what? Not just to keeping the machinery of the C of E going; yours is not to be a maintenance job, it is to be constructive. You are to be builders of the Kingdom, by proclaiming the Gospel of Christ and so leading people to

worship God as Christ reveals him, and so win people from
waywardness and timidity and worldliness to fulness of life
as Children of God and inheritors of heaven. To do this,
God has called you to be *intermediaries*. Now, that can mean
standing between God and your fellow-men; and perhaps the
first thing we've got to learn is not to get in the way – not to
make it more difficult for people to come to a knowledge of
God, but to be intermediaries in the sense of ambassadors,
with a threefold function, priestly, pastoral and teaching.

First, the leading of people in worship. One of the glories
of the Church of England is that its doctrine has never been
systematised but springs out of the Book of Common Prayer.
That is why your assent to the Prayer Book is so important,
granted that the need for revision constitutes a strain for our
conscience as to the precise form in which we interpret that
assent when there is a pressing need for reform. I dislike the
word 'Churchmanship'. It suggests that the Church is a sort
of zoo, graduated from giraffes at one end to mice at the
other. As far as outward forms are concerned, take a lesson
from biology. It isn't a case of building a shell first, and then
finding an oyster to put inside it and chopping a bit off the
oyster if it doesn't fit. The living organism makes its own shell
and its form is determined both by the needs of the organism
and the environment in which it lives. I must leave you to
work out for yourselves the application of that analogy to the
forms of worship of the Church. Never be 'pious' in taking
services; always aim at homeliness provided it doesn't detract
from holiness. The thought of God therefore in the front of
your mind; but also sensitivity to the approach and background of those you are leading in worship; trying to carry
them with you to glorify God. There's one school of thought
which says the minister should suppress his personality –
which if exaggerated becomes cold and hard and mechanical.
Another school of thought understands the need to be expressive – which if exaggerated leads to sentimentality. It is a matter
of being sufficiently expressive to draw people to God,
and sufficiently unobtrusive not to draw them to yourself.

Technique is important – part of the job; your voice clear, natural, sympathetic, firm without being aggressive. Like a singer who studies phrasing, take trouble with technique. And approach every service realising what it is – a new act of praise to God. For someone in the church it may be an event of decisive significance.

Pastoral work. Probably this is what first led you to think of ordination. Vastly important, and an infinitely delicate part of your ministry. You will be a recipient of confidences. Visiting; getting to know people, caring for them. And if you are conscious of being given some power and ability as a pastor, be aware of the danger of manipulating those to whom you minister. Your job is not to get at people, or impress them, or get them into church – but to love them for the Church's sake. Never despair of those who are most difficult. If you believe in the inherent goodness of everybody, you'll be surprised how often you are right. There is no such person as a hopeless case. We have to learn from Our Lord his capacity to see through a person to the point of promise in them, and fasten on that, and be prepared to take a risk. That surely explains Our Lord's choice of Judas. We are never told that He regretted that choice. Always remember that it's not for the under-shepherd to complain about the master's flock.

Teaching and preaching. The most serious attack on the faith today is not that it is unintelligible but that it isn't true. Never allow yourself to whittle God down in your teaching for the sake of simplicity; God is always greater than our understanding. Teaching and preaching must be linked with your pastoral work, for then you can learn to understand how to get alongside those to whom you are preaching. Our Lord's way of teaching was always from the known to the unknown, from the human to the divine, from the natural to the super-natural.

All these functions of your ambassadorial ministry make constant demands on the pattern and discipline of your own personal life; being a man of God, a man of prayer; your reading of the Bible, and theology; so-called secular reading.

Your standards of morality. Being business-like with money – the more necessary when there's little enough of it. Keeping faith with your family and friends. Being sensible with your health – days off, recreation, exercise, sleep – taking your humanity seriously, in fact. Have a high regard for the *status* to which you are called, but never, never stand on your dignity and pretend that thereby you are defending the dignity of the Church; it is the dignity and privilege of the Church always to be humble, always charitable, always ready to serve *everyone* regardless of their position. The fact that you are called to a particular office does not mean that you are therefore to fit yourself into some model ecclesiastical pattern; you are here to be *yourself*; you each bring very varied gifts, all of which God receives in your ministry.

It's the hardest job in all the world: it takes all there is of us. Against the forces of worldliness and indifference, sometimes of open hostility, it will sometimes seem desperately hard to sustain. It can only be sustained by a humbler, closer consciousness of the Master whom we were called to serve. The task is impossible; the resources are infinite.

13

Education and Youth

Education is a drawing out, not a putting in.
(P. G. Wodehouse's Bertie Wooster, quoting Jeeves)

Launcelot did indeed have the 'outside interests' considered desirable for a Bishop of Portsmouth, even if they were not so ecclesiastical as the Archbishop might have wished. He retained his Cambridge links with the Scott Polar Research Institute and Trinity Hall (whose boats he coached from time to time), and with such organizations as the Royal Geographical Society – he also joined the local Portsmouth Geographical Association for which he obtained some first-rate speakers. He was keen for sixth-formers and students to go on expeditions as he had done, through organizations such as the Public Schools' Exploration Trust. More conventionally for a bishop, he was in great demand as a school preacher (the Head of a primary school in Norfolk after Launcelot had been there on a Deanery visit said 'That man will make friends wherever he goes').

In 1951 Launcelot was asked to take over from the Bishop of St Albans, who was much occupied with the new towns in Hertfordshire, as Chairman of the Church of England Youth Council. Under his chairmanship, and with its efficient Secretary Mollie Batten, the CEYC did what it could to promote the Church's work with fifteen-to-twenty-year-olds, but its power was limited since it had no direct financial control over anything and could do no more than encourage and advise, and try to persuade Government that voluntary youth work was vital and should be supported. In this it was helped considerably by Princess Margaret, who was Patron of the CEYC; curiously enough, this was the only field in which she was allowed to do anything on her own initiative, and she was an enthusiastic and effective PR agent.

The Albermarle Committee on the Youth Services, set up in 1958, gave Launcelot an opportunity to lobby for the voluntary sector – it was a piece of luck that he had known Lady Albermarle when they were children. In a House of Lords debate on the Youth Services in February 1959 Launcelot argued for

> a working partnership of all those concerned with the welfare of young people, which . . . will, I firmly trust, include a firm partnership with the Churches . . . [so that] different organisations and groups which are trying to help young people in any locality may understand the particular aims and contributions which the others are trying to make, and not find themselves competing for the same young person's presence at the same time. One cannot of course legislate for awkward and difficult people, and no directions from the top will protect young people from a quarrel taking place over their heads; but effective partnership can do much to prevent wasting resources through competition, and avoid placing a young person in the position of having to decide between the overlapping claims of an organisation and the Church.

He pointed out that besides church youth groups and clubs 'which in the case of the Church of England number around a quarter of a million young people' a great many individual church members ran 'youth rallies, festivals, summer schools, leadership courses, adventure weekends' without any pay and 'on a shoestring budget. That they have achieved a real measure of success is due to the almost superhuman devotion of a very small number of dedicated people. A larger contribution to those organisations would, I am convinced, prove a thoroughly good investment.' That was precisely the point made by Lord Pakenham, who had initiated the debate, but Lord Dundee, winding up for the Government, said it was difficult to make any money available for the voluntary sector, and 'they could not give a grant to any institution which is strictly denominational' (*Hansard*, House of Lords, 4 February 1959, pp. 1166f.).

Even within the Church of England there were differing views as to what the Church should be doing. Many clergy felt that to do any good a youth club or group must be definitely church based, others believed they must be more inclusive. In universities the Student Christian Movement (SCM) was inclusive and aimed to help the young to think about issues like Christian unity, war and peace, poverty and inequality, whereas the evangelical Inter-Collegiate Christian Unions – CICCU at Cambridge and OICCU at Oxford – aimed quite simply at conversions. Launcelot had never liked the CICCU approach, but was also aware of the danger of reducing Christianity to vague do-gooding. Indeed, he had no *theory* of 'work with young people', he simply had a natural gift. As Professor Dean had said, the secret of Launcelot's success was his 'charm and youthfulness, and far more his interest and enthusiasm for all their hopes, ambitions and undertakings [which] make Fleming outstanding to young men'.

It was extraordinary that even when Launcelot was an old man, anchored by infirmity to his chair, the young at any gathering somehow gravitated to him. The young are often unsure of themselves, fearful of being laughed at or made to look silly, but with Launcelot they sensed that they could safely drop their guard. The young also like to be listened to, and to be understood, and Launcelot was a good listener because he didn't have to pretend to be interested – he really was, and had great patience. He also took infinite trouble. How many octogenarians would write in their own hand, as he did, to each member of his old college who had won their oars in the May or Lent races?

In 1945 Launcelot had met Kurt Hahn, who before the war had started a remarkable school at Salem in Germany, and when forced out by Hitler founded Gordonstoun School in Scotland on similar lines. Launcelot found that Hahn's philosophy of how to educate and train the young struck a chord with him; it articulated much of what he had instinctively felt. Critics

said that Hahn simply wanted to toughen up young people by
strenuous outdoor activities and initiative tests – Outward
Bound camps were his brainchild – but Launcelot realized his
ideas went much deeper than that, and after Hahn's death in
1983 wrote to *The Times* to correct what had been written
about his methods:

> Those who knew Kurt Hahn personally think first and fore-
> most of his remarkable and magnetic personality. . . . There
> was something massive, penetrating and incisive about him,
> and yet he was not in the least intimidating. . . . His greatest
> influence was exerted through the force of his personality.
>
> [The article] unfortunately interposes phrases and innu-
> endos which perpetuate ill founded myths that seriously dis-
> tort Hahn's methods and message; allusions to cold water
> and hearty muscularity. He wished to 'molest the contentedly
> unfit' but he was no worshipper of the Spartan ideal, which
> he constantly and specifically repudiated. . . . He sought to
> kindle the whole range of [his pupils'] talents, so helping them
> to realise there was more in them than they knew existed.
> Compassion was a vital quality, to be kindled not by moralis-
> ing but by rescue operations or some Samaritan service.

In a private letter also, Launcelot refuted the notion that Hahn
was really a humanist:

> It seemed to me that when Kurt was confirmed it was not so
> much a case of conversion to Christianity from Judaism, but
> that with the powerful influence that certain sections of the
> Gospels and the example and teaching of Christ had upon
> him, confirmation seemed a natural step to take. I suspect
> that there was also some feeling for Bishop Bell and for Wil-
> liam Temple and other Anglicans [who had helped him come
> to England] . . . but I very much doubt whether he felt any
> allegiance to the Church of England as such. . . .
>
> I would be disposed strenuously to deny that Kurt 'really
> had no faith'. I would describe him as a deeply religious,

deeply spiritual man, and that spiritual vision was the driving force of his work. But he was in no way a churchy man. . . .

Jane and I visited him shortly before he died. . . . He seemed almost put out by seeing us. I then had some time with him alone; and he said he had not been baptised before his Confirmation (I greatly doubt if this was really true), and would I baptise him. . . . The next morning I ministered what is called 'Conditional Baptism' i.e. 'If you have not been baptised already, I baptise you . . .' This seemed to have the effect of bringing the normal Kurt back to life. He was obviously relieved, and instead of being all boxed in he was quite normal and his usual self.

Prince Philip had been Kurt Hahn's pupil at Salem, and asked Launcelot to help set up the Duke of Edinburgh's Award Scheme in 1954. Later on he was also asked to help in inaugurating Atlantic College, the Prince's Trust, Project Trident, Outward Bound, and similar projects, and was always clear that the aim must be to bring out young people's potential; during his time at Portsmouth he wrote a pamphlet that developed this theme, entitled 'Beyond His Grasp':

The value of an Outward Bound course can best be understood, and its spiritual effects assessed, in the part which it can play in helping a boy [*initially Outward Bound courses were for boys only*] discover and grow in the truth. It is important not to make false claims. . . . Outward Bound activities undoubtedly make a powerful, sometimes decisive impact, but this must be seen as only one factor, albeit important, among all those which are contributing to the forming of his character.

The Christian claims that truth has been put within the reach of men by Jesus Christ . . . but the man who is trying to impart religious truth must use the language of poetry. The story of Adam and Eve, the Flood, the Tower of Babel, the parables of Jesus, are all written in the language of poetry; is it not reasonable to claim that Outward Bound provided this kind of imagery in a form which is attractive and instinctively appreciated by a boy? To climb a mountain or sail a boat can provide a release from the artificial conditions in which most of us have to live. Under the right leadership, success in a project of the Outward Bound type breeds not a humanistic sense of self-assurance but a godly recognition of the Giver of all gifts. For Christian humility does not consist of saying 'I am no good at anything', but in recognising what one is good at and at the same time acknowledging that we have nothing except what we have received. . . .

Perhaps the weakness of Hahn's methods was that they depended too much on the character and ideals of those who employed them. Launcelot found as time went by that it became increasingly difficult to find Outward Bound instructors, or teachers for schools such as Atlantic College, who recognized the importance of a spiritual dimension in the work they aimed to do. Kurt Hahn had seen all too clearly the evil of Nazism, but in the wrong hands any youth organization that gives a high priority to physical fitness can degenerate into something perilously like Hitler's 'Strength Through Joy' movement.

On a rather different note, Launcelot made space in his diary for regular meetings of 'Dons and Beaks', a group of (mainly public school) headmasters and senior masters with a sprinkling of university dons who shared a strong Christian commitment. They would meet for a residential conference/retreat in some school or college during the holidays. In 1953 Launcelot gave the addresses, subsequently printed privately under the title 'Humility, Compassion and Courage', which made a profound impression on those who heard them. Like all his sermons, they are less compelling when read than when they were delivered, but they set out what Launcelot considered was the role of a good teacher:

The word 'compassion' implies the idea of being *with* the other person. A teacher imparts his knowledge effectively insofar as he can bring his mind alongside that of his pupil and identify himself with the stage of development which the pupil has reached. But this pastoral approach is fraught with problems. There is the danger of possessiveness; we fail as much by domination, by intrusion, or by pursuit, as we do by aloofness – particularly with adolescents who may develop a sort of protective shell which makes any kind of companion-ship so extraordinarily difficult. Then there is the difficulty of our natural likes and dislikes, our inclination to bypass the indolent, the ungainly, the ungifted; yet those who are most in need of help are the very ones who tend to keep their distance . . .

What was [Christ's] secret? In the first place, no one was ever made to feel he had no time for them. (I have a feeling that Nicodemus not only came to Our Lord by night, but kept him up into the small hours.) If ever an application of Christ's compassion was relevant to the schoolmaster or don, it must surely be to give time, and to be sensitive enough to realise when you have got to drop everything for a pupil who is in trouble and wants your help. Compassion is caught rather than taught; by far the greatest single contribution that any teacher can make is to practise and teach compassion . . .

The talk on Courage was on much the same lines as the sermon he had preached in 1940 at HMS *King Alfred*. A school-master's need for courage was less obvious than it had been for men about to go to war as naval officers, but as Launcelot pointed out,

the ordered rhythm of school or college life can by punctuated by the most unexpected problems which constitute a crisis for which we may or may not be unprepared. . . . Under stress, men will strongly tend to be whatever in quiet hours they have made themselves.

In other words, moral (and nowadays, even physical!) courage can be as necessary for the teacher in the classroom as for those engaged in war. But perhaps the most telling part of these addresses is that on Humility:

> [Compared with] Pride, vices such as greed, anger and unchastity are, as C. S. Lewis put it, mere fleabites. For pride is the complete anti-God state of mind, literally bedevilling everything and everyone it touches. If a man wants to know how proud he is, he has but to ask: how much do I dislike it when other people patronise me, or snub me? And how much do I resent it when they do things more adroitly or effectively than myself – or when they get promotion? Pride is at the root of that competitive instinct which we can all too easily justify as ambition. So long as you are looking down [on other people] you cannot see what is above you. This may explain why some of us find prayer difficult or unreal.
>
> In Christ, we worship one who lacked status or privilege, wealth or position, and what is more important, never sought to possess them. He did possess a sense of divine commission and authority, but how does he express it? He takes a towel, pours water into a basin, and begins to wash his disciples' feet – the most menial service of a slave. But our humility does not begin with the *giving* of service, in which there can be much condescension and pride, but in our readiness to receive it. We must allow Christ to wash our feet, to be clean. Otherwise we become blind to our own need, with nothing to offer those we teach but the product of our own conceit.

It was noticeable that in the Portsmouth diocese and then in Norwich an unusually high percentage of the clergy Launcelot appointed came from public schools, and his involvement with young people was slanted in the same direction; he was a governor of Marlborough, Wellington, Bryanston, Canford and Atlantic College, none of which were within his diocese. For some twenty-five years he regularly took the confirmations at Westminster School and latterly at Radley, besides being in constant demand as a preacher at schools up and down the country. Not surprisingly, he was sometimes accused of elitism, but when taxed with this by an ex-public school master who felt that the whole system of private education was unjust, he replied:

> I would maintain that your use of the word 'injustice' as a form of moral opprobrium is not valid. There is unequal opportunity; so what? Try and improve all schools, and don't set about it by trying to equalise them all in order to eradicate what is spuriously called injustice. . . . Is it unjust that I can have a glass of sherry in the evening and my next-door neighbour cannot afford it?

It is easy to see why he was perceived by some as favouring 'public school types'. Like most people, he found it easiest to get on with those that he had most in common with. As chaplain in a battleship he found it much easier to relate to the wardroom than to the lower deck, but no one who has read the copious letters written, often many years after the war, by ratings who clearly thought of 'the padre' as a real friend could accuse him of snobbery or stand-offishness. He was brought up to assume that gentlemen make the best leaders, and his experiences both during the war and later as a bishop had not made him revise that general assumption, but that did not mean he did not recognize genuine talent from wherever it came. Among the curates he attracted into his diocese were men who were the very antithesis of public school types, including some who had been rejected elsewhere as being too uncouth but whose potential Launcelot had spotted and had snapped them up. His 'elitism' did not mean that he ignored the needs of the less well-off or the less intelligent; it was simply that he did not accept that reducing the standards of the best would improve the attainments of the worst.

Probably his most important contribution to helping young people fulfil their potential was Voluntary Service Overseas (VSO). Dr Alec Dickson, who had worked for the Colonial Service in West Africa and had realized how valuable voluntary work could be in developing countries, gave a talk at Portsmouth Grammar School and stayed the night at Bishopswood. He and

Launcelot discussed how the need for volunteers overseas might
be matched with the need to fill the gap, created by the ending
of National Service, between leaving school and going to university. They agreed that Launcelot should write a letter to *The
Times* ('Alec drafted it, I amended it') about 'The Year Between'
(as VSO was originally entitled). *The Times* rejected it, but the
Sunday Times duly printed it on 23 March 1958:

> A number of headmasters are very much aware that many of
> their senior boys including the most gifted, on leaving are
> having to wait a year (in some cases even longer) before vac-
> ancies become available in universities or technical training.
> So many of these young people have something very much
> worthwhile to give; but where and how?
>
> It is, I submit, the underdeveloped territories of the Com-
> monwealth that today offer opportunities of service that
> would not only make a positive contribution to those coun-
> tries but would constitute an experience of inestimable value
> to many of our young people. . . . I know of urgent appeals
> from Sarawak, from Uganda and from West Africa, not for
> money but for volunteer assistance, in the field of primary
> teaching, youth work, community development, adult edu-
> cation and social welfare generally . . . [projects that] do not
> postulate specialist skills so much as a readiness to work
> alongside the local people.
>
> Equally urgent is the need of the best of our young people
> in their difficult transition before university or career, to have
> the opportunity of doing something worth while, where it is
> most genuinely needed, and seeing a bit of the world into the
> bargain. . . . Is it beyond our organisational capacity to unite
> these needs?

The whole operation was a classic example of how ruthless
Launcelot could be in furthering not his own interests but those
of the good cause he had espoused. The letter went out over his
signature because a bishop was (in 1958) more likely to be
heeded; having thus exploited his position, he then proceeded

to practise some arm-twisting on his friends and acquaintances. He enthused headmasters to commend the idea to their brighter school-leavers, and used the 1958 Lambeth Conference to persuade bishops from overseas dioceses such as Sarawak to set up worthwhile projects for volunteers to go to. He also convinced Lord Dulverton that the Dulverton Trust ought to support such a good cause – and it did, with a vengeance; the first year's accounts of Voluntary Service Overseas consist simply of one very large sum paid in by the Dulverton Trust, a few small contributions on behalf of the first year's batch of fourteen volunteers, and one large cheque for just over £4,000 paid out to BOAC (as the overseas part of British Airways then was).

Alec Dickson became the first Director of VSO, organizing projects, interviewing volunteers before they went and debriefing them on their return. Each of the original fourteen volunteers also visited Bishopswood on their return, and for many years Launcelot wrote to each volunteer while they were abroad. By about 1966 VSO had grown so big that the personal touch was lost – Launcelot wrote 1,100 letters but had fewer replies than he had from the far fewer volunteers in 1961 – but this correspondence made him exceptionally well informed about affairs in various parts of the world. He received a first-hand account of the Ibo–Hausa clashes that started the Biafra war; heard that the Falklands were introverted, that Belize was run-down, that the Anglican Church in one country seemed useless, but that in others the Church (usually but not always Anglican) had made an enormous impression on volunteers who had never before thought much of Christianity. Launcelot often took great pains with individuals; a volunteer who was so impressed with a charismatic project leader in Sarawak that he had decided to read anthropology when he went up to Cambridge received a long letter setting out the pros and cons, and gently dissuading him.

In the early years, having returning volunteers to stay for a night to recount their experiences was the only way to evaluate their projects – it would have been far too expensive to travel out to inspect them on the spot. But the success of VSO meant

that before long the organization had to be put on a more
professional footing, and Alec Dickson (who with his wife Mora
had performed miracles of organization from their flat) left VSO
to start Service by Youth Trust, for voluntary work at home. As
time went by the developing countries wanted trained volunteers
rather than school-leavers who had not obtained any qualifications; this saddened Launcelot because much of his enthusiasm
for VSO had been for what it did to develop the character of
the young volunteers. But by far the greatest good that VSO
did was that it inspired President Kennedy's Peace Corps. With
full government backing from the richest nation on earth, the
Peace Corps has been an enormous force for good in the world;
and its beneficiaries owe a big debt to the founders of VSO.

Chairmanship of the Church of England Youth Council took
Launcelot to Germany on more than one visit between 1954
and 1959. There were large numbers of National Service men
in the British Army of the Rhine, and Launcelot was asked to
report on what he saw of how they were being used and what
effect their experiences were having on developing their skills,
and their character. He was also asked to see how effective
Army Chaplains were able to be (answer: ineffective unless they
were 'essentially Padre of one regiment, and with that regiment
long enough to get on personal and pastoral terms with them')
and advise on their recruitment. Valuable contacts also came
through Kurt Hahn, who introduced him to President Heuss,
showed him round Salem and two similar schools, and enabled
him to meet a most interesting man, Judge Holzchuch. Holzchuch
was a Juvenile Court Judge who tried to make his sentences fit
the crime; thus, a young man convicted of careless driving was
sentenced to a term as porter in an accident ward where he
saw the consequences of such behaviour. On his return from
Germany after his last visit early in 1959 Launcelot was full of
Judge Holzchuch's approach; unfortunately he was not able to
infect others with his enthusiasm as he had done over VSO.

But throughout his time at Portsmouth, what enabled
Launcelot to speak with wisdom and authority about the young

was his own youthful enthusiasm. He turned out regularly for the Bishop of Portsmouth's Hockey Team (not 'Diocesan' team in case, he said, he might not get picked), playing on the right wing which he considered the safest position. He played squash regularly, using the game both as exercise and as a means of getting to know clergy, schoolboys, naval officers and others, with tennis in the summer. The writer also recalls a blistering outing with the Southsea Rowing Club, starting in the choppy waters of Portsmouth Harbour and ending in near-total exhaustion at Fareham with a buffet supper. Many young clergy discovered that their bishop was not only older, but also fitter, than they were.

During his time at Portsmouth, Launcelot visited many State schools, especially the Voluntary Aided (Church), and the few private schools that were in the diocese. These school visits did not make him an expert on education any more than his regular visits to Parkhurst, on the Isle of Wight, made him an expert on penal theory; but when he was later confronted with problems over church schools in Norfolk, he did not find himself in completely strange territory.

14

From Portsmouth to Norwich

The pay's the same.

(Launcelot's response when congratulated on his 'promotion')

At breakfast one morning early in 1959, Launcelot read that the Bishop of Norwich was to retire. He remarked, 'Whoever goes there will have a job on his hands', and when asked 'Might it be you?' replied 'No, it won't be.' But in fact he was an obvious candidate. He had been a bishop for ten years, and his diocese had a reputation for being as well-run and happy as any in England. Those who had known him at Trinity Hall had been doubtful about his administrative ability, but his dislike of spending time on 'admin' had actually proved an advantage. He had refused to attend any diocesan committees except the Board · of Finance, spending the time instead on getting to know people; as a result those who sat on diocesan boards and committees understood and supported his aims. He was clearly on top of his job – so much so that his old Trinity Hall colleague Wansbrough Jones said that Portsmouth had become simply a base from which to pursue his other interests.

Wansbrough's remark was not meant to be taken too seriously, but Launcelot's diary by then had almost as many engagements outside the diocese as in it. In 1956 he made his maiden speech in the House of Lords (on whales – of which more anon), and Bishop Bell had encouraged him to continue to play a full part in the Upper House. It was a forum that suited him, because they liked speakers who were diffident but at the same time knew their subject and had done their homework, while oratorical flourishes, of which Launcelot was incapable anyway, did not impress. But preparing a speech involved an immense amount of reading and asking experts for their views; and as he became better known he was enlisted for yet more good causes.

The Portsmouth diocese was not really a full-time job for an able man once he had learned the ropes (as indeed the Archbishop had realized), and since Launcelot was too energetic and conscientious to sit back and relax, it was inevitable that his list of 'outside interests' would lengthen. It was high time for him to move to a more demanding diocese before he dissipated too much energy on peripheral activities; at the age of fifty-two he was no longer quite so robust as he had been – that winter a bad cold had developed into bronchitis, which when he eventually agreed to see his doctor was diagnosed as ambulant pneumonia. It had been a warning.

For several months Launcelot carried on as usual in blissful ignorance of the fate in store for him. The summer of 1959 was gloriously hot; he chalked up a minor victory over Archbishop Fisher's strict dress code when the Queen Mother said he need not wear gaiters on a visit to Clarence House. Fisher meantime had taken his soundings. On 30 May he wrote to David Stephens, the Prime Minister's Patronage Secretary, with his list of three names for Norwich. In reverse order of preference they were: Jock Henderson, the suffragan bishop of Tewkesbury; Launcelot (who 'had come on a lot lately', but there were doubts about his administrative ability and how he would relate to a 'wide expanse of country villages'); and Gresford Jones (who 'cannot carry this burden of St Albans much longer'). But Gresford Jones made it clear that he did not wish to move; he had important projects in hand and it would be a bad moment to hand over to a new bishop.

That rather stymied the Archbishop. By now he had been told that Jock Henderson was too 'advanced' (high church) for Norfolk; but he was still just as hesitant about Launcelot as he had been ten years earlier. He clutched at a rather wild idea that Maurice Harland, who had moved from Lincoln to Durham, might like to return to a rural diocese where he would be happier than among the miners of County Durham. But not only did David Stephens sit firmly on that idea (to move him from Durham would be an admission of failure), Harland himself indignantly denied that he was finding Durham difficult – 'Percy [Bishop Herbert] had got hold of the wrong end of the stick' as a result of an after-dinner conversation. So Launcelot again floated to the top of the list; 'but he is a bachelor, and are country parishes his natural field?' asked Fisher doubtfully, evidently unaware that Launcelot was at heart a countryman (had he known that his Boxing Day relaxation while at Portsmouth had been going to beat on a local shoot, or seen the pre-war Innerhadden Game Book showing that Launcelot had been just as keen a shot as his father, the Archbishop might have been shocked).

However, on 15 August Fisher wrote to tell David Stephens that Launcelot was the only name he could suggest for Norwich, though in a postscript he did try one more tentative suggestion: 'There is also Owen Chadwick. His claims are outstanding as soon as we can take him from Cambridge. If one can do so *now*, he might become first choice for Norwich. I am making a further enquiry about this.' But the enquiry (to Michael Ramsey, Archbishop of York and a former Regius Professor) elicited the firm response that it would be 'too damaging' to move Chadwick from Cambridge so soon, and in any case Ramsey wanted him for Durham when it became vacant. So on 8 September Launcelot received a letter from the Prime Minister, Harold Macmillan, asking if he would accept the bishopric of Norwich.

Launcelot got the letter while in Scotland on holiday. He did not *want* to leave Portsmouth; nor did he think he was the right man for Norwich. But the bishops he consulted were all 'convinced you ought to go' – Henry Montgomery-Campbell, now Bishop of London, said, 'Of course you have got to go and it's no use consulting the Archbishop because he will say the same.' He was quite right; Launcelot did write to Fisher who replied (in a hand-written letter not marked Confidential) that the three names originally submitted had been whittled down to one, and if Launcelot refused then the whole delicate agreement between Archbishop and Prime Minister about episcopal appointments would be put at risk. That was the message that greeted Launcelot on his return from holiday.

He was still by no means sure that he ought to accept, and consulted several friends. The strong consensus was that he ought to say yes. Ted Roberts wrote:

> On your own principle of filling vacancies with the right man – what does Norwich require? So far as I can judge, someone who is already a Diocesan; someone who can manage a team – a suffragan, three archdeacons and 29 Rural Deans; someone who knows, or is anxious to understand, the problems of the deep country, and the multi-parish benefice; someone to breathe life into and encourage hope in some 400 rustic clergy.

Like everyone else he felt that Sandringham was an important factor – 'a Bishop of Norwich I suppose must in fact try to know [the Queen] and her family more intimately and less officially than any other bishop is able to do'.

Two letters were particularly percipient. Launcelot's brother-in-law Dan de Pass was actively involved as a layman in the Portsmouth diocese; also he came over with Jean to visit her mother almost every Sunday, so saw Launcelot regularly. He wrote:

> a. The Norwich need. On balance, you are considered to be the most suitable man available. In the Service [*Dan was a Captain, Royal Navy, retired*] this would pretty well clinch the argument.
> b. The Queen ... this is the patriotic argument, but on this account is not to be ignored.
> c. The effect on Portsmouth diocese. It would not necessarily be for its good that you should stay on indefinitely ... and in any case I imagine you would be asked to move in the course of the next five years or so.
> d. Your suitability. You are not an intellectual nor have you a forceful personality. On the other hand you have above

average powers of leadership . . . [and] I come back to (a), the powers that be reckon you to be the best man available. e. Mama. This is perhaps the kernel of the problem. You are now very definitely the centre of Mama's life. If she ever heard that you had refused it on her account she would, I believe, spend the rest of her life reproaching herself. On the other hand, if you accept and she goes with you, she would be cut off from Jean and Archie, while if she stays in these parts she would be cut off from you and this is almost unthinkable. . . .

The other particularly well-informed letter was from Wansbrough Jones, a Norfolk man born and bred who stayed there most weekends with his mother and had a shrewd idea of the needs, problems and potential of the diocese.

There will soon be a University at Norwich. Our Bishop must have a part to play in this. The value of having one who knows about universities would be immense.

You may not agree with me that you have a unique gift with young people. I would be so pleased if you had necessarily close contacts with the Heir to the Throne . . . but I do not know if the contact would be a real one.

As to the Diocese: the population is very little larger than Portsmouth but its area and the number of clergy is about two and a half times greater. The clergy are a mixed lot . . . there are some very poor ones in both senses, and some very good ones. A good Rector will get a very good congregation, and an average one, who is also a good person, quite a good one. It would take you several years to sort out the clergy as you would like to do. Norwich itself would probably be no great problem. . . . Nonconformity may numerically exceed the Established Church; even if it does, relations can be improved and good come.

The County is two problems. There is the County, capital C, which is very grand and very well organised and good and loyal but as I think you know has had a little special favour;

and the county itself, large, highly independent, scattered, hard working and sound, which needs more.

The Diocese would particularly welcome, I know, a pastoral Bishop who also upheld the dignity of the See – of which they are very proud – by playing some part in public affairs. Norfolk is not the easiest of places in which to start, that must be admitted. But there are some very sound people in it. I think it would be long before you felt so personally integrated in Norwich as you do in Portsmouth . . . you would be more isolated, I fear. Yet, what can you do? . . . I surmise you would be offered, in the end, something else if you turned this down, but not for reasons you might approve, and nor would I – 'time he was moved'.

Still being objective, my balanced advice must be for you to take it. . . . I know you can manage the business of Norwich. Unobjectively, I do very much hope you will accept. I am sure if you do you will never regret it*, either on public or personal grounds. PS. Thank you for asking me.

*PPS Nor, incidentally, am I sure you would regret declining, but I think you might.

All those he consulted (except Ken Carey, who doubted if Launcelot's health would stand up to it) thought he ought to accept; but still he agonized. What held him back was not his personal desire to stay where he was, strong though that was, but (as Dan de Pass had seen), his mother's situation. During the previous winter a very bad bout of bronchitis had confined her to her room for several weeks, and since then she had only come downstairs in time for lunch, going upstairs again before supper. It was by no means certain that she could stand a move to Norwich, and the alternative would be a nursing home since neither Archie nor Jean could provide the care she needed. Accordingly, Launcelot sent his chaplain, dressed as a tourist and not a clergyman, to spy out the land. In those pre-security days it was easy to have a close look at the new Bishop's House, and when Launcelot learned that it faced south with a glorious view of the cathedral (of which moreover his mother's brother, Bertie

Holland, had once been Dean) he decided that he must accept, and on 4 October wrote to the Prime Minister accordingly.

Disengaging himself from Portsmouth was hard and disagreeable. He always made up his diary for the following year in July so as to keep control of his engagements (and had learned to include, in brackets, any invitations he had declined – there had been an embarrassing picture once in the local paper of him playing hockey having declined some prestigious function nearby), so that well over a hundred engagements now had to be cancelled. Over a thousand files had to be 'weeded' and sorted, some to go to Norwich, some to stay at Portsmouth, and some to be put on the fire. Hardest of all was the business of saying his goodbyes, particularly to clergy who had come to the diocese because he was its bishop – and he was very upset when Michael Peck, who had been a reluctant archdeacon, did not get Launcelot's letter telling him that he would be going to Norwich until he had heard the news on the radio.

Thanks to Jean de Pass's invaluable help, the actual move went fairly smoothly. Some of the Bishopswood furniture was too big for Norwich; the new Bishop's House was very fine but smaller than it looked, since when the estimated cost of the architect's plan exceeded his budget he had hit on the expedient of reducing the size of the house in every dimension. Launcelot's mother went to a nursing home until the house was straight, and then travelled to Norwich by ambulance and was taken straight upstairs to her bedroom. Her presence did give rise to two minor contretemps. Shortly after she had arrived and before a second telephone line had been installed, the Archbishop's Legal Secretary tried to reply to an urgent enquiry from Launcelot only to be told, twice, by his mother that her son was too busy to take telephone calls and he must write; and later, after a meeting in Launcelot's study she reported that every word could be heard in the bedroom above. (The Church Commissioners had to insert about a ton of sand into the study ceiling, which so far as the writer knows has not yet engulfed a bishop.)

Before the enthronement could happen the legal formalities

had to take place. Bishop Herbert had retained the office of Clerk of the Closet, so when Launcelot went to the Palace to kiss hands he was presented by his predecessor; when the Queen, making polite conversation, asked how many parishes there were in his old diocése, 'Can't say, Ma'am, never counted' was the gruff and honest reply.

Launcelot spent the three days immediately before his enthronement in retreat at St Albans where his old friend Kenneth Matthews was Dean. The ceremony itself on 28 January 1960 was a very splendid affair. Norwich was, and still is, much more of a regional capital than most cathedral cities, and its cathedral is one of the half-dozen or so that can vie for the claim to be the finest in England. To add yet further éclat (and some last-minute applications for seats in the cathedral) Princess Margaret asked to attend. As at Portsmouth, there was a Bishop's Company representing different stages of Launcelot's life. Some of its members, like Roddy Maclean from Innerhadden, were the same, but there were inevitably some changes; Claud Barry, Launcelot's Captain in the *Queen Elizabeth*, had died and Admiral Cunningham took his place, and Trinity Hall was represented this time by its Dean, Robert Runcie.

To be the central figure in such a magnificent ceremony might have left some men with an exaggerated sense of their own importance; Launcelot found it awe-inspiring and humbling. The ancient Bishop's Throne had recently been identified as probably the one used by St Felix, and was set high up in the apse behind the high altar; Launcelot later confessed to feeling acutely embarrassed when, as soon as the Archdeacon of Canterbury had placed him on the throne, the choir struck up the Te Deum, 'We praise thee O God'. (His fears that some of his friends might make irreverent comments were justified.) Immediately after the service, there was a civic reception for the new bishop in Norwich Castle – it may have helped that the new Town Clerk, Gordon Tilsley, was an old Trinity Hall man. (Robert Runcie was present as Dean of Trinity Hall; at the ninth centenary celebrations of the diocese, when he was Lord Runcie, he light-heartedly mused that since the first Bishop of Norwich was alleged to have obtained the see by simony, a subsequent Bishop of Norwich had founded Trinity Hall, and no sooner did a Trinity Hall man become Town Clerk of Norwich than Launcelot was made its bishop, the air of Norwich seemed redolent of simony.)

Before he had left Portsmouth, Launcelot had asked his new archdeacons to arrange weekend visits to each of the twenty-nine rural deaneries during his first eighteen months at Norwich. He knew there were problems of clerical poverty and isolation, of tiny populations trying to support large and beautiful medieval church buildings, and of vacant benefices that could not be filled, but before trying to prescribe remedies he wanted to see for himself the situation on the ground. Accordingly, for his first eighteen months at Norwich almost every other weekend was spent on some Deanery visit. He would set off on a Friday afternoon, and during the weekend would visit each incumbent and curate in their own home, eating and sleeping the night in different houses. He would attend three Sunday services, but only preach at one of them (sermon preparation takes time). On Sunday afternoon he would meet all the churchwardens, PCC secretaries and treasurers, and on Monday morning he would attend a chapter meeting, celebrating the Eucharist and talking with the clergy afterwards, before returning to Norwich in time for a couple of hours work before lunch.

This meant that for his first eighteen months he was working at enormous pressure. Besides diocesan work, Bishops' Meetings and meetings of Convocation or Church Assembly each took up three or four days in London, where he always managed to fit in several other meetings and interviews while he was about it. Then there were confirmations, institutions and other services in the diocese, and a number of civic occasions to attend.

A normal day would start with meditation in the chapel at 7.30 followed by Matins. Sometimes Holy Communion was celebrated in the chapel, especially if there were guests; sometimes Launcelot would attend the 8am celebration in the cathedral. At 8.30 or shortly afterwards, breakfast; the chaplain would open the letters (an average of fifty a day) and Launcelot would give them a preliminary glance during breakfast. At 9am there were prayers in the chapel for the household, followed by a brisk five minutes' walk round the garden. After that, there was no let-up, unless it was a day for a game of squash or tennis, until evening prayer and supper (and not always then, since there were often evening engagements that might be an hour's drive away), after which Launcelot would be back at his desk until half past ten or eleven.

Lunch was often an opportunity to talk business with someone – staff meetings usually ended with lunch – or for entertaining. Launcelot preferred asking people to lunch rather than dinner as it took up less time; at two o'clock he would say 'You must put your name in the book before you go'. At Portsmouth guests would usually include someone from the Navy, who knew the form; in Norwich the hint was not always taken, in which case the formula 'You must come for a walk round the garden before you go' was brought into play.

The Church Commissioners paid for official entertainment at a fixed rate according to whether it was lunch, tea or supper, or bed and breakfast (Launcelot was scrupulous about only claiming for genuinely official entertainment), and paid for a chaplain, secretary, gardener and driver; when more help was needed, such as a second secretary, the Commissioners had to be convinced of the need before they would agree to pay, but Launcelot was in the happy position of being able to use his own private means to tide things over until the Commissioners stumped up.

He inherited as secretary the very efficient and totally discreet Ann Warrington, who was shortly joined by Kathleen McEwen. The garden, that of the Old Palace, would be unjustifiably large but for the very full use to which it was (and is) put. To start with, Launcelot jibbed at the idea of an official driver as he disliked the image of a chauffeur-driven prelate and rather enjoyed driving himself. But he soon realized that in a scattered rural diocese a driver was essential; he could read, or dictate letters, while being driven. If the chaplain was going with him, then he would act as chauffeur unless it was to a church

with a good peal of bells, since Spencer Brothers was not only
a first-class driver and mechanic but also a keen bellringer. (He
was an exceptionally nice man, and worked hard in the garden
when he had any spare time.) There was also a living-in married
couple to look after the cooking and domestic side with some
extra help from time to time when necessary.

The contrast between Bishop Herbert's imposing presence and
Launcelot's lack of episcopal gravitas disconcerted some people;
they did not know quite what to make of him. Two anecdotes
illustrate the kind of deference that made Launcelot feel rather
uncomfortable in his early days. Driving back one evening from
a confirmation he came across a man stranded with a puncture
and did the natural thing – stop, and help change the wheel;
to his astonishment, that was newsworthy. And one evening a
Portsmouth curate visiting Norwich was in the study when Ann
Warrington brought in some letters saying 'These are ready to
sign, my Lord'; the curate's jaw dropped, and when Ann had
left he said 'Launcelot, you need to teach her some theology'.
Before long, however, bishop and diocese got used to one
another, and as the 1960s progressed manners, even in Norfolk,
became generally less formal.

Hopes that when summer came Launcelot's mother would be
well enough to come downstairs were not fulfilled. She was by
now very frail; when John Beloe, one of the Portsmouth clergy
who knew her well, called at Bishop's House while on holiday
he was struck by the change in her – 'she is only hanging on to
life by a nylon thread'. By the end of the summer it was clear
that she needed more care than a private house could provide.
Fortunately, there was a very good nursing home within three
minutes' walk of Bishop's House where she could be visited
constantly. She grew steadily weaker, and on 20 October the
matron telephoned to say that she had taken a sudden turn for
the worse. Launcelot was visiting an RAF base in West Norfolk,
and although he hurried home he was not in time to see her
alive; but he had the consolation of knowing that she had died
very peacefully indeed. Her funeral took place in the cathedral,

and the coffin was then taken to be buried in her husband's grave, her four children catching the night train to Scotland at Grantham.

The death of a mother, even if it had been expected and had come as a release from an existence that had become a burden, always comes as a blow; the one person whom one has always known, from the very moment of one's birth, has been removed from one's life. Launcelot felt his mother's death more keenly than his brothers or Jean, because in recent years he had seen so much of her, but any notion that her death was a crushing emotional blow to him is quite simply false. His next Bishop's Letter in the *Norwich Churchman* was entitled 'After Death, What?' and referred of course to his mother's death – which enabled him to write with great sincerity about the Christian doctrine of the life of the world to come in terms that related to the human experience of bereavement. But it does not tell us much about his feelings towards, and relationship to, his mother; much more revealing about that is a Mothering Sunday sermon (often re-used with very minor changes) about 'the generation gap':

In St John's Gospel we are told that as Jesus looked down from the Cross, he saw Mary standing there with John the beloved disciple; he said to Mary 'Woman, behold thy son' and to John 'Behold thy mother' . . . [showing] a deep feeling and compassion. . . .

[Yet] in the few recorded [other] instances of Jesus's dealings with his mother he appears almost off-hand. Remember how at the age of twelve . . . [he stayed behind] in the Temple, and his mother, quite distraught, asks 'Son, how can you treat us like this?' and Jesus replies 'Did you not know that I must be about my Father's business?' A typically motherly anxiety; and a typically adolescent reply from a son who was convinced that what he was doing was right. . . . And when Jesus was running into hostility with the authorities, we are told that his mother and family tried to intervene. When Jesus was told of their arrival he says 'Who is my mother? Who are my brothers?' – then, indicating all the people around him, 'Here are my mother and my brothers; whoever does the will of God is my brother and sister and mother.'

Mary may not have followed Jesus in his mission with the same enthusiasm as his disciples; no doubt she followed his every step, but with perplexity and great anxiety. . . . But when the crunch came, the disciples 'all forsook him and fled'. They were not there when they crucified Our Lord. But Mary, the mother, was there. This was the triumph of a maternal love which had remained constant; the generation gap was bridged by love.

No one who had lived in a house with Launcelot and his mother could read that sermon without realizing that he had his own mother at the back of his mind as he wrote it. He was, as she said, her Benjamin, Bob had gone off the rails, Archie had got engaged to 'an Australian girl' before his mother had even heard about her – and nice daughter-in-law though Cynthia proved, that rankled – so it was left to Launcelot to become the son on whom she fixed all her hopes. Luckily, he was sensitive enough to understand and make allowances for her efforts to direct and mould him, strong-willed enough to resist, and loving and humble enough to do so gently. As his clergy came, sometimes ruefully, to realize, a hesitant and diffident manner concealed a determined will.

Of course he missed his mother, particularly as she died before he had time to make many real friends in Norfolk. But he was too busy to mourn too much – added to which, Kay Leonard, the wife of his suffragan, had that summer presented him with a dachshund puppy who did more than enough to take his mind off things – though she did not hinder his work, and indeed was once very helpful when with brilliant timing she started to be sick on the carpet just as a staff meeting was about to raise a subject that Launcelot had wished to defer until later.

15

The Dead See?

The Dead Sea in Palestine is very buoyant.
*(Bishop Leonard's reply to the jibe that called the
Diocese of Norwich 'The Dead See')*

Norfolk in the Middle Ages was perhaps the richest and most populous county in England. The Black Death hit the county hard but there was still wealth enough to build some fine churches. The industrial revolution passed Norfolk by, and by the twentieth century it had become something of a backwater ('a peninsula, surrounded on three sides by the sea and cut off from the mainland by British Rail') with a population probably no greater than it had been immediately before the Black Death.

Until 1923 the Diocese of Norwich included Suffolk and was far too big to be manageable. The Bishop from 1910 to 1942 was Bertram Pollock, who had been Master of Wellington College* The story goes that Edward VII wanted Pollock for Norwich, and on hearing that he was not considered suitable invited himself to Wellington for a Speech Day and said how sorry they would all be at losing their beloved headmaster as he was shortly to be made Bishop of Norwich. That forced the hand of his advisers. Pollock was indeed much liked by those who knew him well, but he was desperately shy and quite incapable of relating to his clergy. Those who came to see him at the Palace would be proffered sandwiches by the butler as they left and told they might eat them in the garden. The 1914–18 war

* Before going to Wellington he had been a master at Marlborough where an uncle of mine remembered him as a very fine man who typified the best sort of Christian schoolmaster.

reduced the number of men coming forward for ordination, and
the agricultural depression between the wars resulted in severe
rural poverty. Country clergy were not at starvation level like
some of their parishioners, but had to scrape to make ends meet
as they shivered in large vicarages that they could not afford to
heat. Nor could most of them afford to entertain, or run a car;
many became disheartened and demoralized.

When Percy Mark Herbert became Bishop in 1942 he did
much to restore the dignity of the see. A son of one of Queen
Victoria's generals and heir to an earldom, he was well over six
foot with an imposing presence and had already been a bishop
(of Blackburn) for fifteen years. He came from a generation that
believed that clergy should be left free to get on with things
with a minimum of interference from their bishop; and in any
case, wartime conditions followed by years of post-war austerity
made it impossible to do much about clergy stipends or unsuitable vicarages. Herbert was a godly man, totally trustworthy
and absolutely fair, but his lapidary style could make him seem
far less sympathetic than he really was; letters to clergy who
asked for advice seldom exceeded three or four typewritten lines.
The advice was sound, but the style was not such as to make
the recipient feel his bishop loved and cared for him. Herbert
had a dry sense of humour – when the patron at an Institution
muffed his lines and instead of saying 'Right Reverend Father
in God' said 'Dear Heavenly Father', he laconically responded
'Come, I don't think I can quite accept that'; and similar stories
abound.

When Launcelot arrived in 1960 he found a great deal of
goodwill; the welcome he got was warm and sincere. But he
knew he faced a daunting task. On his first Sunday, somewhat
to the Archdeacon's consternation, he celebrated the Eucharist
at the small parish of Fersfield, near Diss, which had felt neg-
lected since its Rector had gone away five months earlier to do
missionary work in Iran without arranging for anyone to take
the duty in his absence. The visit gave a welcome signal that
the new bishop knew that all was not well in his diocese and
meant to do something about it. It also made Launcelot realize

that his profile was much higher in Norwich than it had been in Portsmouth; he drew a far bigger congregation than Fersfield had seen in a hundred years. Yet the fact that people had come, and had given the church a rapid springclean and made a big effort to tidy the churchyard, showed that there was life underneath the surface.

At his first staff meeting the full extent of the diocese's problems was borne in on Launcelot. The Archdeacon of Norwich was snowed in at his country rectory, so the meeting only consisted of the Bishop of Thetford (Pat Leonard, whom Launcelot already knew – he had been on holiday to Innerhadden) and the Archdeacons of Norfolk and Lynn. They were all considerably older than Launcelot; the Archdeacon of Lynn had been ordained in 1921, and the other three before the first world war, in which Pat Leonard had won a DSO. They showed absolutely no resentment towards a new bishop much younger than themselves; indeed they looked to him to solve their problems. But they had been too occupied with day-to-day problems to give much thought to long-term solutions, though the Archdeacon of Lynn did suggest that 'what's wrong with the Church in Norfolk, bishop, is that there's too much Holy Communion'. Over sixty benefices were reported as vacant (one had slipped the archdeacon's memory so it was not until bearded by the churchwardens that Launcelot learned about it). Pat Leonard, who knew how desperately poor many clergy and their families were, had used his powers during the interregnum to move some of them to parishes that had been vacant long enough for the sequestration fund to build up and give them a much-needed windfall; but that had not helped towards any long-term solution.

There were two major problems that had to be tackled if the Church's ministry was to be effective. One was the excessive number of parish churches within the old city-wall boundary of Norwich – this was the problem that the Archdeacon of Norwich wanted to raise when prevented by the dachshund puppy's sudden nausea (she received a charming reply to her letter of apology – 'I too in my youth have sometimes dined not wisely but too well'). The reason why Launcelot did not want it discussed then was that the rural problem was even more urgent. Bishop Herbert had amalgamated some livings, but he could only do so when a parish fell vacant and a neighbouring incumbent was willing to take it on. Even when three or four very small parishes did share an incumbent it was not really a solution; it saved money (and raised money by selling a vicarage) but left the remaining incumbent more isolated than ever.

The Lincoln diocese had pioneered rural group ministries of clergy working together as a team, and Launcelot wrote about this in the *Norwich Churchman* (which he had started so as to have a diocesan magazine lively and readable enough to be an effective channel of communication). This elicited a letter from Hugh Blackburne, the Vicar of Harrow, who had been stationed on the Lincolnshire coast during the war where he had become convinced that the only solution for the remote country parishes in those parts was some form of group ministry. Blackburne said that he must stay at Harrow for a few years yet, but would very much like to be kept in mind for any future rural group ministry in Norfolk. When Launcelot next went to London he asked Blackburne to dinner, and on his return happened to mention their conversation at the very same moment that the ninth contiguous red pin denoting a vacant parish was being stuck into the map on his study wall.

The opportunity was too good to miss. The Bishop of London allowed Launcelot to poach Blackburne, one of his best clergy; the next thing was to persuade the patrons, churchwardens and parochial church councils of nine small parishes in south-west Norfolk (another was added later) to agree to share a Rector and two curates. That was not easy. The Archdeacon warned that two of the parishes could never combine as they had been on different sides in the war (i.e. the Civil War). The wife of one patron did not like to think there would be no resident priest on hand if she was on her deathbed, a reminder perhaps that religion can mean more to people than their actual church attendance suggests. Getting the Hilborough Group off the ground took over a hundred letters (and more than one decanter

of sherry); but it proved very successful, and was the first of
several groups.

In a talk to theological students in 1967 Launcelot explained
their purpose:

> The main problems in [rural] parochial life are the distances,
> the small size of many of the hamlets and villages, and the
> large number of ancient churches, some very beautiful. . . .
> Socially, the parishes [around Hilborough] belonged together;
> most of the children went to the same school. . . .
>   Now, we have eleven groups, comprising 95 parishes with
> a [total] staff of 30 clergy, one woman worker, and one
> Church Army Captain. The groups have been created where
> there seems to be a natural area for social and community
> life, though necessity may mean that a group has to include
> parishes which don't easily fit in, if it's simply too difficult to
> provide for them in any other way for the time being.
>   There is no blueprint, no common pattern. Each group is
> left to develop as seems best; but one feature common to all
> is that the clergy meet together at least once a week for a staff
> meeting. It is here and in meetings of the Group Council which
> includes lay representatives from each of the parishes that
> plans are made. The clergy may meet for worship more fre-
> quently, perhaps daily. Sharing in thought and worship is a
> very important element. In some groups [there may be] a
> deacon being trained in rural ministry. Arrangements for wor-
> ship are planned to suit the needs of the parishes. Initially
> there is no suggestion that any of the churches may become
> redundant; in some cases, after a group has been going well,
> this may begin to happen.
>   Group services where parishioners come from all the
> parishes are planned at varied intervals, and always seem to
> be appreciated. . . . Organisations for all or parts of the group
> [e.g. youth organisations] are planned so far as possible to
> make the special skills of each of the clergy and of lay people
> as widely available throughout the whole area as possible.
>   How successful has the experiment been?

Without exception Church life has shown signs of renewal and development. This is partly due to the calibre of the clergy attracted to the group [*Two of Hugh Blackburne's former curates are today, 2002, diocesan bishops*] and because the teams of clergy include some younger men for whom there would not normally have been suitable appointments in those areas. But I should judge that the spiritual awakening derives partly from the fact that clergy are stimulated and encouraged by close co-operation, their wives and families less lonely, and that lay people are helped to secure a new relationship with the clergy; a change from thinking that their role is to help their clergy to provide religion to the parish, to being helped by their clergy to practise their religion and to be the people of God – to think in wider than parochial terms.

But it does need a lot of organising, and the paternalistic view of the clergy dies hard . . .

That talk was given at Oakhill Theological College, whose Principal, Maurice Wood, was to become the next Bishop of Norwich. A note in Launcelot's hand reads: 'A lot about Group Ministries – perhaps that's why Maurice Wood forsook them! L.F.Aug. 1988'. It does seem that Launcelot's successor did not grasp that the main purpose of group ministry was to 'encourage and stimulate' clergy and counter the bad effects of clerical isolation; like many other bishops, Maurice Wood saw groups simply as groups of *parishes*, so that when runaway inflation and a fall in numbers of ordinands in the 1970s led to a shortage of clergy, the obvious way to save on clerical manpower was to reduce the number of clergy in a group. In fact, although setting up Group Ministries had as a rule led to marginal savings in clerical manpower – in the Hilborough Group a vicar and two curates replaced four incumbents – once a group had been whittled down to just one or two clergy the whole point had been lost. The result was to give Group Ministry a bad name as it seemed to be merely a euphemism for cutting down on clergy. In fairness to Maurice Wood, however, it is arguable that synodical government, introduced in 1970, would in any case have sounded the death-knell of Group Ministry as Launcelot had developed it. Under him, pastoral reorganization was always flexible – if something worked well, it could be built on, if it didn't, it could be modified or scrapped; but under synodical government any linking or severing of parishes must be tied up legally.

Groups were not in any case a universal panacea. Launcelot also countered the debilitating effects of clerical isolation by requiring each deanery chapter to meet at least ten times a year, usually starting with a communion service followed by breakfast and discussion of some theological topic – in other words, the clergy were to share worship, fellowship and study. Launcelot's Examining Chaplains provided a syllabus of topics, and rural deans were given a list of people who were willing (and able) to go to chapter meetings and introduce some subject. They included some very high-powered university professors as well as clergy and laity within the diocese with some particular expertise. Rural Deans were asked to let Launcelot know of any clergy who habitually absented themselves, not because he was developing headmasterly tendencies but because absenteeism could be a symptom of something badly wrong; there had been some serious and tragic cases of clergy going off the rails or having breakdowns, and prevention was better than cure. A few clergy inevitably resented the prescriptive nature of these meetings; Colin Stephenson, a Norfolk priest who had known Launcelot as a fellow naval chaplain, impishly commented that 'they all loved Launcelot when he did something about their pay, but some were less keen when they realised he expected them to work for it'.

Do something about their pay, he certainly did. Almost his first act in 1960 was to set up a small Commission chaired by Timothy (now Sir Timothy) Colman 'to investigate exactly what a parson, curate or incumbent, needs in order to manage' and to do his work properly. A year later Launcelot told the Diocesan Conference that 'it is salutary to remember that although the Commission worked out their figures as a minimum, yet only one in eighteen clergy in the Diocese have an income that they recommend as that minimum' (£975 for incumbents, £550/690 for curates). Unfortunately, inflation meant that the recommended minimum became a moving target and was never completely met, but it is the case that Launcelot found the level of stipends in the Norwich diocese well below the average, and left it above the average. One immediate step he could take was to ask the PCC of each vacant parish to guarantee £200 a year towards a new incumbent's expenses, and if they could not, to ask if they felt the parish justified a full-time incumbent. (One deputation came to Bishop's House to explain that the parish simply couldn't afford £200 a year, but made the mistake of coming in three very expensive motor-cars . . .)

Launcelot made it a priority to attend the Clergy School that took place each July. This had been started during Bishop Herbert's time by the then Bishop of Thetford, Jack Woodhouse, and took place at the teacher training college at Keswick, just outside Norwich. Lecturers were usually of a high standard, and the relaxed atmosphere (the tennis courts were in full use in the afternoons) made it all the more valuable. Launcelot asked parishes to encourage their clergy to attend and did his best to make sure that no one was deterred by the expense.

Clergy housing was a major problem. In those days parsonage houses were a matter for the diocese to deal with, and Norwich had an exceptionally large proportion of houses that were too big, in bad repair, or badly sited. Almost immediately after his arrival Launcelot was asked to confirm a decision to sell a vicarage. He had no hesitation in doing so, but insisted that the house be sold by auction, against the advice of the firm of estate agents who usually acted for the diocese and much to the perturbation of the archdeacon. When the house was auctioned it fetched over 50 per cent more than the original asking price; and Launcelot asked to borrow the files of all parsonage houses sold between 1945 and 1960. They told a sorry tale. Admittedly most houses had needed a lot of money spent on them, but one example of a rectory being sold for £500 and let a year later for £800 a year was not untypical. The root of the trouble was that the diocese had decided it could not afford to employ a full-time professional surveyor, so the management of millions of pounds worth (even at 1960 values) of property was left to a part-time clerk paid £5 a week.

Some felt that a bishop should not get involved in worldly matters like the sale of houses or glebe, but Launcelot's ignorance of the workings of the Church of England before he became a bishop was once more proving an advantage (as was the fact that he was a canny Scot on his father's side!). And in his concern over the design of new vicarages, he was only following in the footsteps of Edward King, the saintly Bishop of Lincoln, who eighty years earlier had insisted that new vicarages must be well designed and get plenty of sun. A man's surroundings do affect his morale, and Launcelot never approved proposals for new vicarages without the plans having been carefully inspected. There were some good architects available, but the Dilapidations Board had lacked a clear vision of how to set about improving clergy housing – they had been too busy with immediate problems such as what to do when an incumbent died and it was found that his house had fallen into considerable disrepair.

Luckily Vice-Admiral Sir Edward Evans-Lombe had retired early from the Navy in order to manage his estate and became chairman of the Diocesan Board of Finance; Launcelot liked good admirals (which Sir Edward was) and they worked together to persuade the Diocesan Conference of the need to raise the Quota, which was as small then compared to today as Mr Pitt's Income Tax was to Mr Healey's. The next move was to give the Dilapidations Board a clearer sense of direction; and since he was determined not to get mired down with Board meetings himself Launcelot appointed a Lay Assistant. Nicholas Crace came with his wife Brigid to work for a pittance in order to do something they felt was really worthwhile, which Nicholas's attendance at Board meetings on the Bishop's behalf certainly was. It was mainly due to him that clergy housing improved during the 1960s, though his attempt to get the Diocesan Conference to adopt agreed standards for parsonage houses was set back when one of the archdeacons who had helped draw up

the plans and endorsed them changed his mind unexpectedly
and persuaded the Diocesan Conference to reject them.*

In 1961 the two senior archdeacons having reached the age
of seventy decided to retire, and the Archdeacon of Lynn
resigned his archdeaconry in order to run the Diocesan Stewardship Campaign – a vital job in view of the state of the diocesan
finances. This meant that Launcelot could choose his own team.
Finding them was not easy, since in such a rural diocese there
were few large urban parishes of the kind where one would find
youngish incumbents of high calibre. Aubrey Aitken, the Vicar
of St Margaret's, King's Lynn, was one such and became Archdeacon of Norwich, but the two others came from outside the
diocese. Bill Llewellyn was Vicar of Tetbury and had spent most
of his ministry in the country apart from the war, during which
he had become Senior Chaplain, Eighth Army. Eric Cordingly
had been a country vicar in Gloucestershire before becoming
Rector of Stevenage as its new town was about to be built; as
an army chaplain he had been captured by the Japanese and
was awarded an MBE for his work in a prisoner-of-war camp.
Both men were outstanding, though neither of them was on the
Lord Chancellor's list of suitable archdeacons; Launcelot was
good at picking winners – and indeed, thanks to his comprehensive 'Patronage Files' there was before long a waiting list of
clergy wanting to serve in the diocese.

Soon after their arrival Bishop Pat Leonard died. Both he and
his predecessor as Suffragan Bishop had got to know the clergy
well through their visits to parishes, but played no part in
diocesan administration. This meant that although they might
know, for example, that a rectory was unhealthily damp they
did not sit on the Dilapidations Board where they could have
got something done about it. The archdeacons on the other hand
were on the boards which made the decisions about parsonages

* Nicholas Crace went on to work, first, for VSO and then for REACH,
which under his direction became a highly successful organization putting professional men and women who wanted something to do in their
retirement in touch with schools, churches, charities etc. that needed the
expertise they could offer.

and other matters that directly affected the parish clergy, but had fewer opportunities to get to know the clergy; they had their own parishes to look after (except for the Archdeacon of Norfolk who was a Canon Residentiary) and they did not of course take confirmations.

The Portsmouth solution of having unbeneficed archdeacons was not feasible in the larger (and poorer) diocese of Norwich, so Launcelot's solution was to ask the Archbishop if his three new archdeacons could be made suffragan bishops as well. They were all of a calibre to make this perfectly appropriate, but Michael Ramsey was only prepared to allow Norwich two suffragans and jibbed at a third one. That put Launcelot in a dilemma. It seemed invidious to make two archdeacons bishops and not the third, particularly since the one to be left out would have to be the Archdeacon of Norwich whose area included the city itself which involved more strictly archidiaconal work than the others, and people might suppose that the two newcomers were thought superior to Aubrey Aitken who was Norfolk born and bred. Launcelot hesitated, but in the end decided that the advantage of having two of the three archdeacons as suffragan bishops outweighed any perceived unfairness. But although he emphasized that the selection had been made for geographical, not personal, reasons, the diocese was still too Barchester-minded for everyone to believe him.

This combining of the role of Archdeacon and Suffragan Bishop was discontinued after Eric Cordingley and Bill Llewellyn had left, so that 50 per cent fewer clergy are now being looked after by three archdeacons and two suffragans, a 40 per cent increase. This operation of Parkinson's Law has come about partly because a bishop can appoint who ever he likes as archdeacons but suffragan bishops have to be approved by higher authority, partly because not all bishops have Launcelot's tenacity (setting up the arrangement took well over a hundred letters and two journeys to London in one day), and also because under synodical government archdeacons have to sit on so many more boards and committees that they could hardly combine that administrative work with the pastoral office of a bishop.

One other aspect of Launcelot's dealings with his clergy was his insistence on their having days off, and holidays. No. 1 of his Bishop's Notices circulated to all clergy and dealing with such matters as marriage after divorce or burial of suicides (never refuse without prior consultation with the bishop – suicide was then a crime) was 'Holidays'. He managed, mainly through the understanding generosity of some wealthy lay people, to build up the Bishop's Discretionary Fund which could help towards the cost of going on holiday – and many clergy who liked the Scottish Highlands used Innerhadden Cottage for holidays, or sometimes took the services for a fortnight in the little Episcopalian palian church at Kinloch Rannoch where a splendid manse was provided for the officiating priest (it was only in the holiday season that any Anglicans were living in the parish).

Launcelot was less clerical-minded than most bishops, and considering how much he achieved on the wider scene – he was for instance the only bishop during the twentieth century to pilot a Bill successfully through the House of Lords – this emphasis on his care for the clergy may seem surprising. But he saw it as a matter of common sense that if you have some four hundred paid full-time agents, then helping them to be as effective as possible will achieve much more than your own unaided efforts could ever do. However, Launcelot's efforts to 'sort out the clergy as you would like to do' (as Wansbrough Jones had put it) were never his only irons in the fire. For example, on the make-or-break day for setting up the Hilborough Group, Launcelot also had three other unrelated matters to deal with urgently: a priest had got into serious trouble; there was a crisis over appointing the first Vice-Chancellor for the University of East Anglia; and a row had to be defused on the other side of the world in Antarctica. That day was exceptional, but gives some idea of the constant pressures he was under.

His ability to get his ideas across and win over doubters by a combination of skill and charm was remarkable – what Owen Chadwick called 'planned incoherence' when chairing a meeting was used to the full. So was his clear-sighted vision of what needed to be done and where the priorities lay. But less apparent at the time, though on reflection very striking, were his sheer tenacity and courage. He hated, even more than most of us, to be disliked; but he never flinched from some very tough decisions that needed to be made if the work of the kingdom of God was to be done effectively. What he did in those first eighteen months, before he had as it were got his own team into place and was very much alone at the wheel, took courage; it also probably took more out of him than he or anyone realized at the time, and it is not altogether surprising that a few years later his health broke down. But before continuing with what he did at Norwich, this is perhaps a good moment to turn to the 'outside interests' that had not entirely been put into abeyance.

16

The Wider Scene

He was concerned for the environment before most of us
were aware that there was such a thing.

(Owen Chadwick at Launcelot's Memorial Service)

Launcelot had made his maiden speech in the House of Lords
on 14 June 1958, eighteen months before he left Portsmouth.
Lord Pethwick-Lawrence had initiated a short debate about
'Cruelty in the Whaling Industry', about which Launcelot knew
more than most. This was long before 'Save the Whale' had
become a popular car-sticker, and when people heard the subject
of Launcelot's speech they wondered why on earth a Scot who
was an English bishop should have wished to talk about the
Principality of Wales.

He took a great deal of trouble preparing his speech, and
thanks to Brian Roberts who had succeeded him at the Scott
Polar Research Institute and Colin Bertram who had been the
marine biologist in Graham Land his was the best-informed
contribution to the debate. The complete speech took twenty-
five minutes, and shows a characteristic blend of Christian
ethical principle, practical knowledge, and common sense:

... As a member of the British Graham Land Expedition, I
spent a month at South Georgia at Leith Harbour, a whaling
station, in 1937, and from there took passage to Las Palmas
in company with several of the Norwegian gunners whose
friendship and stories were greatly enjoyed. ...

There is a general principle which runs through Holy Writ
which applies to this Motion; that man's sovereignty over the

natural creation is to be regarded not only as a right but also as a stewardship for which he bears responsibility to the Creator. Limitation of suffering so far as this is practicable is one important factor in [this] moral responsibility. . . .

I do not think it can be denied that the explosive grenade harpoon . . . frequently involves a great deal of suffering . . . The time taken between the explosion of the charge when the grenade hits the whale and the death of the whale varies a great deal. It depends upon where the whale is hit, and that in turn [depends] on the skill of the gunner, the weather, and the elusiveness of the whale when being pursued. If the whale is hit in the heart, or its back is broken, or if the grenade penetrates its thick skull and explodes inside the brain, it may be killed instantly. If the whale is hit in the stomach, and that quite often happens, there can be a long period, 30 minutes, 40 minutes, sometimes an hour or even in very exceptional cases, four or five hours before the whale dies. A great deal depends on the skill of the gunner, and an estimate of the average time for a highly-skilled Norwegian gunner is probably in the order of five minutes. [But] the proportion of less skilled gunners, particularly among companies and countries new to whaling, is tending to grow. . . .

The infliction of suffering on animals is a subject on which strong emotions can be aroused. I believe that much harm is done to the cause of those who have animal welfare at heart, by ascribing to animals the same feelings and the same reactions to pain as those experienced by human beings, and even sometimes by presenting animal suffering as even more significant than human suffering. We do not live like whales; we do not think like whales; we do not imagine like whales. We can never know precisely what the whale does feel. . . .

[But] all the evidence goes to show that whales, as other mammals, do suffer when wounded. The brain of a whale is larger than that of any other animal and the cerebral hemispheres are elaborately folded . . . [*technical details follow*]. When a grenade bursts within the stomach of a whale the pain suffered as the result of the laceration of the stomach walls must be of a very acute order indeed. . . . Even if it is mistaken to compare the suffering in an animal with that of a human being, this does not exonerate us from taking every possible practicable step to limit such suffering to a minimum. And this for two reasons; first, out of consideration to the creature which is placed under our responsible domination, and secondly out of consideration for the men who do the job. The death flurry of a harpooned whale is a most gruesome sight; to submit men to this experience as part of their daily work is to make them liable to become insensitive, callous, and even brutal. That is a very serious matter.

There is no apparatus which will kill whales painlessly which could be supplied to the whaling companies straight away. But a method of electrocution is far enough advanced to give promise of success, provided some further research is undertaken [*technical details of rockets follow*].

There is, however, one further point. The gunners are immensely proud of their craft and it is not unnatural that a gunner will be reluctant to limit his own inherent skill by adopting new methods until or unless he has been convinced that they are really going to work efficiently, safely, and with a reasonable measure of success. That will not be achieved until further research has been undertaken. . . . With great respect to the noble Lord, Lord Pethwick-Lawrence, an estimate of £10,000 would be over-optimistic for the amount of money that will be required. . . .

[But] in any event, where suffering is involved relief becomes a matter of moral urgency. If whales were hunted in the seas around this country instead of in the distant seas of the Southern Ocean I am sure that public opinion and public conscience would have faced this issue long before today.

It was not a speech that would entirely please either the whaling industry or anti-cruelty campaigners, but it was factual and informative. When taxed with the charge that speeches in the House of Lords were a waste of time since no one took any notice of them, Launcelot insisted that although this might be true of politicians and the media, civil servants took careful note of what was said. Certainly, a glance through the (unreformed) House of Lords *Hansards* shows that while some peers simply aired their own views, others had expert knowledge and spoke very good sense.

On 18 February 1960 Lord Shackleton, son of the explorer, asked when the government proposed to ratify the Antarctic Treaty. Although Launcelot could have wished this had not come up just three weeks after his Norwich enthronement, it was too near his heart to be ignored, and he spoke in support of Lord Shackleton:

This Treaty seems to me to be a most notable achievement. It is not so long since the Antarctic looked as if it would become a source of increasing conflict and dispute, rather than, as this Treaty gives one good prospects of hoping, a continent which offers free scope for a number of nations to co-operate. . . .

It is arguable that such an inhospitable part of the world may best be left to its own devices, now that it has been discovered and roughly mapped and now that the challenge which it presented to man's spirit of adventure has been met. . . . [But] continued exploration and scientific investigation in Antarctica are objectives really worth carrying out; for instance the value of Antarctic weather stations in long-range weather forecasting; a satellite receiving station at the South Pole; studies in the high atmosphere or ionosphere to [improve] world radio communication. . . . It would be wearisome to list all the varied fields of scientific enquiry in which valuable research can be undertaken . . . in geophysics, meteorology, glaciology and biology. . . .

In addition to the historical pioneer expeditions, the British contribution has been notable and we are in a good position to continue and to develop it in the future. . . . Here is a sphere of common interest in which men of different backgrounds, different ideas, different nationalities really can get to know, to understand and to respect each other, working together on a common ground of mutual interest. To foster such co-operation, which as I see it this Treaty will facilitate, is, I believe, to make some contribution to the cause of peace.

The Antarctic Treaty did not come up again for six years, by which time Launcelot was less pressed and was able to make a major contribution.

When he went to Norwich he had to give up being chairman of the Church of England Youth Council, but felt he must take part in a debate on the Albermarle Report on the Youth Service on 18 May 1960. The end of National Service had highlighted the need for young people to have opportunities to develop their character and skills, and this was something he had always felt strongly about:

'They have too much done for them already' is a remark which in certain circumstances may be fair enough. Yet is it really unreasonable that certain facilities should be provided for young people as of right? Imagine what the reaction would be if in all universities, public, grammar and secondary schools and technical colleges it was suddenly decided that all playing fields, all sporting facilities, all premises for concerts, for dramatics, for debating societies, entertainments and the like were to be shut down for reasons of economy. [*Alas, Launcelot lived to see exactly that start to happen in the 1980s*].

I welcome the removal of discrimination against grants to denominational religious youth work. There is a suspicion that when youth work is carried out under Christian auspices there is an ulterior motive, that the young are 'being got at'. There is sometimes a justification for this suspicion, arising from a misapplied zeal, but it needs to be said that the basis of a specifically Christian attitude of mind towards young people is a concern for them for their own sakes, all the deeper because they are recognised as persons who have an eternal destiny.

Two years later (21 February 1962) Launcelot made a rather different plea in a debate on 'The Youth Services'.

> ... Youth Service is widely understood as meaning service to youth, but we do less than justice to young people if we do not also consider service by youth. I do not believe that, in our present conception of the Welfare State, sufficient allowance is made for the particular role that young people can play, in addition to their normal school and their work.... I should like to make a specific proposal – that during the last years at school, the pupils should be encouraged to regard some contribution to the life of the community as an essential ingredient of their own education.

That appeal for the VSO principle to be applied more widely encouraged many schools to do just that. Another less predictable result was that Baroness Ravensdale, one of Lord Curzon's daughters who had for over forty years worked for the Highway Clubs of East London, came to Norwich to discuss the matter more fully. She was well-nigh unique among Launcelot's visitors in managing to prevent him from looking at his post at breakfast time by locking him in conversation throughout the meal – which for her consisted of black coffee and cigarettes smoked though a long holder. (The elderly Canon Edwards, who showed her round the cathedral, found himself on an even sharper learning-curve.)

Archbishop Fisher may have had reservations about Launcelot, but his successor did not. On his side, Launcelot had not been at all sure that he wanted Michael Ramsey to be translated from York to Canterbury, but when that happened in 1961, Launcelot's letter offering his good wishes said, with perfect truth, 'I have come to think that this was the right appointment.' (Ramsey in his reply was 'particularly glad' to get that assurance.) Archiepiscopal approval could sometimes be a mixed blessing; in June 1962, when still very hard pressed with diocesan business, Launcelot was asked by the Archbishop at a few days' notice to speak on behalf of the Bench of Bishops on 'The Probation Service'. He did so, as he admitted, 'without any specialist knowledge'; the facts were supplied to him by the Home Office, and the simple point he had to make was that 'it will be a serious and a tragic matter if there is a shrinkage of the Probation Service . . . or any lowering of its standards'. Even so, preparing the speech properly and remaining in the chamber for as long as polite convention required took up the equivalent of at least one full day's work.

The reason that he always managed to get through so much was partly that he never wasted a minute – for example, when being driven anywhere he took a dictating machine and a pile of letters to answer – and also that he could switch his full attention from one issue to another and then back again with no loss of momentum or concentration. Keeping physically fit with his regular games of squash or tennis also helped; he very seldom gave the impression, except to those working in Bishop's House who knew what was going on, that he was particularly busy. When he went to London for Church Assembly or Convocation he spent as little time as he decently could (if as much!) in the actual sessions which usually bored him stiff, and slipped out to interview some ordinand or potential incumbent, or to attend some meeting – returning to Norwich, as already mentioned, with almost indecipherable notes about people he had seen, which often resulted in bringing good men into the diocese.

In 1961 the British Association for the Advancement of Science chose Norwich for its annual meeting, partly because its new bishop was a scientist. The perceived gulf between science and religion was greater then than now, and Launcelot took great pains with his cathedral sermon on the Sunday.

> Scientists cannot be grouped or classified together as a sort of separate species of the human race, set apart from the rest of humanity, and yet this is sometimes the way they have come to be regarded. A scientist is a person, before and after

becoming a scientist; you cannot climb out of the humanity through which you live and move and have your being. . . .

[But] I seem to be made of several different selves. There is the scientific self, absorbed in some particular area of knowledge; empirical, analytical, selecting only such categories as best serve the purpose of my research. Then there is the administrative self who plans the course of lectures, signs the cheques, arranges meetings; and here rather different qualities come into play than those I need in the lab. Finally there is the social self, involved in relationships of many kinds, at work and at home; and here I am a different kind of person – more emotional though not necessarily on that account less reasonable than my scientific or administrative self.

These three selves appear so often to be pulling in opposite directions. A man may become so absorbed in his work that his home life suffers, or so taken up with his home that his work suffers; ambition for administrative control may affect his relationships or even the integrity of his work. But there is another and deeper cause of tension. The scientist must be detached, dispassionate, and his conclusions provisional. But in his social relationships, he must not remain detached or dispassionate; he must be prepared to stand committed, for better or for worse. Integrity in relationships requires commitment; integrity in the scientific sense forbids it.

Can all three sides of my life be reconciled? Is there such a thing as ultimate truth, a value outside myself to which every side of my personality may be related? Christian teaching about Creation has been the occasion for extraordinary misrepresentations, as past records of the British Association only too clearly demonstrate. The trouble has largely [been] that the first chapter of Genesis has been seen in historical terms, whereas its intention is different; 'Listen,' said the teacher, 'and I will tell you a story about Life with a capital L, and Man with a capital M' – for that is what the words Eve and Adam mean. You cannot prove or disprove the poetic insights of that story by discovering fossils, or the Missing Link, or by finding another man-like species on another planet. There

can be no argument, for instance, about how a baby is con-
ceived or born. The question that remains, though, is 'What
is the meaning and purpose of the life thus born?' The doctor
cannot answer or even ask that question from his scientific
training; but if the doctor also happens to be the baby's father,
then this is precisely the kind of question he will ask. For as
a father he is committed to the child in a way which transcends
his scientific concern for the child's wellbeing.

Sir Wilfred le Gros Clark's Presidential Address stressed the
significance of altruism. This lies at the very heart of Christian
belief about Creation. From the image of God as Creator, the
believer moves into the relationship of a son; a relationship
sustained by love. Love, in the sense of caring, is a unifying
power by which the different sides of our personality at last
fit purposively together. And love is also a unifying power
between individuals, enabling them to sacrifice their personal
interests for the good of others.

The Christian faith not only affirms that Love is at the heart
of Creation, its signature tune; it also discloses in the person
of a man, Jesus Christ, what love means, and offers, and
demands. . . . Pain, death and human sin are facts; and if
Christianity seems sometimes to dwell on these facts, it is
because through Love the power of healing – or redeeming
evil through bearing it – is released. The Christian symbol is
the Cross, because it was on the Cross that the power of Love
was displayed; a power which, in the very act of sacrifice,
sows the seed of new life.

I am part of a Creation made and sustained by Love. But
Love always calls for a response; a response that is never-
ending, that can be painful, and that knows no limits. Only
then is its power released.

A great deal of trouble was taken over that sermon, and true
to form Launcelot read it over to more than one person as
well as consulting Wansbrough Jones who made several useful
suggestions. But the work involved by the British Association
meeting, including a big garden party at Bishop's House, was

more than compensated for by the stimulus and pleasure of being in the company of academic scientists. One of them, Dr Edward Hindle, who had just retired from being Hon. Secretary of the Royal Geographical Society and was a very eminent zoologist (he claimed to have taught Julian Huxley zoology and not to have found him a very apt pupil), stayed for the week at Bishop's House. He was less successful at breakfast-time conversation than Baroness Ravensdale had been; at the end of a harrowing description of the atrocities taking place in the Congo, where he had once studied tropical diseases, he paused; Launcelot, realizing that some response was evidently expected, looked up from the letters in which he had been immersed and exclaimed 'Wonderful!' (When being driven to a meeting and being told by a policeman that only the cars of selected VIPs might park next to the Guildhall, Hindle protested: 'But I am a past Secretary of the British Association.' 'Sorry, Sir, I'm afraid you cannot park there.' But Hindle produced his trump: 'And this is the Bishop of Norwich.' That produced a smart salute, and a wave past the barrier, from the policeman, and acute embarrassment from the back seat where the Bishop tried to conceal himself.)

It was because he felt that this kind of deference was bad for him – it was, in a sense, reflected glory from Bishop Herbert whom a Norwich shopkeeper described with awe as 'a man who never looked to left or right when he crossed a road' – that Launcelot valued and enjoyed his contacts with the young. He continued to take the annual confirmations at Westminster School, and to do a little rowing coaching, and found it refreshing to be treated as 'one of the boys' rather than as the Lord Bishop of Norwich. (The year before leaving Portsmouth he preached the Regatta sermon at Henley Parish Church, and a Westminster schoolboy* was astonished to hear the master coaching his boat hail the bishop who had confirmed the boy two years earlier and say 'Launcelot, remember that there's a right and a wrong side of ten minutes'.)

---

* Dominick Harrod, to whom I am indebted for this reminiscence.

Because he was able to relate easily to the young, even though that mainly meant boys or men since most schools and colleges were then single-sex institutions, Launcelot could and did speak extremely good sense when the House of Lords debated matters concerning young people. Such debates were often initiated by Lord Pakenham (later the Earl of Longford), who despite looking like an absent-minded professor had a great rapport with the young, particularly those who were disadvantaged. Launcelot took part in debates on Educational Policy (24 July 1963), the Problem of Leisure (13 May 1964) and Youth and Social Responsibilities (3 March 1965). If much of what he said now seems platitudinous, that may partly be because he helped make it so. On Educational Policy he said:

> Over too many important issues of right and wrong, of per-
> sonal relationships, of the end and purpose of life itself, a
> large number of [young people] seem to find themselves in a
> state of considerable confusion and uncertainty. In the past
> there was sufficient of a common mind for those responsible
> for education to be fairly sure what were the values for which
> society stood. . . . I am not concerned to argue that the stan-
> dards of today are lower than they were, indeed, some of our
> difficulties are due to our trying to achieve so many good ends
> at the same time. The technical revolution . . . appears to be
> forcing us more and more into a conception of education
> which is essentially one of the imparting of knowledge and
> the training of mind and body in the use of techniques, an
> education for the able. . . . [But] every child has to be educated
> for himself alone and equipped to live as a human being in a
> human society, or, as I should prefer to say, a child of God
> in a world which God has created.

'The Problem of Leisure' was debated on 13 May 1964. That leisure should have been seen a problem may seem strange, but leisure had usually been confined to the 'leisured classes' who had been taught how to employ it with literature, the arts, and games and sports. By the 1960s technology and automation meant that almost everyone had leisure but did not necessarily know how to employ it. Launcelot's main contribution to the debate was a plea to the planners:

> In new housing developments there are in many cases a number of teenagers among the families who first make their homes there. So often the houses are built without any sort of leisure amenities available . . . [and] life in these communities gets off on the wrong foot. . . . The decrease of juvenile delinquency in Liverpool and Birmingham, attributed to the interest teenagers take in the Beatles and in Skiffle groups, is relevant in this connection . . .

His speech on Youth and Social Responsibility (3 March 1965) suggests dismay at some of the theories then coming into fashion:

> The very language employed by psychologists and psychiatrists, and by the earliest social workers trained in those disciplines, lends itself to misinterpretation. The older language of medicine created a technical vocabulary on Greek and Latin models, to serve precise medical purposes. It is wise for a science to do this. . . . Unfortunately, the new psychological sciences were content to re-use words which already had established meanings. The word 'guilt', for instance, was already so charged with meaning and emotion that it would have been wiser for the psychoanalysts to invent a new word to express the new awareness which they had, rather than try to graft new meaning on this old, overloaded word. . . . The words 'accepting' and 'permissive' in the social worker's vocabulary are another case in point . . .

But it would be misleading to suggest that Launcelot was a frequent speaker in the House of Lords in his early years at Norwich, when 'how to spend one's leisure' was not for him a problem that ever arose. There were more direct and practical ways than parliamentary speeches in which his concern and interest in education and the young could find their expression.

17

University of East Anglia

A university is . . . an Alma Mater, knowing her children one
by one, not a foundry, or a mint, or a treadmill.

(*Cardinal Newman*, The Idea of a University)

Education had always been a subject dear to Launcelot's heart.
He had an instinctive understanding of what made young men
tick (he was until later in life less good with women, since Trinity
Hall undergraduates in his day were all male), and the fact that
Norwich was about to have a university had been one reason
for him to accept the bishopric.

But it was schools, not the university, that provided his first
educational challenge. The diocese contained 72 Aided Schools
– those that belonged to the Church but were financially aided
by the State – only one of which was a secondary school. The
rest were primary schools, some in small villages and with very
few children on their rolls. Many needed a great deal of money
spent on their fabric, one-third of which would have to come from
the Church. There was pressure from the Norfolk Education
Authority to close down the smaller schools and for the rest either
to be brought fully up to standard by the Church or handed over
to the County as (State) Controlled Schools. Launcelot put the
issue to his first Diocesan Conference in May 1960:

We must make up our minds whether we wish to retain any
schools as Aided, and if so, how many. There is a very natural
tendency to be a protagonist of Aided Schools if you have
one in your own parish, and unenthusiastic if there does
not happen to be one. . . . [But] the first and all-important

principle is that the Church has an overall interest within the whole field of education – formal and informal, adults and children, universities and schools. Christians see all knowledge of truth as revelation of God. If a school is Aided, then the parish priest can, as of right, freely enter and teach religion in the school; also its Church-appointed governors, being in a majority, have a determining influence in the choice of a head teacher. Perhaps the strongest argument of all is that so long as we continue to keep a large proportion of schools as Aided, the Church has a financial stake in, and can continue as of right to claim a say in, the policies and provisions for State education generally. . . .

Launcelot went on to announce that he soon hoped to appoint a Bishop's Chaplain for Education. Canon Backhouse, the Rector of Caister St Edmund, who had acted for the Diocese over church schools, had exasperated Dr Lincoln Ralphs, the Director of Education for Norfolk, and Launcelot could quite see why – his letters would contain such total irrelevancies as details of his Rugby schooldays. In fairness to Backhouse, though, it should be said that his obfuscation had delayed a reorganization of Church schools which, had it happened earlier, might well have seen the end of them in Norfolk. As it was, some small Aided schools were closed but others were upgraded, and a new Aided secondary school was built.

Launcelot's simple friendliness did more good than any arguments. He got on well with Lincoln Ralphs, and by a stroke of luck was able to enlist the help of a senior official at the Ministry of Education, John Todhunter, a Roman Catholic who was engaged to the daughter of a Norfolk squire and came with his fiancée to talk to Launcelot about their 'mixed' marriage. Not only did their marriage prove a model of ecumenism, it also inspired Todhunter to produce a 'Barchester Scheme' under which government grants could be made on lines analogous to the 'Ported Payments' that had allowed war damage for blitzed London City churches to be spent on churches in new housing estates.

Launcelot also told the Diocesan Conference that he was 'sure the Church has taken the right step in assuming as large a responsibility as possible for training teachers' by funding the expansion of Keswick Hall, the Church teacher training college near Norwich – 'a matter for which we all have a common responsibility, whether one has a Church Aided School in one's own parish or not'. Keswick College, in common with many other Church teacher training colleges, was successfully enlarged, but the tide of 1960s secularism which was about to engulf them diluted their Christian ethos so that they produced fewer committed Christian teachers than had been hoped.

Almost as soon as his appointment to Norwich was announced, the promotion committee for the new university at Norwich had asked their new Bishop to join them (they had felt upstaged when the York deputation to the University Grants Committee was led by the Archbishop). Launcelot thought that it would be a mistake to build a university on Earlham golf course, too far out of the city to integrate with the local community; but by the time he arrived in Norwich the decision had virtually been taken.

It was unfortunate, too, that he was still too new and not well enough known to have much effect on the crucial choice of the first Vice-Principal. The Oxford economist Sir Roy Harrod had got together a group of eminent academics who, like himself, had a house in Norfolk and this became the nucleus of the Academic Planning Board. Sir Solly (later Lord) Zuckerman, who had a house at Burnham Thorpe – was keen to appoint Conrad Waddington, Professor of Animal Genetics at Edinburgh. Launcelot asked some of his academic contacts about him, and their verdicts were unanimous; as one of them put it, 'I am horrified to learn that you are considering Waddington.'

This put Launcelot in a difficult position; he could not pass on what had been written to him in confidence, and yet a simple assertion that the man was unsuitable would carry little weight from a bishop whom they barely yet knew. He decided that he could, in confidence, tell Sir Edmund Bacon what he had learned;

as a Lord Lieutenant with a reputation for being shrewd, well-informed and utterly honest and reliable, his opinion would carry weight. But unfortunately Sir Edmund could not get to the crucial meeting between the academics, most (but not all) of whom felt that to have a geneticist as Vice-Chancellor would be a great coup since genetics were the up-and-coming branch of science, and the local supporters of the University who were more concerned about the character and personality of a Vice-Chancellor than with purely academic credentials.

Richard Gurney, a director of Barclays Bank and an ex-High Sheriff, gave reasons (which were generally known) for opposing Waddington's candidature. According to Launcelot's account when he returned home, Dick Gurney put his foot in it disastrously by saying 'We can't have a man who has been divorced', which did not go down well with academics such as Noel Annan, the well-known agnostic Provost of King's. It appears that Dick Gurney then put his other foot in it even more embarrassingly by saying 'The man isn't even a Christian', at which Zuckerman, a Jew, went ballistic; academic freedom was being threatened as it had been under the Nazis. (Michael Sanderson tells all this in his *History of the University of East Anglia*, a fascinating saga.)

Launcelot tried to save the day by insisting that he was not suggesting any religious test (Gordon Tilsley noted him as saying 'Christian views irrelevant'), but to no avail; the Academic Planning Board decided to go ahead and Waddington was chosen. Mercifully, he turned the job down on the grounds that the pay was not good enough; but in the meantime other high-calibre possible candidates had backed off, and this delay in appointing a Vice-Chancellor put Norwich behind Brighton and York in the race to attract good teaching staff. But Frank Thistlethwaite, a Fellow of St John's College, Cambridge, was eventually appointed, and the new university was spared a Vice-Chancellor who could at best be described as a maverick.

Being a Cambridge don had made Launcelot aware of the pressure universities were under to concentrate resources on areas of learning with an obvious economic spin-off, such as science and technology. Although he was himself a scientist, he agreed strongly with Cardinal Newman's thesis that a university education should be based on the humanities and (as he argued in the House of Lords debate of July 1963) must have a moral basis – not the view of men such as Noel Annan or Solly Zuckerman. He felt uneasy about universities being too dependent on government grants, which he believed threatened academic integrity far more than university authorities in their eagerness for money were prepared to admit. (These qualms did not, however, prevent him from making an appeal in the House of Lords (16 May 1962) in a debate on Government Assistance to Universities: 'The University of Norwich with its splendid site at Earlham is ... greatly concerned to provide the type of community which a university really ought to have ... [its] plans will inevitably be hampered if the money needed for salaries to maintain an adequate staff–student ratio are not met.')

Launcelot would never have had the influence he did but for the fact that academics on the Council, and later on the staff, considered him academically respectable; his views carried weight despite, rather than because of, his being a bishop. He was not always helped by others on the Council who (like Dick Gurney over the Waddington affair) banged the drum for traditional morality so loudly that they could be accused of wanting to undermine academic freedom of thought. Launcelot understood the importance of academic freedom; in his own words on a later university occasion:

Perhaps you take it for granted; but it is a principle that always needs guarding; to follow your thought where it leads, free from political, or social, or institutional pressures ... is one of the most precious assets of university life. At times the Church itself has been responsible for restricting academic freedom, but the freedom of the individual remains a vital principle of the Gospel.

It was because he really believed this that he could convincingly champion the other values he believed were important.

When the University opened in 1963 everything was planned on the Oxbridge lines to which the Vice-Chancellor had been accustomed. The students were to be called undergraduates; they were to dine in hall on most evenings, must either live on the campus or in approved lodgings, had to be in by midnight, and if they were out after 10pm must have their names taken by the porter or their landlady and be reported to the authorities if it happened too often. But all this broke down almost before it had started. So many new universities were being founded that it was difficult to find good staff, let alone staff who shared those ideas of what a university should be. For this was the dawn of the new age of long hair, protest, sandals, the Pill and free love, and most of the newly appointed academic staff had no time for tradition or authority.

In particular, the Church in their eyes stood for all that they suspected and disliked, and they dismissed Christian morality as outworn bourgeois conventions. The appointment of any chaplains was vetoed, and only after hard lobbying did the staff agree to having 'delegated representatives' of the churches, Michael Tyler-Whittle the Vicar of New Buckenham being the Anglican representative. Not until 1965 was Launcelot able to appoint an Anglican chaplain – John Giles, then a curate at Lowestoft, whose account of those early days shows what the Church was up against:

> There was some discussion, not to say uncertainty, as to what my role should be. The student body was very much aware of the conflict felt by the founding members of the University Staff as to the importance of establishing a new ethos and identity for the U.E.A. over and against the 'establishment' of Oxford and Cambridge. Chaplains seemed to be the thin end of the establishment wedge, and had already earned a fairly cynical response in a student publication. Significant points of privilege presented themselves; could a chaplain, for example, have meals in the canteen with the students? (Happily the Vice-Chancellor said they could.)
>
> A second major issue was, could religious services be held

on university premises? At first, the policy was that they could only be held in churches in the town; but pressure for some sort of worship within the university soon arose, and the student Christian Union held a united ecumenical carol service in the Students Union Hall, with the Vice-Chancellor reading a lesson. It was a very successful and happy occasion attended by the great majority of the student body, and after that permission was given for services on university premises at the invitation of the students. . . .

In January 1967 we held our first weekly Corporate Communion in the Students' Union. They were usually attended by 15–25 students, occasionally we reached 40. The sense of reality and common purpose was very impressive; people said it felt like the early Church. Once, the Dean of Norwich arrived to find two students and myself on our knees mopping up the beer and debris of the previous night. He was very sweet about this at the time, but I understand he wrote a pretty stiff letter to the Vice-Chancellor afterwards. This turned out to be one of the most telling shots in the battle for a Chaplaincy Centre.

John Giles remembers the morale-boosting effect of a sermon Launcelot preached at a Corporate Communion in 1966. Its text was borrowed from a sermon by Owen Chadwick at the Cuddesdon Festival a few weeks earlier, which Launcelot applied to the very different circumstances of the new university:

'How shall we sing the Lord's song in a strange land?' This surely is an accurate description of the situation in which we meet. Let me, after the manner of eighteenth-century divines, divide the text and consider it a phrase at a time.

'How shall we sing?' How can we be confident about our faith, be cheerful about it? It's no good substituting a quiet whisper for a song, no good being defensive and apologetic. And yet, we often feel driven into a defensive corner by confusion within the body of Christian believers. The New Theology as well as humanist thought has shaken many in their faith about prayer. They feel that prayer in the traditional sense of personal 'communion with God' is purposeless, a kind of retreat from real engagement and involvement in the world. They forget that we must in a sense withdraw in order to become effectively engaged; as Jesus describes it, 'go into the inner chamber of your heart and be still'. In his case there was an alternating rhythm, of withdrawal and involvement.

A second difficulty in singing the Lord's song arises because some Christians feel that the Church as an institution is an obstacle to faith, and the sooner organised religion collapses the better. This is understandable enough; the Church stands in need of reform. But that is only one side of the coin. The Christian faith as a human movement needs to be incarnate; there must be an institution which will both stand apart from the world and be involved in it and will, like a rock, provide three essentials; Community, Continuity and Stability. Loyalty to Christ would seem to require commitment to an institution that we see as Christ's Body, and therefore we should work for its reformation and renewal.

Then there are the uncertainties felt nowadays about Christian ethics. The argument is that if the cardinal principle of Christianity is Love, one can only decide how to interpret this principle in each given situation; no act can be said to be right or wrong in itself. So you can't have, should not have, any rules of conduct. And very easily, this comes to mean that the distinction between right and wrong doesn't matter any more. All this has led to a certain loss of nerve, and uncertainty. We are well rid of the legalism and sheer insensitivity that so often went with morality in days gone by, but rules, or at least guide lines, would seem to be indispensable in matters of corporate and personal behaviour. We need to rediscover and redefine certain landmarks, rocks on which we can stand when we meet the floodgates of new and radical thinking – and then accept that much of that thinking is like a flood after a drought; it can bring new life to the Church.

This will on the whole make it easier, not harder, to 'sing the Lord's song' – remember, the question is 'How shall we

sing *the Lord's* song?' You can't have a cut-flower Christianity, nor some pseudo-psychological substitute. It must be
rooted; rooted in the Lord whom we can come to know
through Holy Writ, through the tradition of the Church, from
his influence through other people, from the still, small voice
in our own heart.

But can we sing the song 'in a strange land'? – a land
apparently alienated, strange in that it does not recognise
Christ? But during his time on earth, didn't even his disciples
so often fail to see the point? Perhaps we should not be too
shocked or surprised if we today are called to sing the Lord's
song in a strange land, for it is nevertheless still the land that
the Lord loves. For Christ is not only the Lord of the Church,
but the Sovereign of the Universe. He speaks to us through
the world of nature; in man's learning and research; he speaks
to us in films, in novels, in plays, in art; he speaks to us in
the people we know and meet. The imprint of his love is there
for us to see, if only our eyes are open. He is with us always;
and as and when we listen, and respond, so we will endeavour
to the best of our ability, in our lives, to sing the Lord's song
– even though we sing it in a strange land.

The life of a chaplain must indeed have seemed strange. Not
until January 1967 did the Registrar give the chaplains an office
from which to operate – it was being vacated by a department
moving over to the new buildings. John Giles remembers:

It was hard for the students to see how the Chaplains fitted
into the University when they seemed to have so little place
within the academic institutional life. . . . Heated opposition
came as much from disenchanted Christians as from hard line
atheists; I used to be in touch with a number of Radical
students; their principles of naïve idealism were bound up
with a general iconoclasm which rarely lasted after they left
the university. The Staff varied, as one would expect. . . . The
Philosophy Department used a well known introductory text
book which applied the verification principle to religious belief

fairly crudely and found it 'meaningless'. It was eventually agreed that this treatment of religious belief was inadequate and other books were found.

The hardest thing I experienced in U.E.A. was something that did not involve me at all; the treatment of the Dean of Students as a result of the Students' Union taking up the case of an American student convicted of a drugs offence. It was a shock to see how the students could misjudge an official who had their best interests at heart. It was a form of secular crucifixion, only without much sign of resurrection. It was I think a warning for all who work with that age group, that liberal and radical opinions held by students, however attractive those students may be as individuals, can go badly off the rails. In this case they caused much suffering to a man who was doing not only his best, but more than he was called upon to do for them.

John Giles saw from the inside probably more than anyone about the workings of the UEA in those early years. He pays tribute to the Vice-Chancellor 'who guided the University through troublous times', and also to the considerable behind-the-scenes influence of Launcelot on the teaching and administrative staff. Whatever their feelings about the Church, they knew without his telling them that in terms of academic qualifications he was at least on a par with themselves. He could moreover disarm much of their opposition by being able to talk their own language, and having a sense of humour calculated to appeal to the academic mind.

With the student body, Launcelot was less successful. During some 1967 student protest Launcelot was asked to mediate, and invited the ringleaders to Bishop's House. It was a failure. He got off on the wrong foot by offering them sherry, a bourgeois and decadent drink, and there was no meeting of minds. John Giles was probably right; perfectly reasonable individuals, when they became part of a protest group that felt strongly about some issue, tended to go off the rails. As Hitler knew, the herd instinct can be manipulated to cause decent individuals to do terrible things. Certainly those students – and there were several – that Launcelot got to know personally, often through playing squash, found him just as approachable as Trinity Hall undergraduates of old had done; at an individual level he always seemed to get on with the young, and there never seemed to be any generation gap.

Eventually, in 1969, the University agreed to have a Chaplaincy Centre, and to contribute £15,000 of the estimated cost of £41,000. An appeal raised the balance, and in January 1972 the Chaplaincy Centre was formally opened. By this time Launcelot had left Norwich (and his successor felt unable to attend the opening as the Centre was multi-faith so a passage from the Koran was to be read). But there is no doubt that Launcelot's quiet but continuous behind-the-scenes persuasiveness was the main influence behind UEA's becoming the only university of its batch to have a chapel on the campus – though it would not have been possible without the support of the Vice-Chancellor and some of the staff, especially Professor Norman Sheppard, and would have been very much more difficult had not Bernard Feilden become the University's architect after Denis Lasdun had retired.

Three years after leaving Norwich, Launcelot was thrilled to receive a formal letter inviting him 'to receive the degree of Doctor of Civil Law *honoris causa* at a Congregation to be held on Friday 4th July 1975'; and in a covering letter Sir Frank Thistlewaite said what 'great pleasure' it had given him to send that invitation.

18

Marriage

How can a bishop marry? How can he flirt? The most he can say is, 'I will see you in the vestry after the service.'

(Sydney Smith, quoted at Launcelot's wedding reception)

In 1962 Henry and Barbara Brooke invited Launcelot to join them for their family holiday. Dame Barbara (as she then was – she was later made a Baroness) was the sister of Launcelot's old friend and fellow naval chaplain Ken Matthews, the Dean of St Albans; Henry Brooke had just become Home Secretary. They asked Launcelot if he would mind if a friend of theirs, whose husband had died a year earlier after a particularly harrowing illness, came too. She did, but at the last moment Launcelot himself could not go owing to the sudden death of his brother-in-law Dan de Pass. Two years later, however, he did go on holiday with the Brookes, and Jane Agutter was once more one of the party.

Jane had been brought up on the small estate on the edge of the Forest of Dean that had belonged to her father Henry Machen's family for many generations. Her mother was German, and it is a tribute to her character that when war broke out in 1914 and anti-German feeling was so violent that even dachshunds were hissed in the streets, Mrs Machen remained just as respected and liked as ever. In July 1939 Jane married Anthony Agutter, who was working in London for Shell. He had joined the Royal Naval Volunteer Reserve, so when war broke out two months later he went off to be trained as an RNVR naval officer (Jane later recalled that they had both heard Launcelot's sermon on 'Courage' in 1940). After the war he became a shipping broker, but in 1956 fell seriously ill and had to give up work. They moved with their two children, Richard and Margaret, to Gloucestershire, and Anthony Agutter died on New Year's Eve 1960, having lain unconscious for nine months after suffering a severe stroke.

Jane's first sight of Launcelot had not been promising. She had been staying with the Brookes when Launcelot returned in a cheerful mood from a 'Nobody's Friends' dining club dinner, and having put on a motor cyclist's helmet that had been lying in the hall was walking round intoning 'I am a Space Bishop'. This did not impress. But they met again from time to time, and Jane found herself becoming increasingly fond of Launcelot, though without getting a glimmer of any response. However, during the summer holiday of 1964, Launcelot not only noticed her but realized that he was falling in love with her. He did not declare himself, but asked Jane to stay at Bishop's House when his sister Jean was there, and after Jane had left asked Jean what she had thought of her. When Jean replied that she had liked her very much Launcelot confessed that he was thinking of marrying her. Jean asked him if he had ever been in love before, to which Launcelot replied, 'Once, but as she was my tutor's wife that wasn't much good.'

That may well have been true, but not it seems the whole truth. After Launcelot died, Jane had a very kind letter of sympathy from a lady who had been very close to Launcelot when he was a young man; when people used to ask him why he had never got married earlier, his usual reply was 'I didn't have time', but perhaps he should have added '. . . to get married *and* go to Antarctica in 1934'. That expedition took him away from England for nearly three years, and the next two years after that were hectic, as he had to label all his geological specimens and write up his findings for publication while at the same time being Dean of Trinity Hall. Then came the war, and when he returned to Cambridge he became Director of the Scott Polar Research Institute as well as Dean, which would have left little time for other interests. Once he had become a bishop, flirting (*à la* Sydney Smith) would have been difficult. He could, of course, have made time to look for a wife if that had been his priority, but it was not in his nature to be less than 100 per cent committed to the work he was doing. If Henry and Barbara Brooke, knowing that it would be good for Jane to marry again and convinced of Launcelot's need for a wife, had not dangled Jane before his eyes, then he would probably no more have noticed her than he had noticed any other marriageable lady who had happened to cross his path. But once he had noticed Jane, the rest followed.

Need for a wife, there certainly was. The domestic arrangements at Bishop's House were becoming increasingly precarious. With Launcelot constantly out or away for brief periods, and visitors and guests for meals being invited often at short notice, it was not an attractive proposition for a housekeeper – and by 1964 housekeepers had become a dying breed anyway. The difficulty Launcelot had in organizing his domestic affairs was well illustrated by his efforts to plan a suitable time and place to propose marriage. This was something that, like managing his domestic staff, could not be delegated to chaplain or secretary, with the result that the unobtrusive tryst he hit upon was the Leander Club at Henley on St Andrew's Day, when the club was full to bursting of Eton boys being taken out to lunch by their parents. To make matters worse, the Bishop of Willesden (Gerald Ellison, a close friend from naval chaplain days and a former rowing blue) was there, but either he never noticed that the Bishop of Norwich 'had a girl in tow', or was too tactful to draw attention to the fact, so all went well; Launcelot duly proposed, and Jane accepted.

Before the engagement was made public, various people had to be told that Launcelot (to use his own words) 'was contemplating committing matrimony', so that not until 6 January 1965 was the announcement made in the papers. Then, much had to be done before the wedding. Jane had to sell her house, and her two children had to get used to the idea of living in very different surroundings. The wedding trousseau, normally a preoccupation for the bride, was in this instance more applicable to the bridegroom. His sister Jean took sartorial matters into her own hands;

Frank Telfer, who was chaplain at the time, remembers her sitting (by this time she was too lame to stand for very long) in Launcelot's bedroom while his entire wardrobe was brought out item by item and most of it consigned to a heap on the floor for immediate disposal. Thanks to Dan and Jean's generous insistence when he went to Norwich he did already have at least one good suit, but he had never spent more than absolutely necessary on clothes and his underwear in particular was not, in a sister's opinion, a sight to which any wife should be exposed.

Jean also condemned his cassock, a depressing shade of mauve that made it look even shabbier than it really was, and he happened to be wearing the new one when he gave an interview to the local media. There had been some inevitable speculation among its more cynical members that Launcelot must be homosexual since he had reached the age of fifty-eight without a wife, but when Ted Ellis, the Norfolk naturalist who had a regular column in the *Eastern Daily Press*, remarked perfectly innocently 'I like the colour of your new cassock, Bishop; I suppose you'd call it not pansy, but fuschia', that laid the matter to rest so far as the press was concerned. Ted Ellis was probably the only person present who could have said that without being aware of any *double entendre*.

It is a rather sad reflection on the current preoccupation with sex that it seems necessary to point out that Launcelot was not in fact homosexual; if he had been, some hint of it must have been apparent to his chaplains who, before he married, lived in the house and were with him constantly. One attempt to assess Launcelot's make-up labelled him 'an unconscious homosexual', but that oxymoronic description only shows that Launcelot would have been the despair of any Freudian analyst. Roy Jenkins's biography of Churchill calls him (p. 448) 'the least dangerously sexed politician ... since the younger Pitt', and *mutatis mutandis* the same could be said of Launcelot. Despite his experience of Antarctica and the Navy he remained surprisingly innocent of what went on in the world; the bawdy talk on board *Penola* had surprised as well as shocked him, and much later on he was very surprised to hear how many nicely-brought-up young army officers were distinctly unchaste. But just as the sexually promiscuous find it hard to believe that a great many people are chaste, so those who are chaste often do not realize how many people are promiscuous. Jane certainly found that Launcelot was naïve about sexual *mores*, and marriage opened his eyes in many ways – for instance, he had once been shocked to learn that a canon had told his wife of confidential discussions concerning the cathedral chapter; it had never occurred to him that a married couple might indulge in pillow-talk.

The wedding took place nine days after Easter, on Tuesday 27 April, in St Faith's Chapel in Westminster Abbey. Ken Matthews conducted the marriage service and the Dean, Eric Abbott, celebrated the Eucharist. He had also arranged for the ceremony to take place unobtrusively – neither Jane nor Launcelot were the kind of people to welcome the kind of publicity that is meat and drink to some public figures, and which the marriage of a senior diocesan bishop would have attracted. Owen Wansbrough Jones was best man, and the congregation consisted only of family and a few personal friends. When the very moving service was over, any ice was broken when Launcelot failed to realize why the verger wanted him (it was to sign the marriage register) and his much-married eldest brother Bob chimed in, 'They always have this bit, it's when they ask you to pay.' The Brookes gave a wedding reception at their home in Hampstead, Henry Brooke proposing the couple's health in a short speech (during which he quoted Sydney Smith on the subject of episcopal marriages), after which Launcelot and Jane set off on their honeymoon.

If Launcelot had much to learn about marriage in general, Jane had even more to learn about marriage to Launcelot in particular. To start with, they only had one week's honeymoon, as Launcelot did not want to alter the second round of deanery visits that he had arranged before Jane had come on the scene. Then, they spent the week at Innerhadden Cottage, which in Launcelot's eyes was the most perfect place on earth, with the additional advantage of being so well-provisioned that Jane would have to do little more in the way of cooking than open a few tins. Jane saw it differently. Her first impression that the cottage was not very clean was more than confirmed when she surreptitiously ran her finger along a mantelpiece. Much of the contents of the larder looked like an invitation to salmonella; it was before the time of 'best before' labelling, but the rust on the tins told its own story. Afterwards, Jane was very amusing about these discoveries; at the time she had the good sense to keep quiet, do rather more food-shopping than Launcelot thought necessary, and make a mental note of what needed doing to bring the cottage up to standard at a later date. After all, the point of a honeymoon is for a couple to get to know each other better . . . And she was very much in love.

Other adjustments on both sides were necessary. Launcelot had to get used to having two teenagers in the house during the holidays; that came more naturally to him than to most fifty-eight-year-old bachelors, but what he did find hard was to make time in the diary to be with his wife. Frank Telfer was invaluable; he saw the problem, went through the diary with Jane, made 'Keep Free' entries at intervals, and explained to Launcelot why this was necessary. Jane had to make far greater adjustments; she had absolutely no wish to become like Anthony Trollope's Mrs Proudie, but she realized that by marrying a bishop she was marrying into a way of life.

For a bishop, as for a parish priest, his home is his base for work. When seeing clergy couples whom he was going to marry, Launcelot would warn the wife-to-be that in the mornings when she wanted to get on with her work undisturbed her husband would be at home, and in the evenings when she would like him to be at home to talk to, he would be out. For Jane, that situation was compounded by constant entertaining – not on a grand scale, but more often than not there would be a guest for the night or people to lunch or supper, as well as a steady stream of people simply coming to see the bishop. The first two years of the marriage must have been very difficult for her. She had to learn hundreds of new faces and names, and when people wanted to see Launcelot she had to know if they were people he would want to see or not – and since he hardly ever said that anyone was other than an immensely nice person, that took time to learn.

Launcelot meantime was working as hard as ever. The purpose behind his second round of visits to all the parishes was to take the pulse of the diocese, and they were planned to lead up to him delivering a Visitation Charge in the Cathedral to all the clergy and churchwardens in April 1967. During the previous five years there had been a sea-change both in society and in the Church. In 1960 the mood had been one of confident expansion; by 1967 this had become one of self-doubt. The trigger for this change had been the publication of John Robinson's book *Honest to God* in 1963; but the underlying causes had been there earlier.

Robinson had led a very cloistered life; brought up in the precincts of Canterbury Cathedral where his father was a canon, he had missed the war and his experience of 'the real world' was limited to a three-year curacy in Bristol where his vicar, Mervyn Stockwood, had built up such a strong church life that it was very untypical of an urban parish. When Stockwood became Bishop of Southwark he asked Robinson, then Dean of Clare College, Cambridge, to be his suffragan bishop (of Woolwich). For the first time Robinson was in a milieu where the Church cut very little ice in the community, and he was aghast at what he found. *Honest to God*, written while he was lying in bed recovering from a back injury, might have been the work of any impatient young clergyman who felt frustrated at the Church's failure to connect with the masses. But unfortunately Robinson launched his book with a full-page article on the front page of the *Observer* under the headline 'Our Image of God Must Go, Says Bishop'. Launcelot had some sympathy with what Robinson had been trying to say, but thought the book was far too negative, and that advertising it so sensationally showed an irresponsible lack of common sense. He had told the Diocesan Conference in 1963:

A reply from the Bishop of Woolwich [to a pamphlet, 'Images Old and New', by Archbishop Michael Ramsey] said 'I wholly accept the doctrine of God revealed in the New Testament and enshrined in the Creeds.... I reject emphatically any suggestion that what I have written is contrary to the Christian faith.' If some equally emphatic profession of faith had accompanied the Bishop of Woolwich's article in the *Observer* when the book was published, a good deal of the misunderstanding and concern might have been avoided ... although one would like to have a rather fuller account of his views stated in positive terms, if one is to understand better how some of the things he says in his book can be reconciled with the profession of faith which he has made in such clear terms since. But the questions which the Bishop of Woolwich asks are real and cogent.

They were indeed; doubt and scepticism had been brewing for some time, and would have surfaced sooner or later (though perhaps not so damagingly) in any case. When the British Association met at Norwich in 1961, Launcelot's sermon had been able to deal with the apparent conflict between science and religion in terms that an agnostic scientist could relate to. But by 1967 entirely new ways of thinking had thrown up new challenges and problems, which the Visitation Charge addressed:

During the last few years, we have been passing through a dramatic break-up of age-old customs and assumptions on which society and culture were based and by which human behaviour was determined.... The men and women of today have [not so much] rejected the Gospel – they have not known it ... [and] the external trappings of faith appear to them to belong to Victorian or Medieval times. Many of us find it difficult to grasp this. If we are to attempt to teach the faith in terms which apply to the world of today we need to understand the nature of the changes that have taken place and their effects on the way people think and act.

There is the social revolution, the emergence of the Welfare

State, the affluent society, and equal educational opportunities for all. Men now enjoy as of right a security which formerly they did not possess, but which to some extent had been compensated for by the Church's offer of spiritual comfort and her ministry of charity. Social and economic independence have bred intellectual and religious independence.

Then there is the revolution that has taken place in the field of science and technology ... [which] has brought people of all races and religions closer together. Hitherto the main question was whether Christianity was true or not. The question people now ask is whether it is more true than other religions.... [Science] has also made man's environment bigger – more complex, and inevitably less personal. In a world where human activities are estimated by computers and views expressed by public opinion polls, the individual does not appear to count for so much....

Science seems to get things done; it produces results.... Scientists now think in terms of relativity, which in effect means they are less ready to see things in black and white. This has come to mean that many people find it much harder to accept Christian teaching which confronts them with a plain choice – right or wrong, true or false.... It seems as though science may even be able to direct and control man's very nature, through psychology, genetics and brain-washing. This means that a person today may well go to the psychiatrist rather than to the parson. He may think of sin and guilt in terms of the influence of his upbringing and environment rather than in terms of separation from God.

But perhaps the most dramatic effect that science has on people's thinking is [to raise the question], is there room for God at all? This has had one helpful effect; it has helped us to correct the view that God's activity was only seen in that part of the universe which we could not control. Such a view divided the world into two; what was God's, and what wasn't; the sacred, and the secular. But if we look at Our Lord's teaching, all life is sacred. There is nothing secular on earth but the secular heart of man.

To prepare for this Visitation a questionnaire had been sent to every parish, and 'some of the clergy's answers implied that our rural parishes are not yet affected by the changes of which I have been speaking', though the laity had 'indicated that they thought otherwise. . . . [These] revolutions are being brought on everyone, whether in the country or in the towns. Television, with its powerful influence, finds its way into every home.' So Launcelot went on to propose a 'strategy and action':

The laity have been recommending that the clergy be relieved of the administrative work which could be done by laymen, in order that they may be left free for visiting. Visiting is important, but it is equally important that the clergy be free to study. If we are to recover our role as teachers, we must first recover our role as students. . . . In order to help the clergy in their study I want to make a new appointment, of a Director of Training, to be assisted by a voluntary part-time staff of experts in various fields recruited from the diocese, to devise a system of training. . . . I should like to see this linked with the work of training the laity by establishing a study centre with its own library and opportunity for residential courses . . . [and] I ask clergy and churchwardens to arrange a series of open discussions . . . [in which] the role of the clergy should primarily be to listen and to take note of those areas in which there is most interest and most difficulty.

The Charge was comprehensive. Over worship,

we need to remember that the liturgical movement is not primarily concerned with ritual, with aestheticism, or with skill in drafting prayers. It is a pastoral movement, for the renewal of Christian life of ordinary people. . . . We need to take far more trouble, to be more conscious of what it is we are about when we join in worship. . . . In worship we reach out to the love of God. From worshipping together, a congregation breaks out into compassion, into service and into creative living.

Pastoral reorganization had become more urgent than ever –
'until a year or so ago the actual number of men ordained had
been steadily increasing; now, there has come, rather abruptly,
a drop'. There was also a section on 'Relations with other Christian Bodies' – Vatican II had given a great impetus to the cause
of Christian unity. Last but not least, there was a section on
'The Care and Maintenance of our Church Buildings', which
will be dealt with later.

Between getting married in April 1965 and delivering his Visitation Charge in April 1967 Launcelot had not been idle. But
marriage, and the highly necessary 'keep free' entries in his diary
to allow time with Jane, had forced him to moderate his pace
slightly; Bishop's House had become a home, and not simply a
campaign headquarters. Marriage apart, he now had Aubrey
Aitken, Eric Cordingly and Bill Llewellyn to take a lot of the
work and worry off his shoulders. The 'strategy and action'
outlined in his Visitation Charge, and the questionnaire that
had been sent out to prepare for it, had been discussed and
decided at their fortnightly staff meetings which in those pre-
synodical days consisted simply of Launcelot and his three
archdeacons with the chaplain there as minutes secretary.

Alan Webster joined the Staff Meeting when he became Dean
of Norwich in 1970; by then Launcelot was not in good health
but Webster was very impressed with the way he chaired the
meetings and got the best out of everybody. Part of the secret
lay in doing his homework, going carefully through the agenda
the night before, and partly by his warm and friendly manner,
chairing the meeting with a light touch and managing to get
through the agenda quickly and efficiently without bulldozing
anyone. (His 'planned incoherence' was only brought into play
if a meeting looked as if it might make the wrong decision, and
there was seldom if ever need of it with these colleagues.) By
this time it would have been a mistake, marriage apart, for
Launcelot to undertake as many diocesan engagements as he
had been doing, otherwise his two suffragans and Aubrey Aitken
would have felt he was breathing down their necks.

Inevitably, this meant that some clergy felt that he had become less approachable, a feeling exacerbated by a suspicion that he paid more attention to the younger clergy he had brought into the diocese than to those who had been there before he came. And although entertaining was made easier with Jane to act as hostess, informality was more difficult to achieve. For instance, it was Launcelot's practice to have tea parties for all the ordinands within the diocese. During the 1960s this form of hospitality was becoming rather dated in any case, and it was becoming more difficult to put the average ordinand at ease in such a setting; but before Launcelot was married the slightly disorganized chaos of a bachelor household had helped to break the ice – if, for example, by some unlikely chance the best silver teapot had been produced, Launcelot would have reacted with a disarming bewilderment.

There were, however, many ways in which Jane's contribution was very positive. For instance, the old Palace garden had included an orchard on the north side. During the war this piece of ground had been commandeered and the Nissen huts that had been built on it were still there, unused. Before her marriage Jane had been working at the headquarters of the WRVS on various projects to supply affordable homes for the elderly. With Launcelot's backing she persuaded the Church Commissioners to make the old orchard available for such a purpose. Simon Crosse, of the architects Feilden and Mawson, designed flats suitable for elderly ladies of limited means, and the WRVS raised the money to build them. Like so many of Launcelot's own initiatives, this was such an obviously sensible thing to do that it was surprising that nothing of the kind had been done already; but of course it hadn't. And certainly on such practical matters as domestic lay-out Jane had a very much surer touch than her husband – who in any case would not have had the time to devote to it.

Many a happily married parish priest would admit the force of St Paul's blunt words, 'The unmarried man cares for the Lord's business; his aim is to please the Lord. But the married man aims to please his wife; and he has a divided mind.' Yet there is another side of that coin; marriage can widen the understanding of any pastor. Moreover, few men could keep up the pace set by St Paul, whose heroic life was in any case cut short before he reached the age at which Launcelot married. And as it happened, little more than two years after his marriage Launcelot's health suffered a jolt which could well have resulted in total breakdown had Jane not been at hand.

19

Enforced Change of Gear

The spirit is willing, but the flesh is weak.

(Mark 14:38)

One July evening in 1967 John Kirkham, Frank Telfer's successor as chaplain, was playing tennis with Launcelot, and unusually (as he modestly puts it) was winning. After a bit, Launcelot said that his leg was hurting and he must stop playing. That was the last time he ever played tennis.

He had first noticed his leg hurting while he was in London the previous week for Church Assembly. In the weeks that followed it got no better. He tried to ignore it, and insisted that he was quite well enough to travel to Kenya with Jane, on a long-planned visit to hand over a cheque for £50,000 raised in Norfolk for the Freedom from Hunger Campaign, visit the VSO projects in Kenya and the Outward Bound school near Mount Kilimanjaro, and do some sight-seeing. On their return, his leg was no better; he made light of it but one day when processing in the cathedral his leg collapsed, and he could no longer pretend there was nothing wrong. His own doctor was baffled, and referred him to the Hospital for Nervous Diseases in Queen's Square, London for tests. During the next year he had two spells in hospital; they diagnosed the spine as the root of the trouble, but could prescribe no effective treatment.

Some of those who knew him well at this period have wondered why he did not do more in the way of remedial treatment than very occasional vists to a physiotherapist and regular visits to the local swimming baths (where he enjoyed being incognito and would go up to people in his old Trinity Hall manner, saying 'My name's Launcelot, what's yours?'). The probable answer is that he knew deep down that the only treatment that might have done the trick would be a long period of rest and recuperation, which his conscience would not allow, even if the Archbishop would, while he was still Bishop of Norwich. And he still had work to do.

In the years that followed his condition fluctuated according to the pressure of work and stress he was under, but he never again trusted himself to walk without at least one stick. He got remarkably good at concealing this – for instance, he always wore a cope if possible when officiating at services – but inevitably it slowed him down, and he did not get about the diocese as much as he would normally have done. Launcelot's affliction remains something of a mystery. Dr Tom Stuttaford recalls (it must have been between 1960 and 1964) that as he was passing the study one evening Launcelot called out and asked him to switch on the lights, as he couldn't get up from his desk to do it himself because his legs weren't working – adding that this did not worry him because it had happened periodically ever since his Cambridge days and it always soon wore off. No member of Launcelot's household seems ever to have noticed any other instance of this happening, but sitting still on a hard chair at a desk for a long period while concentrating hard (as Launcelot often did) can compress the artery that runs from the sciatic nerve, resulting in 'dead leg' – a variant of pins and needles known in the trade as *arteria comes nervi ischiadici*. Such a condition, however, might or might not have any bearing on Launcelot's later leg trouble, and the diagnosis of 'a rare spinal disorder' is as close as one can get.

One result of impaired mobility was that Launcelot devoted more time and thought to broader issues. He spoke (for him) quite frequently in the House of Lords, where he already had a good reputation. Shortly before his leg trouble started, the Government had decided to stop dragging its feet and ratify the Antarctic Treaty. Lord Shackleton had become a government Minister, and asked Launcelot to pilot the Bill through the House of Lords. That gave him particular pleasure as it had been drafted by Brian Roberts, his friend from Antarctic days, and he introduced the Bill on 1 May 1967:

> My Lords, I have been informed that the last occasion a Bill was sponsored from the Episcopal Benches was in 1927. The title of that Bill was the Liquor (Popular Control) Bill [*and it failed to get through*]. This Bill is of a rather different character, and I hope it will be more successful, and that it will not be thought inappropriate to sponsor from these benches legislation designed to enable international co-operation in scientific discovery for peaceful purposes and to protect wild life . . .
>
> Human activity [in Antarctica] could, if not regulated, all too easily upset the balance of Nature, because so many species are susceptible to extermination. They are so utterly trusting that they lay themselves open to wilful exploitation. For instance, the Adelie Penguin is an inquisitive bird. It does not run away from you; it follows you around. I can recall a day when I was geologising below high-tide mark, when I became aware that I was being observed. I looked up and there were 60 or 70 Adelie Penguins peering over the ice foot. I spent the day hammering the rocks, and their curiosity was constant but evidently unsatisfied.

Lord Wilberforce, who spoke next, said, 'I was asked to say something about the jurisdictional aspect, but there is not a great deal that is necessary to say, because as one would expect the Right Reverend Prelate got the matter completely right in what he said.' It was, admittedly, the charming habit of the Lords to say nice things about one another, but that tribute went far beyond what convention required. The Bill went through to committee and on 24 July 1967 Launcelot successfully moved that it 'be now read a third time'.

Antarctica had made Launcelot aware of the threat to wildlife from human activity long before the phrase 'endangered species' came into vogue. He often wrote in the *Norwich Churchman* and elsewhere about mankind's responsibility towards creation.

At a time when Christian stewardship was much in vogue as a way of persuading Christians to give more of their time, their talents, and above all their money to the work of the Church, Launcelot stressed that 'stewardship' meant something much wider. The book of Genesis tells how God gave Adam dominion over all creation; that means that we are not the masters, or owners, of all that we survey, but are in a position analogous to that of the agent on an estate, who has the power and authority to run it, but must do so in accordance with the owner's wishes. The world belongs to God; we are his agents.

Launcelot applied this principle during a debate on a Conservation of Seals Bill (10 June 1969). As with his speech on whales, he laid himself open to obloquy from anti-cruelty campaigners, pointing out that although 'in concept, clubbing [of young seals] is abhorrent, nevertheless ... if efficiently carried out, it is in fact a humane method of killing, for the very reason that it immediately desensitises the seal', and that 'much harm is done by ascribing to animals the same feelings and the same reactions to pain as those experienced by human beings'. (He seems to have sailed rather close to the wind by saying 'none of your Lordships live like seals, imagine like seals, nor even, I suggest, look like seals'; Lord Chorley commented, 'I am not quite sure whether that was intended as a compliment.)'

Four months later (14 October 1969) came an unusually impassioned speech. The subject was factory farming; the Brambell Committee had recommended regulations to safeguard the welfare of livestock, but the Government was proposing a Code of Practice that watered down its recommendations. Launcelot objected to this.

> My own impression, and my own knowledge of Norfolk farming friends and of stockmen, would support the [Brambell Committee's] opinion that the great majority are concerned to ensure the welfare and health of their stock.
>
> My second interest in this subject concerns the maintenance of a responsible and fruitful relationship between man and nature. This has a significant influence on animal life; it also

has a significant influence on man. The very phrase 'factory farming' seems a contradiction in terms. Farming has to do with living creatures; factories are associated with the manufacture of inanimate objects. It is not only a matter of whether animals are treated cruelly, but whether they are treated as things rather than animals. . . .

The most usual defence in regard to any practice in factory farming is that if the animal keeps in a fit condition this is proof enough that no improper hardship is being inflicted. The Report rejects this argument on the ground that growth rate and condition are not inconsistent with periods of acute but transitory physical and mental suffering. . . . [Moreover,] to make life worth living for an animal goes beyond protecting it from pain and distress. So far as we know, an animal's pleasure in life, in fact the only significant life it knows, is in the exercise of inherited behaviour patterns . . . [in the Commission's words] 'the severely deprived battery hens, white veal calves and immobilised sows and fattening pigs do not live – they only exist'.

The situation regarding veal calves is the one that causes me the greatest repugnance. White veal is dependent on creating an anaemia in the young calf, providing it with only just sufficient iron in its milk to keep it from flagging. It is also denied the normal physiological development of becoming a ruminant by depriving it of all roughage. . . . I cannot believe that people would eat meat produced in this way if they were aware of the conditions under which it was produced.

Unlike the views expressed by the National Farmers' Union, a recent opinion poll of farmers showed overwhelming support for the Brambell Committee. . . . The Ministry of Agriculture has affirmed that any [lowering] of [its] recommended standards arises from new scientific knowledge that has come to light since the Committee wrote its report. I feel it is important that your Lordships should be informed in sufficient detail what these new scientific data are, especially as such reputable scientists as Sir Julian Huxley and Professor W. H. Thorpe are unwilling to accept this ministerial claim. . . .

I should like to end by saying how glad I am to see in the preface [that] 'stockmanship is the key factor in the welfare of all livestock'.... As E. F. Schumacher said, if man thinks he can disregard the truth that 'man does not live by bread alone' and can allow the human sentiment to become brutalised, he does not lose his technical intelligence but does lose his power of sound judgment, with the result that even the bread fails him in one way or another.

That speech clearly got under the skin of Lord Beswick who wound up for the Government, and a combination of government placemen and backwoods farming peers (like one from Leicestershire who argued that 'we are not necessarily being kinder to cattle by allowing them access to the open – cattle pick up all sorts of ailments outdoors, and flies are a thorough pest to them in summer') defeated the amendment. Launcelot had to content himself with telling all his friends that they must ask for *red* veal whenever they went to a restaurant. Since Norfolk was the home of much battery farming, he came in for some criticism of the 'what-can-a-bishop-know-about-it' type, but that did not worry him unduly.

He had learned how easy it was to arouse passionate criticism when, perhaps ill-advisedly, he spoke in a debate on the seamen's strike of May 1966. He happened to be the 'duty bishop' taking prayers that week, and felt impelled to make the point that a ship's crew, unlike a group of workers in a factory, 'will always be a community tightly bound according to the size of the ship that is their world', whose safety 'requires the loyalty of every member of the crew to [that] community'. Accordingly, the terms of reference for a Court of Inquiry 'should be wider than those for a normal kind of industrial dispute and should include human relations as well as wages and conditions'. The Trade Union peer Lord Citrine angrily complained that 'the Right Reverend Prelate seemed very much like appealing to one side in the dispute rather than to the other side'. The fault was not in fact in Launcelot's speech but in Citrine's hearing aid (as Lord Rea emolliently put it, 'There may be something wrong with

the acoustics in this Chamber, but I distinctly heard the Right
Reverend Prelate appeal to the employers as well as to the seamen'), but that did not prevent press headlines about a bishop
being accused of taking sides against the workers. It was a
warning to Launcelot to confine his speeches, as he usually did,
to issues which he had very thoroughly researched.

He intervened more tellingly in a debate on an Abortion Bill
(23 May 1966). He was not totally opposed to abortion, and
supported a clause to permit it if 'the continuance of the pregnancy would involve serious risk to the life or grave injury to
the health of the pregnant woman', but opposed extending that
clause to include '[or if] her capacity as a mother will be severely
overstrained'. He strongly resisted a further amendment to allow
abortion if 'there is a substantial risk that if the child were born
it would suffer from such physical or mental abnormalities as
to deprive it of any prospect of reasonable enjoyment of life',
because in the current state of medical knowledge such 'mental
abnormalities' could not be ascertained beyond reasonable
doubt before the thirtieth week of pregnancy, by which time
any termination was risky:

There is, in practice, a risk that if abortion is induced . . .
three good foetuses will [on average] be killed for every defec-
tive one. My unease can best be expressed by putting three
questions: if that deformed child were born, would you then
hold it lawful to kill it? If not, why not? Is it not a less heinous
thing to kill one deformed child than to kill four, five, six or
seven potential children in the hope of killing one potentially
deformed child? I do not advocate the killing of any newly
born child, but I put it to your Lordships that the principle
embodied in this clause is ethically no more defensible –
perhaps less defensible – than a Bill which permitted the
destruction of a [single] newly born deformed child.

The logic was, and is, unanswerable; but Lord Silkin's amendment was carried. He could say to Launcelot, with truth, 'that
his own colleagues were divided on this issue, so I am sure he

would agree that he is not speaking for the whole of his bench'. It is a sad reflection on the ineffectiveness of the Established Church that Launcelot, who happened to be the 'duty bishop' that day, was the only bishop to be present, let alone take part, in that debate. He was once again the only bishop to speak (and this time he was not 'duty bishop') when the Divorce Reform Bill was debated (11 July 1969). He wanted reconciliation to be given a better chance than the Bill provided, and this time enough peers thought the same way for the Government to say it would at least consider the point.

Launcelot had revised his own views about divorce when he first became a bishop. He had told Archbishop Fisher that he did not think that he could, in conscience, uphold the strict Convocation ruling against the re-marriage in church of those with a previous partner still living. Fisher had convinced him the ruling was right, on the grounds that although in the case of a particular individual there might be valid reasons for allowing a church wedding, that would inevitably send out a general signal that there was nothing wrong with divorcing one partner and marrying another – in other words, 'hard cases make bad law'. Both in Portsmouth and Norwich, the Bishop's Notices made it clear that 'although there are those [clergy] who question the rightness of these decisions . . . no exceptions to the rule are authorised. If the parties concerned want to have any form of private prayers or service in church, the incumbent is asked to consult the Bishop.' If a couple were unhappy about this, then Launcelot would always see them himself; and a letter Launcelot wrote to a married man who had fallen in love with someone else shows the immense trouble he took – the complete letter was at least three times as long as this extract:

I won't answer your theological arguments about the nature of marriage, not because I agree with them or don't think them answerable but because they are at this stage irrelevant and you are quite unwittingly using them as a smoke-screen.

You are faced with three choices. To reject Christianity and follow your own desires; to reject your desires and follow Christianity; or – more subtle – to follow your own desires and persuade yourself that Christianity can be modified in order to allow yourself to continue to call yourself a practising Christian without renouncing your desires.

There is also the point that [your wife] happens to love you, so it is difficult to see that leaving her is the kindest thing for her.

When he spoke on environmental issues Launcelot was listened to with attention – even to the extent that peers were known to emerge from the tea room to hear him. In a debate on 'Development and Threats to Amenity' (19 February 1969) he protested vigorously against 'giving economic factors an absolute priority [while] other considerations are being sacrificed'. That sounds a platitude today but was quite a novel idea then.

His last major contribution in the House of Lords (25 November 1970) was to move 'That in the opinion of this House, it is desirable that the seabed, beyond the limits of national jurisdiction, should be administered as a common heritage of mankind, and a world ocean régime should be created to that end through an international convention'. The impetus for this motion had come from Lord Kennet, Chairman of the Advisory Committee on Oil Pollution of the Sea and about to become Opposition spokesman on Foreign Affairs and Science Policy, Lord Chalfont, who had been Minister of State at the Foreign Office, Lord Ritchie-Calder, who had been a member of the United Nations secretariat, and the veteran left-winger Lord Brockway. Because they were all Labour peers Launcelot, as a non-political figure, was asked to introduce the motion. All three party leaders spoke, and the (Conservative) government ministers recognized that international agreement to control exploitation of the seabed was an urgent matter that transcended party politics.

It was mainly concern about the damage that international competition could do to the seabed that led Launcelot to become vice-chairman of the Parliamentary Movement for World Government in 1969 – and from 1970 to 1973 he was a member of the government standing committee on environmental pollution.

One other aspect of his environmental concerns should be mentioned – his attitude to nuclear power. He first had to study nuclear issues when in February 1959 Geoffrey Fisher asked him to speak in a debate on nuclear disarmament, lest the unilateralist views of some bishops be seen as the official policy of them all. As we saw earlier, in June 1940 Launcelot after much agonizing had rejected pacifism and decided that self-defence could be morally justified; and in the 1959 debate he affirmed that view:

> Warfare can be morally justified, but only if certain conditions are fulfilled. Warfare which goes beyond these limits is to be condemned, not because death is the worst thing that can befall a man – it is not; not for those whose belief stretches beyond this world – but because the indiscriminate taking of life violates the essence of what is properly called humanity, and degrades the perpetrator.

Before that debate Launcelot had spent much time reading the relevant scientific papers and consulting experts in nuclear physics. He concluded that, horrific and indiscriminate though nuclear weapons were, some of the new non-nuclear weapons could have equally appalling effects, and he rejected the view that you could make a clear moral distinction between nuclear and non-nuclear wars.* He also believed that the test ban negotiations in Geneva would be hindered rather than helped if Britain gave up its nuclear capacity; years later, he was exasperated when an official Church of England report advocated unilateral disarmament on the grounds that we could always re-arm if the Russians did not follow suit. Launcelot was often an idealist,

---

* I had recently become his chaplain, and like most young clergy then was CND-inclined. Launcelot did not argue, but asked me to help him with his homework by reading some extremely stiff articles by such experts as Professor Rotblatt – an illustration of his technique of persuading people without arguing with them.

but on this subject his common sense told him that throwing away your weapons would only make an unscrupulous enemy more likely to attack you, before you could pick them up again.

His scientifically trained mind also led him to think that nuclear power was preferable to carbon fossil fuels which polluted the atmosphere and used up non-renewable resources. He believed that powerful lobbying from multi-nationals in the oil and gas industries, combined with pressure from the NUM, was what had persuaded the 'green' movement that nuclear energy was intrinsically unsafe. As he said in that 1959 debate on nuclear warfare, 'the fall-out from misinformed opinion causes widespread contamination'.

During his last four years at Norwich, in fact, Launcelot spoke much more often in the House of Lords than he had previously. He spoke mainly on environmental issues or on youth and education, but occasionally on other matters that he felt strongly about, such as Biafra (where his VSO contacts had made him realize what was going on) and the continued detention of Rudolf Hess, which he felt was morally repugnant. Some speeches seem to have been made simply because some bishop had to speak and the lot fell on him – it is hard to think that the Statute Law Repeals Bill, or even Family Law Reform, were subjects that really gripped him. He had gained his high reputation in the House of Lords because he never said anything that was not sense, and only spoke when he had something worthwhile and well-informed to say. That may not sound a very flattering compliment, but is more than can be said for everyone who speaks in either House of Parliament. When he left Norwich, and therefore relinquished his membership of the Upper House, there was a strong all-party move to secure him a life peerage so that he could continue to speak, but Mr Heath presumably wanted to save his nominations for those who would be politically useful.

Launcelot had always been very fit and wiry. Until his leg went wrong he had not only played squash regularly but had usually beaten people less than half his age – who complained that he seemed able to stand in the middle of the court and make his opponents run round him as they frantically tried to return his shots. Mentally, he was equally alert and energetic; working with him would have been exhausting if it had not also been stimulating. And then in that summer of 1967 he quite suddenly found himself having to live a much more sedentary life than he had ever contemplated.

Richard Hanmer, who at the end of 1969 succeeded John Kirkham as chaplain, found Launcelot in a weak state; he often needed support despite having two sticks, and did not seem on top of his work. That was probably his lowest point. During that year he had spoken in the House of Lords no fewer than thirteen times. He had also undertaken a number of preaching engagements at schools around the country, attended various governors' meetings, conducted a number of weddings and christenings outside as well as within the diocese, and taken confirmation services at Westminster School and elsewhere.

In all these activities he was visiting friends who knew, or could be warned by Jane, of his physical limitations. It was much more difficult to get around the diocese as he used to do visiting the parishes. He spent much longer each day at his desk; going through his correspondence after his death (he seldom threw anything away) left one with a humbling realization that many hundreds of people wrote to him for advice, help, or reassurance, so the time he spent writing letters was not wasted. But nor was it really the right priority for a diocesan bishop.

He had always firmly believed that a bishop should retire at seventy – and when he went to Norwich had actually lodged a Deed of Resignation with Oliver Prior, the Diocesan Registrar, signed and undated, as there had been a recent case of a bishop being so incapacitated by a stroke that he was unable to sign such a Deed so had to remain technically in office. Now, in 1970, it was becoming apparent that he would not recover his strength sufficiently to continue effectively as Bishop of Norwich until his seventieth birthday in 1976.

20

Norwich: What Was Achieved?

He knew so many people and so many were ready and willing
to work with him and for him that once he had made his
choice things somehow happened.

(From Sir Edmund Bacon's Foreword to Friends for Life)

It would be misleading to suggest that Launcelot was just gently
running down during his last year or two in Norwich, like
Barchester's Bishop Grantly (or even non-fictional bishops that
might spring to an uncharitable mind). Much of the driving
force was by now being supplied by his two suffragans Eric
Cordingly and Bill Llewellyn and by his non-episcopal archdeacon Aubrey Aitken, but Launcelot's was the directing mind
that guided their regular staff meetings. Michael Mann, who
became a canon of Norwich and the Bishop's Adviser on Industry in 1969, affirms that Launcelot 'always supported my work
in a role with which rural Norfolk was totally unfamiliar', and
did so effectively; and when Alan Webster started to attend staff
meetings in 1970 he was amazed by Launcelot's thorough grasp
of the agenda.

Moreover, there were some things that only the diocesan
bishop could do; for example, although a Deanery is a Crown
appointment the bishop has an important say in who should be
nominated. In 1970 Dean Norman Hook retired; a godly man,
and quite exceptionally kind, he had been a good administrator
(as he had shown as Vicar of Wimbledon where he successfully
ran no fewer than fifty parish study groups!), but the world had
changed since his appointment in 1953 and the choice of his
successor was of key importance to the diocese. Alan Webster,

the Principal of Lincoln Theological College, was appointed, and remembers Launcelot writing to say that he wanted the cathedral to be more 'user-friendly' (though that jargon word was not in vogue then) both to visitors and worshippers, and – most important – that he was anxious that it should be a diocesan resource for theological discussion and study. (A year later, after considerable voluntary work re-decorating and re-ordering some vacant premises in the Close, Centre 71 was duly established.)

From the very first Launcelot had been keen to instil in church people a stronger sense of belonging to a diocese and not just to a parish. This was harder to achieve in a large and scattered diocese than it had been in Portsmouth, but was even more important because so many country parishes were very small and isolated (which was why he promoted Group Ministries). One of the first things he had done on arrival was to invite about forty young men from rural parts of the diocese (in retrospect, how extraordinary that neither Launcelot nor anyone else at the time thought that women should be invited – but then, of course, who had then thought of men belonging to the Mothers' Union?) to Bishop's House and ask them to start up groups of their own age to discuss the meaning of the Christian faith. He felt that since a small parish might have only one or two young people in its congregation, they would benefit from linking up with others of their own age in other parishes; but the idea never really took off. People were much more reluctant then than now to talk about their faith, and many clergy resented anything that might siphon off their young people into some extra-parochial organization. However, 'Norwich Young Churchmen', as this idea was called, did do some good by broadening the outlook of people who before long would find themselves churchwardens or other key figures in their parishes. It also proved that it was no good trying to bypass idle or ineffective clerics; Launcelot must (in Wansbrough Jones's words) 'sort out the clergy as you would like to do', which would indeed 'take several years'.

By the time of his Visitation Charge in 1967, Launcelot had undoubtedly transformed the morale of the clergy as a whole. Courses of study for deanery chapters, his own friendliness and

approachability, and the trouble he took over clergy appointments (not to mention his occasional unscrupulousness – as Sir
Edmund Bacon commented, 'as a picker of people, or, if necessary, as a poacher of people from others, Launcelot was in his
element') had changed Norwich from a diocese with over sixty
unfilled benefices to one where there were more clergy wishing
to come into the diocese than there was room for.

But one problem still had to be tackled. There were 628
churches in the diocese but only 326 clergy including those
in non-parochial posts, and some 60 vacant benefices (1961
Diocesan Directory figures). Only 87 parishes had a population
of more than a thousand, and 69 (not counting the Norwich
ones) had less than a hundred. Launcelot pointed out that

> on the basis of population we have thirteen times the national
> average of historic churches; taking their size into account, it
> would be twenty times. The fact that [about 75 per cent]
> appear to be in good repair shows what they mean to the
> people. That makes it all the harder to discuss the next ques-
> tion: which churches in your deanery you considered to be
> redundant.

Unpalatable though that question was, Launcelot insisted
that

> it has to be tackled. . . . [The question] is not so much 'What
> shall we do with St X's?', but 'What pattern of Church life
> is right in our contemporary society?' When we can see the
> answer to that question, we can more confidently face the
> other problems.

He was convinced that if resources could be redirected from
maintaining church fabric into pastoral work and evangelism,
the Church would be reinvigorated; congregations would
increase in numbers and vitality if they joined forces instead of
each one worshipping in its own vast (and often freezing) parish
church, and clergy would not have to duplicate Sunday services
or spend so much time on administration. (When notices for
the week are given out in many country churches today, it is

quite common to hear that three or four evenings will be taken up with PCC meetings; when, one wonders, can the vicar find time to visit any parishioners other than those who are retired and at home during the day?)

However, Launcelot could hardly persuade any parishioners to agree that services need not be held in their own church, though he certainly did not fail for want of trying. He even persuaded an old Trinity Hall man (John Kitching) who ran a firm of management consultants to carry out a thorough survey of distances between churches, communications, river or railway barriers, bus timetables, local authority boundaries, school catchment areas – everything, in fact, that would indicate which churches could be closed with a minimum of disruption. But closure of any village church was fiercely resisted.

In the ancient city of Norwich, however, something simply had to be done. It contained thirty-one medieval churches, more than London, York and Bristol put together. Some were outstandingly beautiful, but their populations were minute – St-Martin-at-Palace-Plain, a fine church just by the entrance to Bishop's House, boasted thirty-two resident parishioners most of whom were in a Salvation Army Hostel. Launcelot had put off tackling the problem of the Norwich churches, but he knew how bad things were. He had visited St Edmund's Church and was aghast at what he saw; it was being used as a shoe store, and another church, St Swithin, was a furniture store. By 1967 twelve other churches were no longer being used for worship, and the remaining seventeen (not counting the cathedral) were struggling to attract congregations – though St Peter Mancroft, the magnificent city centre church whose large pre-war population had shrunk almost to nothing (today, in 2002, the resident population of the parish is just 59) flourished by extending its 'catchment area' into surrounding country parishes.

So in November 1967 Launcelot appointed a Norwich City Commission as 'an advisory body to report' to him, chaired by Henry Brooke, no longer a minister or MP but Lord Brooke of Cumnor. It was a high-powered body whose members included both radicals and conservatives. The members were: Aubrey

Aitken, Archdeacon of Norwich; Miss D. F. Bartholomew, Headmistress of Norwich High School; Bernard Feilden FRIBA; the Revd James Fraser, an Ipswich vicar; Leslie Hunter, the retired Bishop of Sheffield; the Bishop of Huntingdon; Basil Roberts, the General Manager of Norwich Union, and Neil Wates, Director of Wates Ltd. The Secretary was Michael Elliott-Binns, Legal Secretary to the Church Assembly. When the Commission reported two years later, it made various suggestions for improving the Church's ministry to the city (some of which were later taken up by the Cathedral), but its core message was stark:

> The churches which it is likely to be justifiable to retain permanently for public worship are St Peter Mancroft, St Giles, St George Colegate, St John de Sepulchre and St Peter Parmentergate, together with St Julian for special use [as a shrine]; in addition, St Stephen, St George Tombland and St Andrew might continue in use for the time being.... [For the other churches], if the church is of outstanding historical and architectural merits, it is possible that it may be deemed worthy of vesting in the Redundant Churches Fund.... Should [it] not be of such outstanding quality as to merit national preservation by the Fund, the only course remaining is demolition.

The law laid it down that before approaching the Fund, the diocese must try to find an 'appropriate and serviceable' use for a church, such as 'use by another Christian church; by the University; as a health centre; a headquarters for Church societies or voluntary organisations; a bookshop; a diocesan printing centre; a concert hall, theatre or arts centre; a meeting-place for old people; a refectory; a depositary for archives'. But '[i]f no reasonable alternative use for a medieval church building emerges, and if no money is available for its future upkeep, then the only course would be to demolish it. That would be a sad day for Norwich.'

The Report caused something of a storm. The idea that the diocese should simply give away or demolish churches steeped

in history and consecrated by centuries of Christian prayer and
worship seemed a betrayal – a letter in the *Eastern Daily Press*
commented that Judas at least got thirty pieces of silver but the
Bishop of Norwich was *giving* his churches away. Lady Harrod,
who was deeply committed to the Christian faith and also cared
very much about old buildings in general and Norfolk ones in
particular, bearded Bernard Feilden in his office and accused
him of being a traitor to the cause – he was Surveyor to Norwich
Cathedral and York Minister and architect to many Norfolk
churches, though he sat on the Commission not as an architect
but simply as a layman giving advice to the Bishop. Feilden
defended himself by pointing to a passage of the Report that
she had not read, and although he may not have been completely
forgiven, the Report, by insisting that the Norwich churches
must be considered as a whole and not picked off one by one,
saved many that would otherwise have had to be demolished
as their tiny congregations dwindled to nothing and repair bills
soared.

Dorothy Bartholomew, another member of the Commission,
thinks that it was never Launcelot's intention for any church to
be demolished, and this is borne out by the fact that the initial
report drafted by Henry Brooke, who as a close friend of Launcelot could read his mind as well as anyone, was far less radical
than the one that the rest of the Commission insisted on. It
would have been churlish for Launcelot to reject that final
Report after all the work that had gone into it, and after ten
years getting to know Norfolk people he could have calculated
that its effect would be to galvanize people into action.

He was right; the head of steam raised by the Report did
harness itself to constructive ends. Gordon Tilsley, the Town
Clerk, realized at once that the Church could not raise the money
needed, and that for the Norwich skyline to lose its medieval
towers and spires would indeed 'be a sad day' for the city. The
City Council agreed that they must take responsibility for the
upkeep of those redundant churches which English Heritage
rejected. In May 1971, the Town Clerk and the Conservative
and Labour leaders on the Council went up to London and

persuaded the Church Commissioners to transfer the freehold of these churches to the City Council, which would then grant ninety-nine-year leases to a charitable trust. And six months later Tilsley was able to report that the Norwich Historic Churches Trust had been set up.

However, none of this made Launcelot very popular; it is bound to jar to see a church that was built to the glory of God and worshipped in for centuries being used for secular purposes. But better to use a church for teaching young offenders computing skills than for storing shoes. Moreover, on the evidence available it seems certain that if things had simply been left to the local clergy and their congregations to do what they thought fit, some churches would have fared far worse. Before the Commission reported, one church, cut off from its parishioners by a new road, had been turned into a shelter for down-and-outs. In theory that was an admirably Christian use, but with neither expertise nor money the result was disastrous. Similarly, a church handed over to another Christian body received no maintenance at all, and with buddleias running riot and percolating walls and roof, had to be taken back by the Norwich Churches Trust and a more conservation-minded tenant found before something collapsed.

There seems little doubt that Launcelot, being a pragmatic Scot, did not fully recognize the extent to which a church building might itself be an inspiration that could evoke faith. Although he did not, like so many in the 1960s, speak dismissively of a church building as 'plant', as if a church that had been loved and prayed in for centuries could be treated as if it were a factory for which there was no further use, he could not have subscribed to the church architect Sir Ninian Comper's assertion that a church ought to be 'a building which prayed of itself'.

The report on the Norwich churches did not only galvanize Gordon Tilsley and the City Council into positive action; it also spurred Lady Harrod to enlist John Betjeman, Paul Paget FRIBA, who lived in Norfolk and was a member of the Redundant Churches Fund, David Mawson FRIBA, who was a partner of Bernard Feilden, and other local enthusiasts, in the cause of saving country churches. Lady Harrod recalls that in their enthusiasm they arranged their initial meeting before they thought of informing Launcelot, and by the time they realized this his diary made it impossible for him to come. He was (she thinks!) rather cross; and it was a pity. Had Launcelot been there – and, perhaps more to the point, had he still been as vigorous as he had been five years earlier – a certain amount of friction would probably have been avoided. As it was, there was a period when the Norfolk Society's Committee for Country Churches was at odds with the Norwich Churches Trust, and indeed with the Diocesan Pastoral Committee – people even spoke of Billa's diocese and Launcelot's diocese. In the end, the Norfolk Churches Trust (as Lady Harrod's Committee became) proved brilliantly successful in voluntary fund-raising for church repairs – in 2000 it gave grants totalling £258,000; but if it could from the start have been co-ordinated with the Diocesan Pastoral Committee, energy spent in tugs-of-war might have been devoted to pulling together.

Perhaps, however, some argument was inevitable anyway. Launcelot's successor Maurice Wood wrote in 1972, in a Foreword to *Norfolk Country Churches and the Future* (privately printed by the Norfolk Churches Trust), that 'some people feel that buildings are less important than people ... others, that every church should be maintained for the worship of God if it is even remotely possible. This book will make a significant contribution to this urgent ongoing debate.' Launcelot could never have brought himself to be quite so emollient; as he told the Diocese in 1967:

If you feel that [to close any church] is a betrayal, consider whether your feelings about what the Church exists for are the feelings of the New Testament. The Church is Christ's body. Its members – clergy and laity – are in the world to continue Christ's work of healing, teaching, forgiving, reconciling men to God; and we must be careful to give this first place and not to put buildings before people.

The present (2002) Bishop, Graham James, has summed it up well:

> Such negativity about Launcelot as I pick up comes from some of those associated with the Norfolk Churches Trust . . . who look upon him as a church closer. I expect that is where I would differ from him most, in that I think he believed that redundancy of buildings was a solution to some of the problems of pastoral strategy that we possess in the Church of England. I regard that as too simple an answer to much more fundamental problems.

Although by mid-1970 Launcelot was in better shape physically than he had been a year earlier, he realized that he could not do justice to his work as a bishop (if he had been on top form, some of the negative fall-out over redundant churches might have been avoided). That autumn the Dean of Windsor, Robin Woods, was made Bishop of Worcester. Since one of the duties of the Dean is that of Senior Domestic Chaplain to the Queen, her views are naturally taken into account when making the appointment. In 1959 Macmillan, while staying at Balmoral, had discovered that the Queen admired Launcelot and wished for him at Norwich, and in 1970 it seems that, realizing that his leg would soon make him resign that see, she wished for him to go to Windsor.

When the letter came inviting him to become Dean, Launcelot did not hesitate as he had done before accepting Portsmouth and Norwich. Leaving Norwich was a wrench, but he knew he could not carry on much longer, and to put it at its lowest, the offer of Windsor extended his active ministry for five years further than would otherwise have been possible.

Before settling down to St George's, Windsor Launcelot and Jane went abroad for a much-needed holiday. One day they bought an English paper which they took up to their hotel room and read that Maurice Wood was to be the new Bishop of Norwich. Launcelot liked him, and had made him one of his Examining Chaplains; but he was an extreme Evangelical – even

to the extent of being strictly teetotal. Launcelot sat down on
the bed with a bump; said nothing for a minute; and then
announced, decisively, 'We will take the wine rack with us after
all.' It had been tailor-made to fit under the circular staircase
at Norwich . . .

Bishop Graham has generously written an appreciation of his
predecessor-but-two (part of which has already been quoted
above).

> One of the things that has struck me is that Launcelot's name
> is mentioned more frequently than I would have expected for
> a bishop who left a generation ago now. My impression from
> what people say about him is that he was a great friend and
> befriender of clergy and lay people alike, and especially the
> young. It is clear he brought new energy and vision to the
> diocese, drawing younger clergy into the parishes and through
> his schemes for a more sensible deployment of the clergy,
> releasing fresh energy.
>
> That is my other great impression of him – energy. If I've
> got his measure right it is that his greatest contribution was
> the energetic way he gave himself to his ministry and to all
> the schemes in which he was involved. No one tells me that
> he was a wonderful preacher or a great theologian, but the
> breadth of his sympathies seems to have been enormous and
> about him there was a huge humanity. . . . I have met just one
> or two people who clearly think that I might be able to do
> what Launcelot did all over again and bring lots of young
> clergy into the parishes to rejuvenate them. I envy the
> resources from the Church Commissioners which were at the
> disposal of the Bishop in Launcelot's days and the greater
> freedom it gave to him. In general, however, I think the legacy
> from Launcelot, so far as it can be discerned in such rapidly
> changing times, is one that I value and is not the least bit
> difficult to live with.

21

Dean of Windsor

I exhort that Supplications, Prayers, Intercessions, and giving
of thanks, be made for Kings, and for all that are in authority,
that we may live a quiet and peaceable life, in all godliness
and honesty.

(First Epistle to Timothy, quoted in the Accession Service in
The Book of Common Prayer).

St George's Chapel, Windsor, is a breathtakingly beautiful building. It was and remains the focal point of a religious foundation;
King Edward IV wanted Church and State to interact in order
to promote good government, and the centre of government then
was the Court, based on Windsor Castle. St George's Chapel, to
which the Deanery is physically attached, is within the Castle
walls, together with the rest of the collegiate foundation. This
consists of the Dean and four Canons, minor canons, the organist and lay clerks, vergers, and their families; there are also the
Military Knights, retired senior army officers aged 65 or over.
In the Chapel are the banners of the Knights of the Garter, of
which the Dean is Register.

St George's Chapel, in fact, is steeped in history. It is probably
the only Anglican church in which the Blessed Sacrament has
been reserved continuously, except for the dozen years of Crom-
well's rule, for over five hundred years. In its glorious west
window six popes are commemorated together with the kings
and saints one might normally expect, and still in Launcelot's
time the annual commemoration of benefactors included the
Pope who advised the Bishop of Winchester in drawing up the
Statutes 'by which we are still substantially governed' (the list

of benefactors goes on to commemorate those 'of more modern times', starting with Henry VIII).

There were three aspects to Launcelot's new office. First, the Dean is responsible, together with the four Canons who with him constitute the Chapter, for ordering the worship in the Chapel. Secondly, he is the senior domestic chaplain to the Queen. Thirdly, there is St George's House, the conference centre housed in what had been two minor canons' houses (as it sleeps twenty-four and still has room for a dining room and large lecture room, one can see that the original Foundation was built on a generous scale).

Launcelot was installed as Dean of Windsor on 16 July 1971. The difficulty in arranging an earlier date gave him a foretaste of the problems that lay ahead; the Canons had found it difficult to find a convenient date that fitted in with the Queen's engagements. But on the day, the sun shone, and the Queen, the Queen Mother, Princess Margaret and Prince William of Gloucester were there together with the rest of the Windsor community and Launcelot's own friends and family, who between them filled the chapel.

We can allow him to give his own description of what 'being at Windsor' was like, since that is the title of a talk he gave to Sherborne Rotary Club a few years after he retired – the invitation to speak came from his bank manager so he felt it was 'of the nature of a royal command'.

I am all too conscious of the pitfalls of a talk on this subject. It was, I think, a former member of the Royal Household who said 'There is one thing that the Queen and I cannot stand, and that is name-dropping'.

When my wife and I moved from Norwich, it meant moving to a bigger, not smaller, house; Dean Baillie in the late 1920s said it could be managed with a staff of nine. There is the Drawing Room, where we decided to hang the most eminent portraits of former Deans (rather than the portraits of the most eminent Deans), assigning the remaining portraits to the Long Gallery which would have made a splended bowling

alley. On one wall of the Dean's Study are panels bearing arms
of Knights of the Garter dating back to the foundation of the
Order in Edward III's reign. There is a vast 14th century stone
fireplace with a picture over it of St George slaying the dragon,
and an oak gate-leg table on which the headless body of
Charles I lay before being interred.

Two features of living in the Castle were, the noise of aero-
planes – it is on the Heathrow flight path – and the stream
of tourists from all over the world. It was fun talking to
tourists, though sometimes after some minutes one realises
they don't speak any English! I was very pleased at getting
tipped 50p by an American until it dawned on me that this
was his only way of getting rid of me. . . .

In 1475 Edward IV built a new and magnificent Chapel, of
Cathedral proportions. It is noted for being a masterpiece of late
Perpendicular architecture and for its musical tradition through
five centuries. There are three organists, twelve lay clerks, and
22 choristers all living on the premises; the boys are scholars
of St George's School. Sunday morning service is picturesque,
with the Military Knights, originally called the Poor Knights
whose duty was to attend Mass daily and pray for the souls
of the Knights of the Garter. They are retired senior Army
officers (there were Naval Knights in Queen Victoria's day,
but they were disbanded for being drunk and disorderly).

In 1966 Prince Philip and Robin Woods my predecessor had
some of the Canon's houses converted into a Conference Centre
where clergy and laity, Christians and non-Christians, men and
women of diverse skills and callings, could consider issues of
current importance where value judgments are specially
involved, and could seek to rediscover the unity of truth and of
human society. This Centre, known as St George's House, was
to provide for two interconnected types of gathering:

1. Conferences and in-service training for selected clergy of
the Christian churches;
2. Consultations of leading representatives of different walks
of life.

As Dean I was ex-officio Chairman, assisted by a most distin-
guished Council including Knights of the Garter, of whom
Prince Philip was one. This was a fascinating aspect of 'being
at Windsor'. Outstanding consultations included: Trade
Union leaders, Shop Stewards, and Shop Floor representatives;
Artists – in which my co-chairman was Yehudi Menuhin;
Sportsmen (before the Olympic Games); Interfaith leaders;
Senior Church Leaders (chaired by Basil Hume, Abbot of
Ampleforth). Also there was a consultation on Legislation on
the Sea Beds, sponsored by the Inter-Parliamentary Group
for World Government, and two consultations under Lord
Ashby's chairmanship to identify the questions that should be
being asked by society today. The method was to invite up
to 30 persons, who could be divided into three discussion
groups. The planning required skill; and the proceedings were
private, which meant that the participants could talk freely
and frankly.

Then there is the ceremonial side of Windsor. On Garter
Day, when the Knights worship in the Chapel with the Sovereign of their Order and new Knights are installed, the pro-
cession from the Castle must be the most splendid annual
pageant anywhere; but the atmosphere has the intimacy and
happiness of a parish fete.

It has been the custom for members of the Royal Family to
be buried at Windsor. During my time we had the funeral of
the Duke of Windsor; that of Prince William of Gloucester,
tragically killed in a flying accident; Prince Henry Duke of
Gloucester; a moving service for Haile Selassie, Emperor of
Abyssinia and an Extra Knight of the Garter; also the military
funeral of Lord Montgomery of Alamein.

At Christmas and Easter all the Royal Family came together
at Windsor, and the Queen spends many weekends there. As
Domestic Chaplain to the Queen, being careful about protocol
and at the same time being relaxed and natural can sometimes
be a problem; but the Royal Family are well aware of this
and will always help one out. Besides, when off duty its

members are very much personalities in their own right, in touch with a whole range of life – well-informed, possessed with a wonderful sense of humour, and with a deep sense of responsibility and care. If there is one reaction which grew in me more strongly, it is that we are singularly fortunate in our Sovereign, her Consort, the Queen Mother, and other members of their family; and of their Christian influence.

But my time is up. As the geologist said to his exploratory team, 'If you haven't struck oil you'd better stop boring.'

As Chaplain to the Royal Family there is no doubt that, in the words of Michael Mann, his successor as Dean of Windsor Launcelot 'did brilliantly and was much loved and appreciated'. He claimed to have persuaded Prince Charles, not long down from Trinity College, Cambridge, that he must turn and bow to the print of Trinity Hall hanging near the bottom of the stairs. He shared with Prince Philip an informed and deep concern for the environment and for Outward Bound kind of activities for young people; he had known him ever since helping to plan the Duke of Edinburgh Award Scheme nearly twenty years earlier. (Another small but striking indication of his influence on members of the Royal Family, heard quite by chance on a car radio, was when Princess Anne was being asked how she could support both the Wildlife Fund in Africa and Save the Children, since wildlife competed with undernourished children for scarce land resources; the Princess in her reply used some of the identical phrases that Launcelot had been wont to use twelve years earlier in arguing that the wellbeing of human beings was inextricably linked with that of the environment.) And at times of stress or tragedy, such as the death of Prince William of Gloucester, Launcelot was as wise, sympathetic and helpful a parish priest as anyone could wish.

With St George's House, too, he was in his element. He did not play so dominant a role as Robin Woods, but he kept in close touch with what was going on and played what Kenneth Adams, who was Director of Studies at St George's House during Launcelot's time there, describes as a hosting role – 'which he did very well indeed'. Much of the hospitality fell on Jane, who certainly had her work cut out at Windsor, often having to improvise and adapt at short notice – as when Launcelot came in at half past twelve on a bank holiday, when the larder was almost empty and the shops were shut, to announce that he had asked Prince Philip to lunch as they wanted to discuss something. Kenneth Adams considers that Launcelot made two major contributions to St George's House, apart from oiling the wheels very effectively by his friendliness and hospitality; he instituted the courses for senior churchmen (all Christian churches, not just Anglicans), and he placed the environment firmly on the agenda.

Previously the 'secular' courses had concentrated on such issues as relations between people at work, business ethics, and what motivated, or put off, people in the workplace. But in the 1970s the world was beginning to wake up to the need to conserve the environment – whales were starting to swim into the public ken, and people were starting to quote E. F. Schumacher and to think that Small is Beautiful. Launcelot's membership of the Parliamentary Group for World Government and of the government standing committee on environmental pollution gave him a good grasp of the issues and also meant that he could call on leading authorities such as Barbara Ward of the Club of Rome to address the Windsor conferences.

He usually chaired these conferences on the environment himself, as he did the courses for church leaders. Those courses, and ones for up-and-coming clergy recommended by their bishops as possible future leaders, were based on the theme: What is the world of today telling us? What theological thinking does that require? What kind of Church, therefore, and what kind of minister, should we be trying to have? Canon Stephen Verney also developed courses for clergy who around the age of fifty were experiencing mid-life blues; he recalls that they would arrive looking depressed and go away with a spring in their step. There were also inter-faith conferences, at one of which the Dalai Lama was present.

During one senior clergy course, Basil Hume, the Abbot of Ampleforth, had to take an urgent telephone call. He apologized to Kenneth Adams, but said he must go up to London at once and would have to miss the evening session. Everyone assumed that there had been trouble at the abbey, but on his return he confided to Launcelot that he had been told he was to be the new Roman Catholic Archbishop. Launcelot invited him to say Mass the next morning in his private chapel in the Deanery, so the future Cardinal's first Mass after he knew he was to be Archbishop of Westminster was served by the Dean of Windsor. No doubt they are both continuing to pray that the divisions that hamstring the Church's mission may be healed.

A Dean's main responsibility is St George's Chapel itself. With five centuries of tradition and large endowments behind it, the regular pattern of worship could of course carry on with no help from the Dean. Any change was bound to take time – rather as it takes at least a mile before a large super-tanker starts to respond to an alteration of course or speed. There was one change that Launcelot did want to make. The Sunday congregations were growing, and he thought that the main Sunday service ought to take place in the nave, which would accommodate all who took part, rather than in the choir from which the general public was excluded and which was hidden from the nave by the screen. Strong opposition to the proposal, however, came from the Military Knights who enjoyed stumping up the length of the Chapel in their picturesque uniform on a Sunday morning, and from the two senior Canons who opposed all change on principle. Launcelot failed to implement the change, but it very quickly happened under his successor.

It must be admitted, in fact, that Launcelot did not find the Canons easy. Until Anthony Dyson arrived in 1974 there were just three; Canons Bryan Bentley and Jim Fisher took a consistently conservative position, Stephen Verney was very much more progressive. Bentley and Fisher had both been born in 1909 and had been at Windsor since 1957 and 1958 respectively. They both had good academic brains; Bentley had been a Scholar of

King's, Cambridge and had then gone on to take an Oxford degree, winning the Carus Greek Testament prize; Fisher had won a scholarship to Cambridge and obtained a first in theology. Verney was younger, ordained after war service, and had worked in the Coventry Diocese under its charismatic (in the best sense of the word) bishop Cuthbert Bardsley in 1958 as Diocesan Missioner, and had been made a Canon of the new Coventry Cathedral; he had come to Windsor just a year before Launcelot, in 1970. Dyson was also on the progressive side; he was under forty when he came to Windsor in 1974 from being Principal of Ripon Hall theological college.

If four intelligent men with well-developed views are asked to work together with no clearly defined duties or objective, some friction is likely to occur. All that was officially required of the Canons was to take duty in the Chapel every fourth week. Before pronouncing sententiously that the devil always finds work for idle fingers, it must be pointed out that the Canons wrote books, sat on committees, played a part in the work of St George's House, advised on divorce reform law in the case of Canon Bentley and acted as Treasurer in the case of Canon Fisher. But such disparate activities required no common discipline, and Stephen Verney, the only surviving Canon from those days, admits wryly that 'no, we really didn't work as a team; you couldn't say that'. Until Dyson's arrival made up the full complement of four canons, there was always a two-to-one majority against change, and even after Dyson's arrival Launcelot would not use his casting vote to push through reforms such as moving the Sunday morning service into the nave.

Verney comments that it was not in Launcelot's nature to be decisive and drive measures through, which shows the extent to which physical disability had blunted Launcelot's cutting edge. He had never been confrontational, but Verney's Dean sounds very unlike the Bishop who without fuss or bludgeoning managed to appoint three new archdeacons within two years of arriving at Norwich. But perhaps Launcelot did not think that these issues mattered enough to fight over; he knew he would be retiring when he became seventy, and that having made the case for change he could leave it to a successor to implement it. Sure enough, Michael Mann, whom Launcelot had appointed to advise him on Industrial Relations when he became a Canon of Norwich in 1969, did institute the nave service – not for nothing had he been a Colonel of Dragoons.

It is no use concealing the fact that Launcelot was taken aback by what he felt was the unreasonably obstructive attitude of the Chapter. But the unhappy atmosphere was not entirely due to the personalities of the individuals concerned. The trouble was long-standing* and systemic; Windsor as a religious foundation was not designed for married clergy. Even in a community of celibate monks with a strong common purpose and the highest ideals there are considerable strains – imagine having to watch and listen to Father So-and-So eating his soup day after day with no escape – and when priests in a religious community (which is what St George's is) are married, it is even harder to maintain a good 'common life' because each member has his own family life separate from that of the Community itself. And it may not have helped at Windsor that the Dean was a member of the Royal Household and the Canons were not, so that they

---

* In January 1827 the Duke of York's funeral at Windsor was grossly mismanaged; the congregation had to stand for two hours on wet flag-stones in bitter cold, and Canning wrote to Wellington, 'I presume that whoever filched the cloth or the matting from under our feet in the aisle, had bets or insurances against the lives of the Cabinet.' The only actual fatality was the Bishop of Lincoln, though Canning and Wellington both caught severe colds which in Canning's case, thanks to two of the Canons, turned to pneumonia and probably caused his premature death six months later as Prime Minister. Canning's aunt wrote that he had declined the offer of a comfortable bed at Eton 'being engaged to Mr Long, a Canon'; Long turned out to be away but 'promised him a bed near him at Mr Stopford's, another canon whose house had not been lately occupied. I feared it must be cold and damp and that GC would probably suffer from it. Next day his indisposition was announced in the papers ... actually the house was so forlorn that there was no pen and ink in it, he was obliged to send out for some.' (Giles Hunt, *Mehitabel Canning* [Rooster Books, 2001])

and their wives were not invited to as many social functions as the Dean and his wife. Michael Mann sums up Launcelot's relationship with the Chapter by saying:

> When Launcelot went to Windsor he was not well and had only five years to do before retirement. . . . St George's, unlike Westminster Abbey, has Statutes which makes the Dean only 'primus inter pares', and the Canons determinedly and consistently outvoted him. By this stage Launcelot was too tired and was there far too short a time to have the energy to take on what was a formidable consortium, so the Chapel and the Castle community went into 'suspended animation' during his Deanship. . . . In succeeding Launcelot at Windsor I could not have had more help from him and Jane, and frequently in my early years there I sought his counsel and advice, which was always given most helpfully.

There was one initiative of Launcelot's that the Chapter did welcome. The Military Knights had their grace-and-favour apartments for their lifetime, but when they died their widows had to move out, which was very hard. Launcelot had plans made to provide homes for these widows so that they would not have to leave Windsor, where housing would otherwise be too expensive for them to afford. The actual work was not put in hand until after he had left, but the plans were all there and the project ready to go ahead as soon as his successor was installed. (The Military Knights were gallant old gentlemen; one of them told Canon Verney how the Queen, knowing he had recently had an operation which made standing difficult, invited him to sit at a tea party. When he replied 'But I cannot sit in Your Majesty's presence', the Queen knew exactly how to persuade him, and said 'I order you to sit'.)

Perhaps the most time-consuming event during Launcelot's time at Windsor was the 500th anniversary of the foundation of St George's Chapel in 1975. The celebrations began on St George's Day, 23 April, and continued during most of the summer. There were exhibitions of illuminated manuscripts and other treasures, a series of concerts reflecting five centuries of English church music, special services. It was exhilarating, but exhausting; and retirement before his seventieth birthday became an increasingly attractive proposition – not least for Jane. Towards the end of their time at Windsor, when she was arranging flowers against the clock a friend remarked 'After you have left, you will look back on your time here with enormous pleasure; but now, it is very hard work.'

Launcelot's Windsor years cannot be acclaimed as being such an outstanding success as his time at Trinity Hall, in the Royal Navy, at Portsmouth or at Norwich. One of the Military Knights commented that 'Dean Fleming was like a stone dropped into a pool which made no ripples'; but since both his predecessor and his successor were very much men of action, St George's (as Michael Mann has suggested) 'probably needed a period of quiet'. It was said of a Bishop of Oxford that 'under him many things went quietly right that could have gone noisily wrong'. Even if that were all that could be said of Launcelot's time as Dean of Windsor, it would represent no mean achievement; few men could have managed, as he did, to prevent the tensions within the Chapter breaking out into open acrimony. But a great deal more can be said; Launcelot was superbly good pastorally, his scientific and environmental interests helped to enhance the reputation of St George's House, and he managed to find time for his multifarious concerns in the field of youth and education, geology and exploration. For a man who was by no means in good health when he went there, it was no mean achievement.

22

Poyntington

There are three ages of Man, and of Woman: Young, Getting
On, and Wonderful.

(an oft-repeated saying of Launcelot)

The first thing that Launcelot did after leaving Windsor in July
1976 was to go to sea for five weeks; he had been invited to
act as honorary Chaplain in HMS *Kent* during her summer
cruise. Jane may have been rather glad to be on her own while
she got the house straight, with no risk of Launcelot coming in
to tell her that he had asked people to lunch or dinner or to
stay the night.

Their new home was a converted tithe barn nestling just
beneath the small village church of Poyntington. The village,
little more than a hamlet, lies about three miles north of Sherborne in unspoiled countryside but with good road communications, and with a reasonable train service to London. They
had rather hankered after Norfolk, but felt that to go and live
in Launcelot's old diocese would not be fair on his successor.
They had converted the tithe barn themselves, and although it
was not very convenient for someone with a bad leg, as the
ground floor was split level so that you had to go up half a
dozen stairs to reach the drawing room and study, their own
bedroom and bathroom, and the kitchen and dining room, were
on the ground floor.

Poyntington was to be Launcelot's home for fourteen years,
longer than he had ever lived in one place before. Since the
parish was one of half a dozen looked after by one rector,
each being separated from the next by narrow winding lanes,

Launcelot found himself largely fulfilling the role of parish priest. He always made himself pastorally available and took a great many of the services; the church registers show that between 1977 and 1988, when physical infirmity made him give up doing so, the average size of the congregation increased from four to thirty. He and Jane were thoroughly integrated into the life of that small village community, and made many friends in the neighbourhood.

They also went away a great deal. Launcelot often visited the Outward Bound school at Brathay and the Atlantic College at St Donat's, and remained actively involved with the Duke of Edinburgh Award Scheme, the Jubilee Trust, the Prince's Trust, Endeavour Training, Ocean Youth Clubs – the list seems endless. In 1984 (at the age of 78) he became President of the Trident Trust, and his description of its aims illustrates the philosophy of many of the organizations which he supported:

Trident arose in the early '70s as the outcome of a Conference held at Ditchley Park. Sir Robert Birley [*one time headmaster of Eton*] was the Chairman; Alfred Blake [*Director of the Duke of Edinburgh Award Scheme*], Sir John Nelson [*Deputy Chairman of the National Playing Fields Association*] and I were among its members. The Trust was established with the aim of helping young people, when leaving maintained schools, to be better prepared for working life. An immediate and practical result . . . [was a pilot scheme] for pupils during the last year at school to be attached to local industrial organisations as part of the curriculum. This idea soon spread . . . and led to the Education (Work Experience) Act of 1973. But the other two 'prongs' of Trident are important; first, a period of residential training involving personal challenge (such as Outward Bound) and secondly, Community Service.

Launcelot tried hard to keep the original spiritual aims of these organizations alive as the personnel changed and became more secular-minded. In 1988 he was pleading:

Could we not commend for adoption at other UWC Colleges the Religious Studies Course that the multi-faith panel [at] Atlantic College considered had been sufficiently tested to justify its extension to other Colleges. This would of course mean the appointment of a teacher qualified to teach the course. The course has been funded by a charitable Trust; I think the grant could be extended. . . . There is a need to identify and clarify what characteristics distinguish United World Colleges from the large number of international Colleges which have sprung up all over the world. . . . I am worried about basic principles and the way in which the original dream-concept has been watered down by human incapacity.

The United World Colleges (UWC), of which Atlantic College at St Donat's on the coast of Wales was the British example, had been founded by Kurt Hahn. Their international character enabled their adolescent pupils to get to know others from different countries and cultures. This was something that Launcelot had become increasingly keen on – as evidenced by his involvement with the Parliamentary Group for World Government, which might seem at first sight uncharacteristically idealistic and impracticable, but which his concern for the future of this planet had led him to support. He had more and more come to realize that the measures needed to conserve the environment were too economically unpopular for any sovereign state to adopt unless all the others did too; if ecological disaster was to be avoided, therefore, there would have to be some supra-national body with the power to control exploitation of natural resources worldwide. (Perhaps Prince Charles's support for the Rio conference on climate change might have had something to do with Launcelot's influence.)

Kurt Hahn's educational theories were, as we have seen, very much in tune with Launcelot's own ideas – and he firmly believed that the continental baccalaureate was a far better system of examinations than the O levels and A levels in most British schools – but it would be most misleading to dwell on Launcelot's *ideas* about education. They were sound enough, and his advice on how to run a school (or university, come to that) would always have been sensible; but his real strength was his extraordinary personal ability to relate to people of all ages – and now that he had retired, he had much more time to visit schools.

It seems extraordinary that a septuagenarian – indeed, latterly an octogenarian – retired bishop should have been in such constant demand not only to preach or give talks to sixth-formers in grammar or secondary schools, but also to pay visits of three days or more to boarding schools to give a series of talks, or simply be available to any who wished to have a talk with him; but his diaries show that he was very much in demand. As he grew older he had to curtail the number of school engagements that he could accept, but he continued to make visits to Bryanston, where he had been a governor and which was within easy reach of Poyntington, and to Atlantic College at St Donat's, one of whose pupils wrote:

I know your visits to Atlantic College have always been of great value and are very much appreciated and enjoyed by all; I am also convinced that it's one of the things that does allow you to retain the air of a teenager, and prevents you from getting out of touch with other people especially the younger generation.

The very fact that an eighteen-year-old should feel free to write like that to an eighty-year-old retired bishop speaks volumes. Launcelot had never lost his touch with the young – Simon Crosse, the architect who designed the homes for the elderly in the grounds of the Palace at Norwich, was deeply impressed by the way that he had 'entranced the young' on his (invariable) visits to the Norwich Rowing Club regattas. And despite the weakness in his leg, he still rowed occasionally even in his retirement. Some years after he had gone to live in Poyntington, a Bryanston boy wrote a longish letter full of his hopes and fears for some coming exams, and saying:

We were all very honoured to have you rowing with us and the boat felt much better before you got out. . . . Before I end I must just say how glad I am I became confirmed, by you especially. Because I think I can now realise how much it means.

The Antarctic lecture and slides were always a useful ice-breaker if Launcelot was giving a series, say, of Lenten talks. But the reason why his talks and sermons were effective was mainly because of his personality, and because he always seemed to know what things really concerned his hearers. Just as he had preached on 'Courage' to naval officers in 1940, so forty years later he would preach on such topics as 'Tolerance' or 'Failure':

You may well think that failure is a very strange subject. But whether we like it or not, we all fail, and it is important to see this in a positive rather than a negative way. . . . A sense of failure is one of the commonest recipes for depression; but I say a '*sense* of failure' for at the end of the day much depends on where you have set your sights. I may regard myself as a failure because I've set my target too high – or regard myself as a success because I've set my target too low. . . . Failure is not always the tragedy which at first it may have seemed. Maybe the aim we didn't achieve was wrong. In any case, what matters is how we respond to failure. . . .

The worst sort of failure is a failure in one's relationships. But if we fail even in this most critical area – a failure in love – all is not lost; such failure is never absolute. The love of God goes more than half way to meet us – and that love, as Christ has shown, is utterly dependable and re-creative . . .

Tolerance, he argued, 'springs from a recognition of the sanctity of human life, the equal worth of each individual, and the respect due to each individual in his/her own right'. Like 'Failure', it was not an obvious choice of subject, but touched the spot for many a teenager. He was good, also, at finding some more-or-less relevant anecdote to catch his hearers' attention; 'Failure' was introduced by the pedigree cow who saw a van driving past her field advertising extra vitamin-rich milk and turned to her companion, saying 'Makes you feel kind of inadequate, doesn't it', and a sermon on 'Faith' at Loretto School in June 1988 was introduced by his bevy of 'fifteen great aunts . . . best encountered one at a time'.

Visits to schools to take confirmations or preach, longer visits to Bryanston, St Donat's or Brathay, taking friends' weddings (and, increasingly, funerals) all took time. Talks and sermons had to be prepared as well as delivered, and Jane often found herself protecting him from demands on his time that she feared would overtax him. Then there were trips abroad: to South Africa where there were VSO projects to see, to New Zealand for the opening of the Polar exhibition at Christchurch, to the USA and Canada to visit the Atlantic Colleges there. His correspondence shows a bewildering mix of tours of inspection, of giving talks or sermons (one at St Thomas's Church on Fifth Avenue New York produced a remarkable letter from a complete stranger saying that Launcelot's sermon had a most profound effect on him although he could hardly remember a word that he had actually said), and of fund-raising – with great success, since St George's House had put the coping stone on his already remarkable network of influential people. And wherever he went, old friendships were cemented and new ones made.

The most remarkable feature of the archive that Launcelot left behind him was the number and variety of people who wrote to ask for advice of every kind. Long after he retired he continued to be asked about church appointments; it was natural that he should have been consulted over the appointment of a new Archbishop of Canterbury in 1974, for he was at that time Dean of Windsor, but the only possible reason for consulting him in 1979, eight years after he had ceased to be a diocesan bishop and three years after he had retired completely, was that the powers that be valued his good judgment. (In 1979 he backed the winner, though with some misgivings that his 'altogether delightful wife' would find being an archbishop's wife almost unbearable.) When people wrote asking if they should accept a job, or get married, or become a Roman Catholic, or take any other important step, Launcelot hardly ever gave direct advice. Just occasionally he did: 'Don't go to that parish; it is a grave-yard for any priest', or 'you would find the ethos of the school simply too uncongenial'; but almost invariably his advice con-sisted of helping people to see the pros and cons and weigh them for themselves. A letter to Alan Webster (who has kindly allowed it to be quoted here), who had just been invited to become Dean of St Paul's, is a typical example of the way Launcelot gave advice:

I'm tempted to start by saying 'How difficult' but that doesn't help very much. Let me first make these two comments.

1. I don't know whether you feel your present job is beginning to run out of steam. My own observation, limited as it is, would lead me to think this is *not* the case. . . . But I don't think you ought to go to St Paul's for the sake of getting away from where you are now – and I'm quite sure you ought not to say to yourself 'if I don't accept this, perhaps I will never be offered anything else'.
2. It will not be surprising if you feel a bit flattered to be asked . . . (it is after all rather upstage to be Dean of St Paul's), but [you can] come to terms with these false lures by recognis-ing clearly that they must have absolutely no bearing on whether you should accept or decline.

Obviously you need to assess the nature of the job – what it looks like currently and what in your view it should be. . . . In making such an assessment you obviously would need to consider the likely snags, for instance in connection with your family responsibilities. Then, I understand that St Paul's has had very considerable [financial] problems . . . it would be well for you to try and discover what the present position is. Furthermore, St Paul's has had the reputation at some times in recent years of a difficult Chapter. This may or may not be the case now, but I would have thought you could, without allowing it to be known that you have been offered the job, find out how things stand at present.

Your appointment to Norwich has been a tremendous God-send to the Cathedral, the City and the Diocese, and the experience you have gained would be an immense help if you decided to say Yes. Oh – and one more thing – it would mean a lot if you felt you could get on happily with the Bishop. . . .

These are some of the factors which occur to me . . . it's no bad thing to write down the pros and cons and then see what they look like on paper. Sometimes this will clear out of the way considerations which really aren't important. . . . Do you want – not so much to be Dean of St Paul's, as to be doing the kind of things that someone in that position should in your view be doing? Don't hesitate to get in touch if you want to talk . . .

He always emphasized that any move should be made for positive reasons, and not in order to escape from an uncongenial situation. To a priest who felt frustrated in his job and was unhappy about current trends in the Church of England he wrote:

I'm sure you are wise to look around for possibilities. Mean-while it seems to me of very great importance to battle on with your present job as if you were going to be there for ever. . . . But I would couple with the 'soldiering on' the need to continue to think and pray and write . . . P.S. I think a move to R.C. would be a case of out of the frying pan into the fire.

But it was not only clergy or teachers, or people wanting advice about a job or career, who wrote about their personal problems. 'Why do I continue to confess myself to you?' asked a nineteen-year-old; this copy of a letter Launcelot wrote to someone else of the same age group suggests the answer:

Chastity really is a virtue and I believe that the self-discipline to achieve it is not only right but deeply rewarding. At the same time, I do want to make the point that, as I understand the teachings of Christ, he saw the sins of pride and avarice as far more damaging than the warmer-hearted 'sins of the flesh'.

The fact that in the 1980s Launcelot could get away with commending chastity, and usually have his advice accepted, says a great deal for the influence of his personality. It was not so much the words he wrote that were persuasive, but his own character. Older men might sometimes jib at unwelcome advice (a recently divorced priest was contemptuous when Launcelot demurred to the proposition that his first step must be to find a new wife), but younger men and women, including those who were by no means inclined to accept 'the Church's teaching', did not seem to resent being told they should aim at chastity. Some failed to follow that advice, but all seem to have seen the point of it, and respected it. Launcelot had a way of putting his finger on the real issue which was either consciously or subconsciously being evaded, but doing so in a way that would not cause resentment or make anyone feel they were being put down.

A draft of a (very) long letter to someone engaged to a Roman Catholic illustrates how much trouble he took with individuals; and parts of it are worth reproducing because they set out his considered opinion on several matters.

The doctrine of Papal Infallibility . . . has unquestionably produced a great solidarity among Roman Catholics and made it a strong church – but Our Lord redeemed us by weakness and was most redemptively powerful as a helpless babe. I firmly believe that the Anglican position that Doctrine should evolve through the combined sources of scripture, tradition, reason and experience is sound. Unhappily, the Anglican position has been compromised through Synodical Government resulting in a confidence-sapping bureaucracy wanting to be politically powerful and by its awful concern with success and statistics ... dividing authority between bishops and a democratically elected Synod has created confusion and muddle. ...

Immaculate Conception. I find this hard to accept ... incidentally, this whole area [including the Virgin Birth] would appear to lend itself too easily to the view that there is something intrinsically wrong about sexual intercourse as the means to the conception of children. Assumption ... I find myself in total agreement with you. I am baffled by what it is meant to mean ... Celibacy of the Clergy. One can see the purely practical advantage where a priest does not have to cope with family responsibilities of his own. I also find it impressive that so many celibates give the impression of being fulfilled, as if their sexual appetites have indeed been sublimated.

The ordination of women. I can see no theological ground against [it]. Unfortunately this issue has become entangled with somewhat aggressive women's lib campaigns and with inter-church politics. Some priestly roles are performed better by women than men, and others by men rather than women. I think it is a matter of time. ... But reforms require carefully prepared safeguards.

Birth control. The primary trouble which has emanated from ... [the Pill etc.] is that because it makes promiscuity easy and intercourse before marriage 'safe' – and because [homosexual] relations between consenting adults in private is legal – therefore many people can see nothing wrong in such practices. It needs to be made clear that such practices separate us from God, and they demean human nature. The remedy lies in repentance. Contraception within marriage between husband and wife is a very different matter. ...

Divorce. One of the most difficult problems with which I was confronted as a Bishop was in respect of the remarriage of divorced persons, and when the Archbishop (Geoffrey Fisher) asked me if there were any matters on which I would particularly value his advice, I immediately mentioned this matter.

And thank God I did. For over an hour he gave me the distilled products of his theological learning and his pastoral experience – and produced specific advice which I adopted as I readily accepted the principles and reasoning on which it was based. I personally handled all the cases in the two dioceses of which I was bishop for 23 years, of couples who wished to re-marry after divorce when the partner of the previous marriage was still living. The couples concerned in every case bar one undertook the nature of the discipline and the type of arrangements for a private service of blessing after their marriage in a Registry Office – all with a view to strengthening the sanctity of marriage as a lifelong commitment.

(In a nutshell, the Archbishop's policy was to ask the couple to accept that even if they were entirely 'innocent parties', a marriage in church would send a signal that divorce and remarriage were acceptable, and that would weaken the resolve of those whose marriages were going through a bad patch to remain faithful. By the time that changes to divorce law had made that argument unsustainable (because the horse had bolted) Launcelot had ceased to be a diocesan bishop, so the pastoral problems raised by divorce were no longer a priority in his thinking.)

His letter concluded by agreeing that 'the Anglican and R.C. traditions are more similar than not and I think each of you would be likely to find it more natural to grow in your spiritual life and enquiry within the tradition in which you have grown up'. He never shared the visceral anti-Roman prejudices of many of his contemporaries, but academic freedom of thought was very important to him, and he believed that would be compromised by accepting the authority of the Pope.

Soon after he retired, Launcelot preached a sermon in Westminster Abbey that reveals an aspect of his episcopate that was not widely known. In 1960 he had been asked to profess an Anchoress. He was hesitant, but after more than one long talk with her and after consulting the Bishop of Exeter (Robert

Mortimer) he agreed to profess her, and to the end of her life she continued to look to Launcelot as her spiritual director. He arranged for her to celebrate the Silver Jubilee of her original profession as a nun in St Faith's Chapel, Westminster Abbey, and in his sermon said:

Dame Mary Lioba ... felt the call to devote herself to an enclosed life of prayer as an Anchoress. This meant living in circumstances which from a physical point of view are not unlike those of prisoners condemned to solitary confinement. A cell was set aside for her at the shrine of Our Lady of Walsingham. A year later she took her vows. In 1968 she was taken ill and to hospital in London. When she was well enough to leave hospital she was given a room where despite her physical handicap she could still continue her ministry in the home of her principal benefactress, where she is living now.

And today she has come to this Abbey with its long history as a home of a Benedictine Community within whose precincts Anchorites have lived from the 10th century until well into the 18th century. She has come to give thanks to Almighty God for the joy of twenty five years in the Religious Life. We who are sharing this Eucharist with her are some of the many who over the years have been strengthened and supported more than we can ever know by her ministry and her prayers. It would scarcely be in keeping with a life which is deliberately 'hidden' to attempt to describe her work of prayer. Let me simply read you some extracts from the Prologue to the Rule by which her life is governed. ...

There are four features of this Rule which have much to say to the life of our own society and our own lives. First; obedience to Christ ... prayer, the Practice of the Presence of God, is the prime activity by which we may grow in that obedience. Secondly; self-denial, on which total obedience must depend. Thirdly; simplicity ... to be set against the duplicity of our minds, cluttered up and confused as they so easily become by serving too many masters. Lastly; Wisdom. Not intellectual prowess, but the perception which drives to the heart of things, to be contrasted with worldly wisdom. Today is April 1st – April Fools' Day. And I want to say to you, my dear Dame Mary Lioba – April Fool! Your Ministry will appear as folly to many, but 'the foolishness of God is wiser than men; the weakness of God is stronger than men'.

Jane stoutly maintained that the most significant and valuable years of Launcelot's life and ministry were his time at Windsor and in retirement. That view was a natural reflection of the fact that the formative years of his episcopate were over before she got to know him, but there is an element of truth in it. The real influence of any diocesan bishop is exerted not directly, on the individuals he himself meets, but indirectly by his imprint on his diocese. Launcelot was a diocesan bishop before the wings of bishops had been clipped by synodical government. By the time he left Portsmouth, and then Norwich, most of the diocesan clergy had been appointed either directly by him, or through his influence – he was brilliantly successful at persuading all but the most intransigent of private patrons to heed his advice. Even today, the general character of the Church in any diocese is very much influenced by its bishop, and before synodical government started to bite that was even more true. After he had ceased to be a diocesan bishop Launcelot continued to have a good deal of indirect influence, for instance, by being consulted on various appointments. But the main difference, especially after he retired, was that once more he had time for the kind of personal, one-to-one ministry to individuals that he had exercised as a chaplain at Trinity Hall and in the Navy.

Retirement gives time to think, and reflect; and if, as with Launcelot, retirement does not remove the stimulus of meeting fresh people with fresh ideas, then the results can be fruitful. In 1983 he attended a Conference on World Religions chaired by Rabbi Hugo Gryn, as a result of which he gave a talk to Atlantic College on 'What I Believe'.

It's no good saying 'I'm a Muslim', or 'I'm a Humanist', or 'I'm a Christian'; nor, I think, can you get away with saying

'I'm an Agnostic – I don't know'. That's probably true of us all, but you must believe in something, have some sense of what you think to be worthwhile, some view of things. What then do you believe about your own nature? about your destiny? about the point of life, if there is one?

My father was an Elder of the Presbyterian Church of Scotland – a wonderful man and a much respected physician. My mother was the daughter of a Church of England parson – so the Christian religion ran strongly in the family. . . .

But the process of belief was, for me, greatly helped by three years in the Antarctic, isolated from the outside world and living for most of the time with eight other men. I would take services for such of my colleagues who wanted to attend. To preach in these circumstances naturally led to discussions of the faith I was attempting to expound – and that was a stimulating opportunity for me to come to terms with, and test out, basic matters of belief. But in addition . . . this was in the years 1934–7, the years when Hitler came to power, the years that heralded World War II. It was a tragic, divided, belligerent world, uncertain of its aims, ideals and beliefs.

All this helped to strengthen my conviction that the nature of the beliefs you hold matters a very great deal; and it drove home one basic aspect of belief which I find myself holding with increasing conviction – namely, the Sanctity of Human Life – that every being is sacred and of priceless worth, each with his or her own distinct potential of excellence. Let me put it this way. I think each one of you is terrific. In saying this I'm not being extravagantly polite – or asking you to lend me money. I say this, and mean it, because each of you is a human being. And every human being, I believe, has personal and creative possibilities of priceless worth . . .

After quoting St Paul ('the Spirit of God dwells in you'), the Parable of the Prodigal Son, and that of the Good Samaritan that 'lay at the heart of Kurt Hahn's belief in founding this college. . . . The man who came to [the wounded man's] rescue was an alien', Launcelot continued:

But what of the animals? Or indeed the whole natural environment? Who is my neighbour? Is it to be supposed that we draw the line at man? Jesus taught that the whole world is God's world; it is sacred. We are short term occupants, responsible for how we treat the premises – the earth, as Barbara Ward once said, is 'a partner to be cherished, not a captive to be raped'.

I find that this teaching of Jesus – that God is presumed to exist and can be understood as a God of Love – is authenticated in the life of Jesus Christ. . . . With astonishing consistency, he practised what he preached. This, and the way in which as a young man he met a form of dying ghastly in its cruelty, pain and injustice, has had a profound effect on me – well expressed in the words of a Christian hymn, 'Love so amazing, so divine, demands my soul, my life, my all'.

Many aspects of the Church of England did increasingly disturb Launcelot, and this was not simply the result of old age finding new ideas difficult. He had supported the idea of synodical government, which he had hoped would free the Church from the stranglehold of Parliament that had thwarted attempts to update the Prayer Book; and although his recipe for better church government was 'More power to the Bishops' (enunciated in a strong Scots-Presbyterian accent), he had, more than most bishops, trusted and enlisted the laity. But the way that synodical government developed depressed him very much; he spoke quite bitterly of 'the extraordinary and suicidal policies of the Church' such as the 'enormities' of the Sheffield Report on 'rationing' clergy, the Tiller Report on their deployment, and the crippling growth of a centralized bureaucracy.

But luckily these things had come too late to affect his own ministry as a bishop. A poem called 'The Gap' which Launcelot often quoted at school confirmations showed what he thought were the things that really mattered:

> Did Jesus live? And did he really say
> The burning words that banish mortal fear?

And are they true? Just this is central, here;
The Church must stand or fall; it's Christ we weigh,
All else is off the point; the Flood, the Day
Of Eden, or the Virgin Birth – Have done!
The Question is: Did God send us the Son
Incarnate, crying 'Love! Love is the Way!'

What mattered to him infinitely more than church politics were individuals who needed encouragement, consolation, advice. And there were friends – not just hundreds, but thousands of friends. On his eightieth birthday (6 August 1986) his neighbours put on a party with a hilarious floor-show depicting all the stages in Launcelot's life, from childhood through Cambridge, Antarctica, the Navy, the bishops' bench, and Windsor, to Poyntington.

Although by that time he was finding it harder to get about, the flow of letters between the Tithe Barn and every corner of the globe did not diminish; his legs might be giving trouble, but his hand could still hold a pen (and the writing was no more indecipherable than it had been fifty years earlier). Overseas travel was no longer to New Zealand or South Africa, but to Madeira in February or March to ward off bronchitis – he had shrugged off his bout of pneumonia in 1959 but these things catch up in later years. When in company he perked up, and his friends noticed no difference apart from his having to sit when normally he would have stood. He continued to come up to London for various meetings and dinners – including a Trinity Hall dining club, the Aula Club (whose members had clubbed together to present the portrait of Launcelot that now hangs in the College). At one such dinner someone mentioned in conversation that she thought it was mainly due to Launcelot that at Trinity Hall, unlike many colleges, the Boat Club had made women members like her feel really welcome from the word go.

But when Launcelot was at home with Jane and without the stimulus of company, it was all too clear that he was not at all well.

23

The Last Chapter

> Between the probable and proved there yawns
> A gap. Afraid to jump, we stand absurd
> Then see *behind* us sink the ground, and, worse
> Our very standpoint crumbling. Desperate dawns
> Our only hope; to leap into the Word
> That opens up the shuttered universe.
>
> *(last verse of 'The Gap', already quoted)*

Those lines, whose author Jane later tried hard but unsuccess-fully to trace, evidently expressed what Launcelot felt as he approached the 'gap' between this known world and that of the life to come. Perhaps one reason why the poem spoke to him so powerfully was that, consciously or unconsciously, it brought to mind those treacherously shifting ice-floes of Marguerite Bay when a gap of open water yawned ahead that had to be crossed because, *behind* the traveller, the firm ice over which he had come was now submerged. That is conjecture; but it would be surprising if, as he began to know that the end of his mortal life was not far away, he did not recall those Antarctic days when he had first looked death in the face.

A few months before he died Launcelot was asked by the Arch-bishops' Adviser for Bishops' Ministry to suggest how bishops and their wives should plan and prepare for retirement. His reply shows how he had tried to use his own retirement:

The very word 'retirement' is apt to create a false and damag-ing image, as if to suggest that it consists largely of withdrawal. When a bishop retires he and his wife can enjoy a new freedom from pressures, enabling them to apply their gifts, experience and vocational aptitudes to particular fields of their own choosing. . . . However, the change of circumstances can come as something of a shock . . . the Bishop loses the secretarial help to which he has become accustomed, and his wife will have less help in the house [*would Jane, thinking of Windsor, have agreed?*]. I would strongly urge a bishop to retire outside the boundaries, or close proximity, of the diocese he is leaving . . . [and] leave the way clear for his successor. In planning where to live it's worth bearing in mind the approach of old age [so as] to be saved the trauma of a double move. Presuming that they will be moving into a smaller house, he and his wife will almost certainly need to dispose of many books – but amongst those which bishops will need to consider retaining are reference books, with which they will have been well supplied when in office.

He will need to consider what advice it will be appropriate for him to pass on to his successor. Clearly it will be the greatest help to a successor if he can be given factual information . . . but when it comes to opinions, this is a more delicate matter. . . . There may be individuals whom the outgoing bishop has found to be unreliable or unbalanced, but in general it is well for the new bishop to come to his own judgments. A change in a diocese provides a good occasion for reassessment.

It might be wise for the Bishop and his wife to consider acquiring a Word Processor and learning how to use it. This should help them cope with correspondence, and as they grow older to avoid inflicting on correspondents handwriting which with increasing old age is liable to become increasingly illegible (mea culpa) and in some cases increasingly small.

The 'mea culpa' was justified; the carbon copy shows that this letter was hand-written and its perusal may have taken time; but his writing was no more illegible than it ever had been.

He had, however, become physically less and less able to remain active. The way he faced the trouble with his leg was an inspiration to many; at some function where Launcelot was sitting down, surrounded as usual by a throng of (mainly young) people, someone was heard to say 'What a man! I should go under; I just couldn't take that kind of disability.' So long as he possibly could, he forced himself to take exercise – mainly swimming as that exercises the leg muscles without putting any weight on them. And each morning at Poyntington he would walk the hundred yards or so with the help of two sticks to where he collected the morning paper, and bring it back in a satchel on his back so as to leave both hands free for his sticks.

Shortly before leaving Windsor he had undergone a minor but painful operation for piles, and in 1980 he had an operation for hernia. In 1987 a cataract was removed – and to his relief his driving licence was then renewed. In 1989 he felt he had to turn down, with great regret and for the first time ever, a request to be Patron of an Expedition because he 'couldn't do the job properly'. And asked in that same year if he would give a reference to a schoolmaster applying for a new job he declined – 'I am now 83 and am getting rather doddery (my memory is in fact disintegrating) and I think your referee should be more compos'. That disclaimer, however, should be taken with a pinch of salt.

Most people who saw Launcelot were unaware how difficult life had become for him; he always brightened up when stimulated by company and only Jane fully realized the strain he was under. In 1989 Atlantic College gave him a 'leaving present', and in his speech of thanks he said:

Nine months ago I gave a talk here about the need to *let go* when one stage of one's life comes to an end to be succeeded by another. Now I have to remind myself of that same principle. Letting go of something you have greatly valued and enjoyed isn't easy, especially when you don't altogether know what the future has in store. But it's made much less difficult by two compensations. First, the benefits you've gained in the period you are leaving have become a part of you which you can develop in the time ahead. And secondly, the friendships you have made can deepen; the friends remain.

Launcelot preached for the last time in All Saints' Church, Poyntington, on Easter Day 1988. A note pinned to a sermon he had preached in Norwich Cathedral on Easter Day 1964, and which formed the basis for that Easter sermon of 1988, says 'This pretty well expresses my belief about the Resurrection'.

For the events of the first Easter morning, we can only take the Apostles' word. Their experience not only changed the rest of their lives but had a profound effect on the course of human history. . . . Mary Magdalene who thought he was the gardener, or the disciples on the road to Emmaus . . . were not seeing a ghost, but seeing him as it were in a new kind of existence. The Risen Christ was not a corpse re-animated . . . although he was recognisably the same person, body and soul, he belonged more to the invisible world than the visible – no longer confined to our framework of space and time. . . .
What does all this mean? Jesus had not been defeated by the hatred, the brute force, the intrigue and cruelty which had brought about his death on the Cross. His goodness, his courage and his love had triumphed after all. It also made clear the relationship between life and death – and how life is renewed through life laid down – 'a grain of wheat remains a solitary grain until it falls into the ground and dies, but if it dies, it bears a rich harvest'. Look chiefly to your own interests and either they turn bad on you or they will be taken away from you when you die. Look to the interests of God, which means loving and serving others, and you'll find him and everyone else as well.
We all have to die. The choice is between the death of extinction, where all the energies have been spent on getting and keeping; or the death of a letting go where the energies have been spent on living and giving – a death which is followed by Resurrection. . . . During our lives there are

innumerable little deaths (some of them not so little) which are a pre-condition for something new that lies ahead. Failing an exam, which may mean a fresh start on a new course. The break-up of a love affair – always painful; the loss of a childish faith, where one must be prepared to let go some childish ideas in order to adjust to a more mature understanding. Seeing a son or daughter leave home for the first time. And, of course, retirement.

Cling to all you have at such moments and you're lost. If we can learn the habit of letting go from such occasions of 'dying' as these, then, when the last letting go is called for, it will be familiar and confident. Death followed by Resurrection is the principle of all existence. Our formation of the habit of being prepared to let go will be immeasurably strengthened if we respond to the life and teachings of Jesus; for we are the children of God, heirs of that more abundant life which Jesus has revealed.

In April 1990 Launcelot and Jane were able to celebrate their silver wedding, albeit quietly. But later that month Launcelot went into St Luke's Hospital for the Clergy for a prostate operation. The surgeon was astonished to discover what appallingly bad shape his body was in; only sheer will power could have kept him going for the last year or two. Although the operation itself was successful and he was able to go home, he did not recover his strength and soon had to go into the local Sherborne hospital. Less than three months later, on 30 July 1990, he died peacefully.

He would have celebrated his eighty-fourth birthday on 6 August, the day his funeral took place at All Saints' Church, Poyntington. The Rt Hon. Peter Brooke, son of Henry and Barbara, gave an address, and the blessing was given by the Bishop of Sherborne, John Kirkham, who many years earlier had been Launcelot's domestic chaplain. Later on, his ashes were interred in the churchyard at Poyntington.

On 25 October, at the service of thanksgiving for Launcelot's life at St George's Chapel, Windsor, Dr Owen Chadwick, who had been his colleague at Trinity Hall and a close friend ever since, gave a memorable address; Princess Margaret and the Duke and Duchess of Gloucester were among the members of the Royal Family who attended, and St George's was, not surprisingly, full to capacity.

His old diocese of Norwich insisted that they too must have a thanksgiving service, and although it was over twenty years since he had left, the nave of the cathedral was full. The address was given by Bishop Hugh Blackburne who had been Rector of the Hilborough Group, the first rural group ministry in the diocese.

Epilogue

The parishioners of Poyntington were very keen that Jane should commission a memorial tablet to Launcelot in the parish church. As it happened there was a memorial on the north wall of the chancel commemorating the last Rector (who was likely to continue being the last one for the foreseeable future), and a large blank space on the opposite wall. Not only had Launcelot been a person of note of whom the village had been proud, but he had also been *de facto* their beloved parish priest for many years. Jane agreed to the proposal, and applied accordingly for a Faculty.

What happened then was an object lesson in how the Church is not immune from 'the insolence of office and the law's delays'. The Diocesan Chancellor refused to grant a Faculty, couching his letter in terms that could hardly fail to cause distress. In the long run, however, all turned out for the best. Jane was not one to sit down under such treatment, so that after the initial hurt her determined efforts to put things right did much to help her cope with the sadness of bereavement.

In due course the Chancellor retired, and on Sunday 5 October 1997 the memorial to Bishop Launcelot Fleming was dedicated during Evensong by Lord Runcie. His address on that occasion provides a fitting summing-up of this portrait of Launcelot.

This is the end of a long road. Never was a plaque more pleaded for. Never was its placement more popular, and now we rejoice in the only visible memorial that commemorates Launcelot's whole life. Others are limited to his work in those particular places; some, as he would wish, are embodied in causes and the careers of young people. Poyntington is the place of harvest. In the happiness of his home with Jane, in the letters and visitors and the familiar figure moving round in torn guernsey and flannel trousers, you could see his whole life gathered – and here his ashes rest.

There is a sentence of St Paul that I treasure: 'Godliness with contentment is great gain.' Godliness is an old-fashioned word but it fits Launcelot. Holiness – yes, but that has a touch of churchliness about it. Spirituality was not a word in Launcelot's vocabulary; it has something of the specialist about it; he wouldn't care for that. Godliness, if I dare say so, is a manly word. Contentment has for its opposite sourness or envy and there was no hint of sourness or envy at all in the Launcelot we knew and loved. The world may associate him with Cambridge or Antarctica, with Portsmouth, or Norwich or Windsor. But we know that the nearest this rolling stone came to some sort of halt, was here. Astonishingly he lived longer and more consistently in this village than anywhere else in his life. Three years in Antarctica as an explorer revealed the man and literally enlarged his horizons. Naval action in the Mediterranean put him to the test which he passed with flying colours. For years he was part of the fabric of Trinity Hall; my wife bit his ankle when she was three and he married us when she was twenty-seven (an age from which she has never moved). Portsmouth and Norwich quietly discovered they had a bishop whose planned incoherence as a chairman and his remarkable ability to be in the right place at the right time created dioceses where any young man would want to start his ministry. At Windsor no head was ever less turned by the various privileges and intimacies, but with Launcelot that was ever so; ask a porter at Trinity Hall whose son had gone to the bad – Launcelot cared for them as much as for the professor who was past it and going slightly dotty.

It is surprising how many movements for the young which we now take for granted had the hand of Launcelot upon them. The Duke of Edinburgh Award Scheme in 1954, Voluntary Service Overseas in 1958, the Atlantic College, the Prince's Trust, Outward Bound.

He seemed the least likely person to be a parliamentarian but he had the unique advantage of a bishop in the House of Lords who actually knew something – that nobody else did. He piloted a Bill (the Antarctic Treaty) through the House of Lords. Well in advance of his time he pressed for environmental and ecological issues to go up the agenda. His maiden speech was about cruelty to whales. He spoke with authority about the need for a law about the sea bed.

His desk was a mess, his letters charmingly un-word processed. How on earth did he achieve it all? Let me tell you a few parables from my own experience.

First. If you put him in a room full of students, at the end of an hour or so each of them would tell you they had a memorable personal conversation with Launcelot. Yet there will be little evidence that he ever finished a sentence. It was simply his friendship and his ability to listen – they were truly charismatic.

Second. When I was a tutor at Trinity Hall there was much competition to get into the College and much special pleading. We were fierce about academic achievement; but we did have a little column which was headed 'Launcelot's Lambs'. These were people that Launcelot had met in railway trains or had played squash with at a public school. Launcelot had seen something special about them and had suggested that if they worked hard they might go to Trinity Hall. If you will forgive the mixed metaphor – not all his Lambs were swans but he spotted some real winners to our great advantage. He was always optimistic about people and often they were determined to prove him right.

Third. There was a man who wanted to give up rowing. He felt his work was suffering. Launcelot loved the Boat Club. It was grief for him to lose a good oar. He produced a wonderful argument. He said that if you give up rowing you might think that automatically you are doing more work. On the other hand if you continued to row you would have a tremendous sense of urgency and that might make you work much harder. Launcelot was right. He was always good at helping people to a wise decision though it was not imposed. It was modestly drawn out of a discussion.

My last example is of the wonderful confirmations he conducted in college chapels. They were quite without oratorical sparkle. They always spoke very simply about the laying on of hands with prayer. The address was short and to the point, unadorned. There was no self-promotion or publicity. Yet in the quietness people knew they had been in the presence of God.

These are hints of his genius; but it was here in the parish that these gifts could be tailored to anyone's understanding. A generous Rector, Claude Rutter who is with us today, points out that Launcelot was far more the faithful parish priest than he could be as the incumbent of six parishes. He was a quiet and humble source of Christian strength to those who were bereaved, an inspiration to those he married, and ever interested in the progress of those he baptised. Children adored him and as always young people were blessed with his sensible wisdom and advice.

The days at Poyntington, however, not only disclose the secret of his vast influence despite his totally unassuming ways. They also say something very important about the life of a priest. It is widely believed (rightly or wrongly) that the attitude of a vicar (and that's the general term, except in Liverpool where everyone is called 'father') is a living symbol – faint and imperfect but the only living symbol we have – of the attitude of God himself. So his presence and attentiveness, or his absence and seeming indifference, is likely to affect a person at a deep level in times for them of acute sensitivity and concern. The movement of a human soul or a whole human family towards or away from God may well be determined by the minute particular of whether the vicar calls or does not call on a parishioner who is gravely ill, or whether he is accessible or inaccessible to an unhappy youngster or a proud parent.

The attitude of most people to God which affects all other attitudes is determined for good or ill, not by general ideas or intellectual formulations – certainly not by news in the papers about synods or archbishops – but by concrete signs and evidence of the nearness and care of God in those commonplace yet sensitive situations to which I have just referred. And of such evidence the parish priest is an available and effective symbol.

Godliness with contentment is great gain. That is not only a statement about the personality of our beloved Launcelot. It explains his influence in the corridors of power and how it was marvellously seen, scaled down and tailored to our understanding in the houses and in the Tithe Barn and in the worship of this church of All Saints' at Poyntington.

Index